Sean Finnigan

GW01066457

ICSA Study Text

Diploma in Offshore Finance and
Administration
Portfolio Management

ICSA Study Text

Diploma in Offshore Finance
and Administration

Portfolio
Management

Tony Kilmister, Coventry University

icsa.
Publishing

First published 2013
Published by ICSA Information & Training Ltd
16 Park Crescent
London W1B 1AH
© ICSA Information & Training Ltd

All rights reserved. No part of this publication may be reproduced, stored in a
retrieval system, or transmitted, in any form, or by any means, electronic, mechanical,
photocopying, recording or otherwise, without prior permission, in writing, from the
publisher.

Typeset by Paul Barrett Book Production, Cambridge
Printed by Hobbs the Printers Ltd, Totton, Hampshire

British Cataloguing in Publication Data
A catalogue record for this book is available from the British Library.

ISBN 978 1 86072 536 4

Contents

How to use this study text

ICSA study texts developed to support ICSA's Diploma in Offshore Finance and Administration (DOFA) follow a standard format and include a range of navigational, self-testing and illustrative features to help you get the most out of the support materials.

Each text is divided into three main sections:

◆ introductory material
◆ the text itself
◆ additional reference information.

The sections below show you how to find your way around the text and make the most of its features.

Introductory material

The introductory section of each text includes a full contents list and the module syllabus, which reiterates the module aims, learning outcomes and syllabus content for the module in question.

Where relevant, the introductory section will also include a list of acronyms and abbreviations or a list of legal cases for reference.

The text itself

Each **part** opens with a list of the chapters to follow, an overview of what will be covered and learning outcomes for the part.

Every **chapter** opens with a list of the topics covered and an introduction specific to that chapter. Chapters are structured to allow you to break the content down into manageable sections for study. Each chapter ends with a summary of key content to reinforce understanding.

Features

The text is enhanced by a range of illustrative and self-testing features to assist understanding and to help you prepare for the examination. Each feature is presented in a standard format, so that you will become familiar with how to use them in your study.

These features are identified by a series of icons.

The texts also include tables, figures and other illustrations as relevant.

Reference material

The text ends with a range of additional guidance and reference material, including a glossary of key terms and a comprehensive index.

Stop and think

Test yourself

Worked examples

Making it work

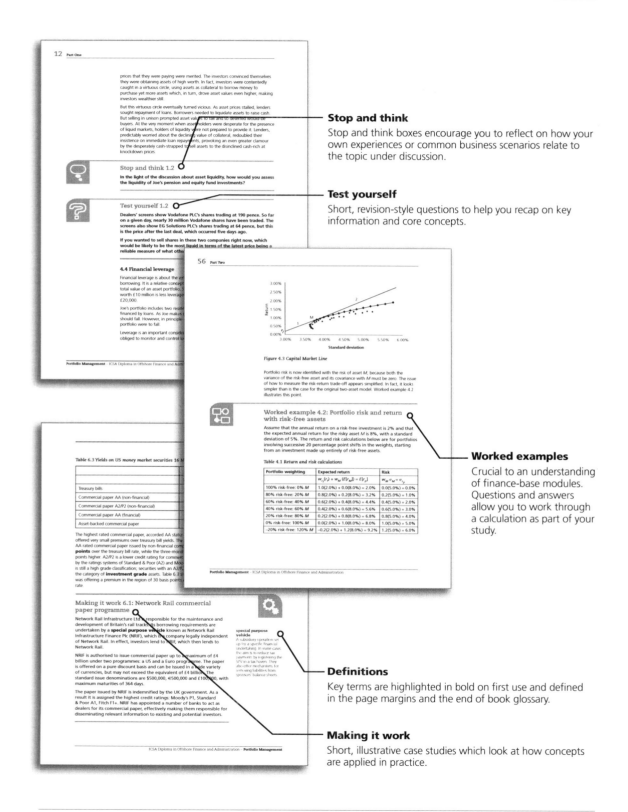

Stop and think

Stop and think boxes encourage you to reflect on how your own experiences or common business scenarios relate to the topic under discussion.

Test yourself

Short, revision-style questions to help you recap on key information and core concepts.

Worked examples

Crucial to an understanding of finance-base modules. Questions and answers allow you to work through a calculation as part of your study.

Definitions

Key terms are highlighted in bold on first use and defined in the page margins and the end of book glossary.

Making it work

Short, illustrative case studies which look at how concepts are applied in practice.

The Portfolio Management syllabus

Aims

This module focuses on the practice of managing an investment portfolio, covering portfolio risk, performance and the different management styles and asset classes used to manage an investment portfolio.

Learning outcomes

On successful completion of this module, candidates will be able to:

◆ demonstrate an understanding of the techniques required for effective portfolio investment;

◆ identify and describe the different classes of assets used in investment portfolios;

◆ understand and evaluate the risks associated with different investment styles;

◆ explain asset allocation with due consideration to risk and return;

◆ understand how returns are measured and the range of options for conducting measurements;

◆ understand and explain the techniques employed in the analysis of an investment portfolio;

◆ understand the risks associated with international investment; and

◆ discuss portfolio management fees and charging structures.

Syllabus

1 Introduction to portfolio management

Importance of portfolio management in creating wealth through investment

Challenges of portfolio management – risk versus return

Relationship with clients

Liquidity and time horizons

Discretionary and non-discretionary management

Active and passive management

Ethical and socially responsible investment

2   Portfolio risk

Implication of investment styles on portfolio risk and return

Asset allocation and investment styles

Portfolio objectives and associated returns

Discussion of modern portfolio theory

Capital Asset Pricing Model – assumptions and limitations

Forms of the efficient market hypothesis

International investment risks

Protection against risk with the use of options, hedging, sector weightings and counterparties

3   Portfolio performance

Measurement of performance by using returns and ratios

Benchmark indices

Yields and earnings measurements

Calculation of present and future values

Importance of annual and periodic reviews

4   Portfolio investments

Asset classes, including bonds, equities, property, collective investment schemes and derivatives

Corporate actions

International markets

Charging and fee structures

A note on calculation in the Portfolio Management syllabus

The Portfolio Management study text contains examples of investment calculations and these are included to provide students with a full view of the issues in Portfolio Management. The main requirement is for students to understand how and why such formulae are used in the financial markets.

Although the calculations shown here are not considered complex, the exam will not focus on testing students' ability to perform these calculations. Where there are such exam requirements, relevant formulae will be included with the question.

Past papers and practice questions

Students can access past papers for this module by logging into the MyICSA area of www.icsaglobal.com.

Acronyms and abbreviations

ABCP	asset-backed commercial paper
AMC	annual management charge
BIS	Bank of International Settlements
CAPM	Capital Asset Pricing Model
CME	Chicago Mercantile Exchange
CML	Capital Market Line
DMO	Debt Management Office
DVM	dividend valuation model
EBITDA	earnings before interest, tax, depreciation and amortisation
EMH	efficient market hypothesis
ETF	exchange traded funds
Euribor	Euro Interbank Offered Rate
FCA	Financial Conduct Authority
FRA	forward rate agreement
FRN	floating rate note
FSA	Financial Services Authority
FTSE	Financial Times and Stock Exchange
FTSE-AS	FTSE All Share
GDP	gross domestic product
ICMA	International Capital Market Association
IPMA	International Primary Market Association
ISF	Institutional Secured Funding Ltd
ISMA	International Securities Market Association
Libor	London Interbank Offered Rate
LSE	London Stock Exchange
M&As	mergers and acquisitions
NASDAQ	National Association of Securities Dealers Automated Quotations
NAV	net asset value
NRIF	Network Rail Infrastructure Finance Plc
NYSE	New York Stock Exchange
OEIC	open-ended investment company
OTC	over-the-counter
PAL	provisional allotment letters
PBV	price to book value
PER	price-earnings ratio
PRA	Prudential Regulatory Authority

ROCE	return on capital employed
SEC	(US) Security and Exchange Commission
SEDOL	Stock Exchange Daily Official List
SPV	special purpose vehicle
SSE	Shanghai Stock Exchange
STIR	short-term interest rate
TER	total expense ratio
TERP	theoretical ex-rights price

Acknowledgements

This study text was funded by the ICSA Education and Research Foundation.

Part One

The portfolio management environment

Overview

The purpose of Part One is to outline important characteristics of investment and portfolio management practice, and to highlight aspects of the environment in which they occur. Chapter 1 examines the principal motives behind investment and suggests that a portfolio approach to investment is deeply ingrained. It goes on to outline key facets that make up asset portfolios.

Chapter 2 focuses the broader market context within which investment and portfolio management activity is undertaken. It suggests that the modern financial markets are in many ways quite different from those of a generation or two ago and that the ways that investors seek to pursue their objectives have been affected by the altered environment.

Learning objectives

At the end of this part, students will be able to:

◆ understand the key objectives informing the desires of individuals to invest wealth;

◆ appreciate the importance of economic circumstances and uncertainty in framing individuals' attitudes to investment opportunities;

◆ be able to identify and explain the essential characteristics of what makes up an asset portfolio;

◆ understand that there have been major economic, operational and cultural shifts in financial markets, some of which are subjects of controversy;

◆ define terms relating to a range of financial securities and financial market procedures;

◆ demonstrate an understanding of the difference between exchange traded and over-the-counter methods of dealing; and

◆ appreciate the opportunities and pitfalls of leverage though an understanding of margin trading.

Chapter One
Asset portfolios and portfolio management

List of topics

1   Investment
2   Investment behaviour and the banking crisis
3   Risk, return and portfolios
4   Asset portfolios
5   Client-centred portfolio management

Introduction

People earn and spend money. They do so for private reasons like supporting a family, and as participants in goal-driven associations such as business enterprises, civic institutions and clubs. The money earned and the money spent by individuals over a given period seldom equates. Some spend more than they are earn and must borrow. Others earn more than they spend and therefore save.

This is a simple depiction of the interaction between earning, spending, borrowing and saving. Individuals routinely save and borrow at the same time. For instance, many people owe money on mortgages secured by property while also holding funds in savings accounts. The more meaningful distinction is between net savers and net borrowers. Furthermore, individuals' financial situations alter. It is surely true, for instance, that with age we tend to shift from being net borrowers towards becoming net savers. Most of us, after all, fear the prospect of reaching retirement burdened with large debts while possessing few assets. Hence we incline towards fiscal adjustments that facilitate increased saving.

What do people do with savings? They invest them. Furthermore, they invest in portfolios of assets. Let's start by examining investment behaviour in its own terms.

1. Investment

The analysis of investment is generally not concerned with the details of why people save. One reason is that the motives for saving are obvious. We could cite any number: keep cash in reserve for a 'rainy day', save to pay off a loan in the future, save for a holiday, car, education, and so on. They explain why individuals save but do not require explanation themselves.

Secondly, motives are subjective and psychological. They operate as impulses, attitudes and plans that are expressed, articulated and organised by autonomous individuals. There are, to say the least, huge difficulties in devising universally applicable systems for quantifying things (aggregates, averages, distributions, etc.) as subjective as individual motives.

People are disposed to save – not all at the same time, to equal degrees or for identical reasons – but they do save. We will discount the proverbial money 'under the mattress' or 'buried in the garden' methods of saving and assume that individuals prefer to deploy savings productively. Saving productively is investing.

The aims of investment are:

◆   to sustain the purchasing power of saved wealth;

◆   to augment wealth as a reward for saving; and

◆   to compensate savers for the uncertainties associated with investments.

1.1 The protection of purchasing power

Individuals measure monetary wealth in terms of its purchasing power – the quantity of goods and services that a given sum of money buys. Imagine that you put aside £100 for a year. If the prices of goods in general rise, then the £100 will buy less by the end of the year. You are worse off. If prices rise by 3%, you need £103 in a year to buy the same amount of goods that £100 buys today. In effect, you need investment yielding 3% merely to preserve wealth in real terms. With inflation, even the simple preservation of wealth requires investment.

1.2 Wealth enhancement and time

Wealth that is saved is wealth that the owner refrains from consuming in the present. Saving, therefore, involves inconvenience and hardship associated with forgoing the benefits of consumption. As a result, schemes that promise no more than the mere preservation of wealth will be unacceptable because they offer no reward for the sacrifices. People will choose to forgo consumption for periods of time only if there is the prospect of gaining additional wealth to consume in the future. It follows that the longer the investment period, the bigger the sacrifice, and so the greater the required addition to future wealth.

The preferred investment period is mainly influenced by the motives informing a particular investment. Someone in their mid 40s is unlikely to make three-month treasury bills the centrepiece of a retirement fund. But a company looking to earn a return on a temporary cash reserve may well consider treasury bills a convenient option. In effect, investment decisions normally involve, at least in some approximate sense, the matching of asset maturities to the planned investment term.

In practice, maturity matching can be a complex issue for a number of reasons.

◆ In many circumstances it is impossible to be precise about when investors will liquidate assets. For instance, a manager of an equity fund cannot know exactly when investors will decide to cash in and, therefore, cannot be precise about choosing assets with matching maturities.

◆ Secondary markets in which assets are traded make asset maturity, in principle, more flexible. Take the example of company shares which characteristically do not have maturity dates but exist 'in perpetuity'. Many of these shares are publicly traded on stock exchanges, meaning that individual investors can determine the maturity at any time by simply selling the asset.

◆ Maturity matching is liable to occur as some form of term averaging procedure. For instance, an investment with a five-year maturity could consist of two equally weighted components, one with a maturity of two and a half years, the second with a maturity of seven and a half years.

◆ Situations of mismatched maturities can often be very profitable and, therefore, attractive to investors. In the years preceding the 2007–8 banking collapse, many investors were able to borrow money on a very short-term basis at exceptionally low rates. They used the funds to invest in longer-term assets offering higher yields. The trick was to renew the short-term loans repeatedly and, thereby, retain ownership of the higher-yielding assets. It worked very well – for a time.

1.3 The uncertainty of returns

Investors go without to invest. But rewards are uncertain because the future course of events is unknown. Investments come with a warning sign: return not guaranteed. This means that investors expect compensation not merely for the period of sacrifice but also for the degree of uncertainty attached to compensation itself. The less certain a reward, the larger it must be relative to the capital invested.

Investors can choose how much uncertainty they are prepared to tolerate. Those with low risk thresholds tend towards safer investments. These are safe in the sense that actual returns tend not to differ much from expectations. The cost, not surprisingly, is that predictable returns also tend to be modest returns.

Other investors have higher risk thresholds, favouring investments offering more impressive rates of wealth accumulation. The salient point, of course, is that the actual results of risky investments are more prone to deviate significantly from initial estimates (they wouldn't be risky if this were not the case). Sometimes risky investments produce pleasant surprises (big payoffs well above expectations), but at other times they result in unpleasant shocks in the form of significant losses of wealth.

Financial theory states that all investors are 'risk averse'. This should not be interpreted in the everyday sense of investors being unwilling to take risks, as this is a plainly absurd notion. The classic formulation of risk adversity is that *all* investors, faced with alternative assets offering the same return but with contrasting risks, will choose the lowest-risk investment. No investor in possession of the necessary information would prefer the higher-risk alternatives.

To recap, investment is the productive employment of savings to enhance the wealth of investors in an inherently uncertain economic environment. Investment analysis involves the meticulous scrutinising of different investment opportunities, the objective being to provide the best possible assessment of their risk and return attributes so as to maximise the likelihood of making good decisions. Portfolio analysis focuses on the risk and return attributes of groupings of investments.

Test yourself 1.1

You are given a choice of three investments, which are:

1   **shares in a biotechnology company that has been trading for two years;**

2   **bonds issued in the name of the US government; or**

3   **an asset management fund that focuses on companies included in the FTSE 100 index.**

   a)   **Which do you imagine would be the safest, the next riskiest and the most risky of the investments?**

   b)   **The investments offer expected returns of 3%, 7% and 12%. Which of the investments is likely to be associated with each return?**

2. Investment behaviour and the banking crisis

treasury bills
A type of financial security issued by central governments seeking to borrow funds on a short-term basis.

Sometimes investors' behaviour seems at odds with the characterisation outlined above. A striking case in recent years has been the willingness of investors to buy **treasury bills** offering close to zero rates of return. For instance, in the final week of July 2012 the US government auctioned $124 billion of treasury bills. The bills offered an average annual return below 0.14%. At the time, the annual rate of inflation in the United States stood at 1.7%, with forecasters expecting it to be around 2% over the next year. The willingness of investors to buy treasury bills on these terms contradicts the argument that they seek, at the very least, to preserve purchasing power. Buyers of treasury bills were willing to lend the US government $124 billion and charge virtually nothing (a yield of 0.14% is practically zero) while facing the likelihood that over the investment period consumer prices would rise. They were set to lose wealth in real terms.

Worked example 1.1: The yield on the one-year US treasury bill

The US government sells treasury bills on a weekly basis via an auction system. They are issued with maturities of 4, 13, 26 and 52 weeks. The US government promises to pay bill owners $100 per bill on the maturity date. Investors paid $99.823 for the 52-week bills auctioned on 26 July 2012. This represents a gain of just $0.177 over 52 weeks, and an approximate annual rate of return of:

$$\frac{\$0.177}{\$99.823}\,(100) = 0.1773\%$$

Why are investors prepared to spend billions of dollars on assets that promise a zero rate of return? To answer the question we need to look at the issue from a different vantage point. US treasury bills offered miniscule returns because investors were desperately keen to acquire them. Demand by investors drove up bid prices at auction to a point where yields ended close to 0%. For instance, tenders for 52-week bills totalled nearly five times the amount issued in the final week of July 2012. It was investors exercising the spending power that drove yields down.

The backdrop to this unusual state of affairs is the seismic crisis that hit the international banking system in 2007–8, and which continues to reverberate to this day. The shock was so devastating that even bank deposits and term accounts, assets normally deemed risk free, were at risk. Without worldwide government and central bank schemes to inject massive amounts of capital and liquidity into the banking system, personal savings would have disappeared on a systemic scale as banks folded. Governments around the world also bolstered **deposit insurance schemes** designed to protect savers in the event of localised bank failures. For instance, in 2008 the Federal Deposit Insurance Corporation, a United States government-sponsored agency, increased the level of savings protected by statute from $100,000 to $250,000 per depositor, per bank. This covers accounts offered by more than 4,900 deposit-taking institutions operating the US.

deposit insurance scheme
A mechanism, normally government sponsored, for protecting depositors' funds in the event of a bank failure.

Those at the centre of managing the crisis recognised that savings could not be considered immune to risk. Saving personal savings was, arguably, the most compelling influence guiding their efforts to support the banking system.

Savers are lending money to the US government at close to zero rates of interest because of highly exceptional circumstances. The usual mechanisms of investment, primarily operating through the banking system, have malfunctioned and persuaded many that it is best for now to safeguard wealth rather than risk it. They see lending to the government as the safest haven. Indeed, with US inflation running at around 2%, buyers of US treasury bills are demonstrating that they are prepared to pay the US government for keeping their money safe. It is a striking testimony to the scale of the financial crisis and the depth of the fears it has engendered that savers are effectively hoarding rather than investing savings.

3. Risk, return and portfolios

The factors driving individuals to invest are myriad and intricately intertwined in complex, contingent, often contradictory, ways. Age, education, family obligations, accumulated wealth, employment status, career, commercial connections and many other considerations are plainly important influences on individuals' investment decisions. However, pondering these influences does not yield much beyond schematic, mostly self-evident, generalisations.

By contrast, careful reflection on investment behaviour in its own right has proved enormously significant, offering up vitally important insights that have demonstrated their worth in the improved quality of investment decisions. This, at least, is the claim made by portfolio theory and portfolio managers.

Portfolio theory starts from a remarkably simple postulation: all investments are in essence a trade-off between risk and expected return. Despite the unique perspectives and temperaments of millions of investors, despite the multitude of different things that they invest in, it all comes down to a binary interaction. Investors with a preference for safe, low-risk returns will find themselves forced to accept low levels of return. Investors seeking high returns will find that they are also less safe, higher-risk returns. Of course, as with all rules, it operates with exceptions.

The notion that the quest to increase rewards invariably means a willingness to take bigger risks is hardly a revelation. The real significance of portfolio theory lies in its systematic efforts to investigate how the trade-off can be improved (the more technical term is 'optimised') through the use of insights into how different investments can mutually counteract the risks of others when they form components of a portfolio. The really important claim of portfolio theory is that investors can add assets with high expected returns to their portfolios without increasing the total risk of the portfolio. In some circumstances, the addition of high risk assets offering the possibility of higher rewards can result in a *reduction* of investors' exposure to risk.

The implication is that investors will necessarily seek to acquire portfolios of investments. Individual investors have different outlooks regarding how much risk they are prepared to take on. But all are better served holding portfolios of assets with the desired risk because they offer superior returns to those of individual assets of comparable risk. Portfolios are part of the innate order of investment.

This paradox of risk lies at the heart of portfolio theory and is of primary interest in this module.

Stop and think 1.1

Why might we expect an investor who owns shares in a rail operator *and* a motor vehicle manufacturer to face less risk than investors who own shares in just one of the companies?

4. Asset portfolios

Meet Joe. He's a fairly typical investor residing in the UK. He has money in a savings account with a well-known high-street bank. The house in which he resides was purchased in 2003 using a 25-year **capital repayment mortgage** on which he makes monthly payments. Joe works in the private sector and invests a portion of his monthly salary into a **defined contribution pension** through a company scheme. A few years ago he contributed a lump sum to an **equity growth fund** run by a major fund management institution. The fund invests exclusively in UK company shares but is structured to provide some protection against capital losses. Joe recently took on a second capital repayment mortgage to purchase and renovate a property in France which he plans to use for family vacations and to let out at other times. The mortgage payments are in euros.

Joe has an investment portfolio. In comparison to the 'high finance' conducted on global capital markets, by banks, insurance companies, investment funds and brokerage houses, it's humdrum stuff. Nevertheless, it contains all of the key characteristics of an investment portfolio. Let's examine each in turn.

4.1 Ownership of diverse assets

The most rudimentary attribute of an investment portfolio is a combination of different assets. In Joe's portfolio there are 'bricks and mortar' assets in the form of the properties in the UK and France. The manager of the equity growth fund purchases, on Joe's behalf, ordinary shares of companies listed on the London Stock Exchange (LSE). The pension fund will also invest Joe's contributions in a range of financial securities, including ordinary shares, central and local government bonds, and investment grade corporate bonds. The individual securities contained within these categories will themselves have distinct characteristics. For instance, the ordinary shares in Joe's portfolio will be in companies operating in different sectors of the economy, exposed to different market pressures and prospects, and guided by distinct management styles. Joe also holds a cash reserve in a savings account.

4.2 Different degrees of risk

The assets contained in a portfolio display differing degrees of risk. Fundamentally, risk is the possibility that the outcome of an investment turns out differently from what the investor expected. Savings accounts are generally considered among the lowest-risk investments, not least because deposits are, in

capital repayment mortgage
A mortgage payment method where the monthly instalments include two components, one directed to repaying the debt and the other to paying interest on the debt.

defined contribution pension
A type of pension scheme in which payments into the plan are specified, but the scale of benefits depends on the returns accruing to the scheme's assets.

equity growth fund
An asset management fund that places particular emphasis on the objective of acquiring shares deemed likely to offer significant capital growth.

many jurisdictions, guaranteed by the state. This doesn't mean that savings are perfectly risk free (no investment is). Even assuming confidence in government guarantees, the returns on savings accounts and similar investments are affected by uncertainties relating to inflation and the rates of interest offered by banks. Nevertheless, these factors do not significantly jeopardise the capital invested, except in extremely exceptional circumstances. The motives of protecting and preserving capital, rather than risking money in the quest for gain, figure more prominently in decisions to deposit funds in bank accounts.

Joe has been making repayments on a mortgage for nine years. At the start he might have expected to become wealthier as the amount owed against the property declines with each mortgage payment. Indeed Joe would probably have accepted the conventional wisdom that property values tend to rise more rapidly than inflation and, therefore, anticipated being better off still.

But property investment is riskier than depositing funds in a bank account. According to data from the Nationwide Building Society, the average house price in the UK fell by 10.4% in absolute terms between June 2007 and June 2012 – or 23.4% after taking inflation into account. Indeed, in real terms, the average house price in 2012 is similar to the price in 2003 – when Joe bought. We don't know if Joe has bought an 'average house'. Maybe he wisely (or luckily) bought better than average. But he might have bought worse. If he has bought the average, the subsequent increase in the value of the property has been sufficient only to compensate for the erosion of wealth due to inflation between 2003 and 2012. In this case, the property component of Joe's portfolio would have risen in value solely as a result of Joe making payments against the mortgage. It would be as if Joe has deposited the mortgage payments in an account that promised a return equal to the rate of inflation. Hardly disastrous, but not exactly what most property investors hope for or expect.

The other key component of Joe's portfolio consists of indirect investments in financial securities, via a pension fund and a managed equity fund. The values of these investments depend upon the market values of the constituent parts together with any income streams accruing to the securities. The values of publicly traded company shares can be subject to considerable uncertainty even when stock markets as a whole are relatively calm. On occasion, investors experience catastrophic losses or astonishing windfalls. Dividend payments on shares are also unpredictable. All in all, investing in company shares entails more immediate exposure to the vagaries and uncertainties of commerce and, therefore, depends on investors' assessments regarding future returns.

principal
In the case of bonds, the principal refers to the amount repayable on the maturity date of the bond.

The pension fund also invests in bonds offering pre-determined income streams (the most common form being a regular series of fixed interest payments over the specified period together with the return of the **principal** on the maturity date of the bond). Generally, bonds are less risky investments than shares. For instance, in a case of corporate bankruptcy, holders of a company's bonds have stronger claims to its assets than do its shareholders. Put simply, bondholders can generally rely on receiving what they are due from companies operating as going concerns and are more likely to recoup at least something in the event of bankruptcy.

The value of the pension fund to Joe will depend on factors other than the values of the underlying investments, including fund-related actions by his employer and the level of interest rates (more specifically, annuity rates) when he retires. Low interest rates are bad news for retirees. The demonstration of this point requires familiarity with a few technical issues addressed later.

In the later chapters of this book we will address the issue of risk in considerably more detail, highlighting in particular its impact on asset values, investors' reward expectations and portfolio management practice.

4.3 Liquid and illiquid assets

The assets contained in a portfolio differ in terms of their liquidity. The liquidity of an asset refers to the ease with which its value can be realised as money. In common parlance we talk of liquidating assets when referring to the act of selling them for cash.

Take the case of Joe's savings account. He can instruct the bank to close the account and hand over the cash or credit the funds to another account of his choosing. The process can be concluded immediately. There is little prospect of either Joe or the bank questioning the value of the asset since the account balance is known and adjustments for accumulated interest are routine. The savings account is, thus, very liquid. It is, for all intents and purposes, cash.

What about Joe's house? There are clear technical reasons why it takes longer to sell property, to do with the time needed for conveyance, surveyance, marketing and the arrangement of funding. Technical factors are pertinent to the understanding of liquidity of different asset classes, but they are not the most important considerations. The more significant sense in which property is a less liquid asset is that there is much more scope for disagreement over value. A particular valuation is an estimate of what the market (i.e. prospective buyers) will be prepared to pay for a property. Of course, we can expect estimates to be influenced by the prices at which comparable assets have recently traded. Yet circumstances can change quickly enough to make even the latest prices poor indicators of value. This is certainly the case with property if only because there is plenty of time from the start to the conclusion of the vending process for would-be buyers to reconsider.

The problem of liquidity has been a hot topic in reflections on the causes of the international financial crisis. The story, in concise terms, is as follows. The securities profession focused its talent for innovation on devising novel and eye-catching investment opportunities calculated to appeal to high-end investors such as fund managers (we'll take a closer look at some of these newer investment products later on). A recurrent problem was how to value these assets given that for many there was no active market from which to extract guide prices. The solution was to employ abstract models of asset prices in conjunction with powerful simulation software to produce theoretical values.

While financial markets boomed, the valuation problem didn't cause much concern. Many dealers appeared to welcome model-dependent asset valuation, viewing its apparent objectivity as useful in persuading investors that the high prices that they were paying were merited. The investors convinced themselves they were obtaining assets of high worth. In fact, investors were contentedly caught in a virtuous circle, using assets as collateral to borrow money to purchase yet more assets which, in turn, drove asset values even higher, making investors wealthier still.

But this virtuous circle eventually turned vicious. As asset prices stalled, lenders sought repayment of loans. Borrowers needed to liquidate assets to raise cash. But selling in unison prompted asset values to fall and so deterred would-be buyers. At the very moment when asset holders were desperate for the presence of liquid markets, holders of liquidity were not prepared to provide it. Lenders, predictably worried about the declining value of collateral, redoubled their insistence on immediate loan repayments, provoking an even greater clamour by the desperately cash-strapped to sell assets to the disinclined cash-rich at knockdown prices.

Stop and think 1.2

In the light of the discussion about asset liquidity, how would you assess the liquidity of Joe's pension and equity fund investments?

Test yourself 1.2

Dealers' screens show Vodafone PLC's shares trading at 190 pence. So far on a given day, nearly 30 million Vodafone shares have been traded. The screens also show EG Solutions PLC's shares trading at 64 pence, but this is the price after the last deal, which occurred five days ago.

If you wanted to sell shares in these two companies right now, which would be likely to be the most liquid in terms of the latest price being a reliable measure of what other investors will be prepared to offer?

4.4 Financial leverage

Financial leverage is about the extent to which investments are financed from borrowing. It is a relative concept, whereby the level of debt is compared to the total value of an asset portfolio. Someone who owes £1 million and owns assets worth £10 million is less leveraged than a person owing £10,000 with assets of £20,000.

Joe's portfolio includes two residential properties, both of which are partially financed by loans. As Joe makes mortgage payments the level of leverage should fall. However, in principle it could rise if the value of the assets in his portfolio were to fall.

Leverage is an important consideration for portfolio managers. They may be obliged to monitor and control leverage for regulatory reasons. They may regard the use of leverage as potentially shrewd and profitable. For instance, if you are optimistic about a particular asset, you will wish to invest in it. Borrowing money to increase your stake still further could turn out to be an astute move. Of course, you could end up looking foolish if your optimism is misplaced. Leverage also affects investors' tax liabilities because interest on debt is treated as a business expense for tax purposes.

Leverage may be present in a portfolio in less noticeable forms than loans. Derivative securities such as futures and options contracts can be used to create commitments that closely resemble assets acquired with loans. Other devices – generically known as shorting or short selling – enable investors to sell assets that they do not own. Short selling is the use of financial leverage, but instead of borrowing money to purchase assets, the investor borrows assets to purchase money. It's not as strange as it sounds. Short selling has come to feature more prominently in portfolio management over the years. We will have more to say about it later.

Worked example 1.2: The costs and benefits of financial leverage

Assume that shares in a company are trading at £1.00 and you expect the price to be £2.00 in a year. You have £10,000 in savings and a bank will permit you to borrow another £10,000 for one year at an interest rate of 10%. If you restrict the investment to the amount of savings and the share price rises as expected, your wealth increases from £10,000 to £20,000 – a return of 100%. But if you borrow £10,000 you can buy a total of £20,000 worth of shares, potentially worth £40,000 in a year. What is the rate of return on your capital of £10,000?

You have £40,000 worth of shares. Some must be sold to repay the loan. The total repayment is £11,000 (the £10,000 principal plus interest of £1,000). That leaves you with £29,000 – a return of 190% on your capital.

But what if you're wrong and the share price falls to £0.50? The 20,000 shares that you own are worth only £10,000. You must still pay the bank £11,000. Your capital has gone and you still owe the bank another £1,000. The upshot is that the scale of leverage affects portfolio performance, making it more volatile than it would be in the absence of leverage.

4.5 Structured products

Joe's portfolio includes a stake in an institutionally run equity fund that invests in UK company shares traded on the London Stock Exchange. If shares prices fall, this ought to cause a decline in the value of Joe's investment. Yet the fund offers some protection of capital (we are not told the precise details). How can this be the case? How can the fund protect Joe, and its other investors, when the sole source of wealth is the risky assets acquired using the financial contributions from those investors?

One possibility is that the fund manager invests in a mixture of low-risk bonds and FTSE 100 index options. The idea is that the bonds provide capital protection while option contracts offer the growth potential. It is an example of a structured product.

The importance of structured products in modern portfolio management is much greater than many investors appreciate. Numerous apparently straightforward investments, some targeted towards retail investors, are in essence complex structured products – products that rely on derivatives to reproduce a specific risk-return combination.

4.6 Hedging

As a UK resident, Joe is paid a salary in sterling. However, he is also obligated to make mortgage payments on his French property in euros. He acquires the necessary euros by purchasing them with sterling. There is a risk that the value of sterling will fall. This would make the euro-denominated mortgage more expensive because Joe would need to spend a greater amount of sterling to obtain the necessary euros.

Let's imagine that Joe plans to rent out the French property to holidaymakers when not using it himself. Furthermore, let's assume that he plans to charge rent in euros. In the event of sterling weakening, Joe's mortgage would still be more costly but the rental income would be worth more in sterling. The rental proceeds *hedge* (guard against) the effects of a weaker sterling on the cost of the mortgage. Admittedly, he could have avoided the currency risk at the outset by taking on a sterling-denominated mortgage to pay for the property. However, he may have found it much cheaper at the time to borrow euros than sterling and judged that the resulting currency risk was manageable in other ways.

Hedging is an integral feature of portfolio management. Investors take risks. They accept uncertainty in the expectation of being rewarded for doing so. They appreciate that sometimes the rewards are not forthcoming – the occasional failure is integral to risk taking. But investors should not be prepared to accept unnecessary risks, or risks for which there is no economic rationale for rewards. Such risks ought, in principle, to be hedged.

Joe's entry into French property is illustrative of the core purpose of hedging. The aim is to acquire ownership of a desired asset, not to speculate on the vagaries of exchange rates. Joe is at liberty to choose to do nothing and hope that sterling does not weaken. But this amounts to a gambling decision, not an investment decision. We expect investments to yield returns because investment is the application of savings to productive uses with the intention of generating increases in aggregate wealth. Using money denominated in one currency to buy money denominated in another currency is not investing but trading pure and simple. If the motive is to increase wealth, it is gambling because a 'win' can only occur as another's loss. The purpose of hedging is to protect investments from being undermined by the random, noisy, facets of functioning markets.

5. Client-centred portfolio management

Investors invest to realise objectives. The objectives differ. They may be specific or diverse, clear or ambiguous, fixed or changeable. Whatever the details, investors generally:

◆   prefer to receive more rather than less in return;

◆   have an impression of how much risk they are prepared to (or should) take on, and the riskiness of different investment options; and

◆   have some perspective about how long they wish to invest.

One problem facing investors is that these considerations produce complicated trade-offs that may be difficult to assess or may remain elusive. Investors face a further difficulty – the sheer scale of investment opportunities on offer. Savings accounts, government securities, corporate securities, investment trusts and funds, property, precious commodities, artistic works and many more things offer prospects for investment gain. The range of options within just a single category is daunting. We routinely use instinct, common sense and other heuristic methods quite successfully to screen out much of the information. Even so, the scale of choices remaining can still be intimidating.

The fundamental role of portfolio management is to help investors negotiate these difficulties and develop investment portfolios that minimise the cost of the necessary trade-offs and, in doing so, maximise the likelihood of investors realising their aims. It is no insult to suggest that many investors, probably even the majority, possess only a rudimentary sense of the benefits of adopting a portfolio approach to investment decision-making. Fewer still will be familiar with the technical terminology, theories and practices of portfolio management that have emerged from many decades of effort to understand and resolve complex investment problems. Indeed, a thorough grounding in this knowledge and a reputation for utilising it skilfully and discerningly in the sometimes charged environment of finance is scarce. It's a skill-set that offers a reasonable prospect of a well-rewarded career.

The roles of investment advisor and portfolio manager entail having a great deal of power *vis-à-vis* clients. The very act of consulting another party about investments or delegating to another party the management of investments implies great trust in that party. Clearly, advisors and managers have significant influence. Investors, therefore, face a perennial danger that the trust proves misplaced and is wilfully exploited by professionals for ulterior motives. (It should be stressed that this is different from managers recommending investments in good faith that subsequently fail. That's called risk.) In 2008 financier (now felon) Bernard Madoff admitted defrauding clients of billions of dollars. Of more concern is the suggestion by many biographers of the financial crisis that a culture of contempt towards clients has become more pervasive in some recesses of the financial markets, especially where fees and commissions are strongly dependent on continual product turnover.

Investment and portfolio management is not a one-size function. Some investors have great faith in their own expertise and might be interested in the opinions of others primarily as useful insights into market sentiment. We might refer to them as 'execution only' investors in that the financial services they are prepared to pay others for, often begrudgingly, do not extend much beyond the dealer-broker charges that are part of the institutional fabric in many areas of banking and securities trading.

Other investors routinely consult financial professionals on issues such as sourcing loans, trading financial securities and risk when seeking to decide on the best course of action. They welcome advice, and are prepared to pay for it, but retain control over the execution of investment decisions. A third group go further than advice-influenced investors, choosing a full portfolio management service. In this case, managers use their discretion to undertake and manage investments on behalf of clients. They do not consult clients on each and every decision, instead being guided by a broad understanding of clients' needs. In many cases, discretionary portfolio managers, rather than *respond to* clients, promote particular investment strategies with the intention of attracting clients. An obvious example is that of pooled investment funds, of which there are many thousands in the UK alone, offering all manner of distinctly constructed investment portfolios.

The enormous responsibilities on the shoulders of portfolio managers are reflected in codes of ethics, rules of disclosure and systems of compliance. Some operate as systems of behavioural standards articulated and applied by professional associations to their members and by market institutions to their participants. Other codes have statutory status and are operated by state, or state-sanctioned, bodies. For instance, both the Bank of England and the Financial Conduct Authority have regulatory oversight responsibilities for financial institutions operating within the jurisdiction of the United Kingdom.

Of course, the extent of both statutory and non-statutory codes varies across jurisdictions and is a cause of intense debate. Critics of tight government regulation argue that draconian rules, vigorously enforced, stifle business and ultimately involve high costs in terms of lower investment, leading to lower economic growth, lost tax revenues and so on. They also add that tight regulation encourages institutions to invest time and talent in devising compliance window-dressing initiatives and regulatory avoidance schemes. Advocates of tighter rules argue that light regulation is a charter for fraud and corruption which is costly far beyond the sums defrauded because the ensuing loss of confidence in financial institutions lowers investment, again leading to lower economic growth, lost tax revenues and so on.

Test yourself 1.3

In the United Kingdom the Financial Services Act 2012 resulted in the abolition of the Financial Services Authority (FSA). Its responsibilities were split between the Prudential Regulatory Authority (PRA), controlled by the Bank of England, and the Financial Conduct Authority (FCA).

a)   Identify the specific areas of financial regulation for which the PRA and the FCA are responsible.

b)   What were the arguments for abolishing the FSA in the aftermath of the banking crisis?

c)   In what ways does the new system of financial regulation introduced under the Financial Services Act 2012 differ from the old?

Chapter summary

◆   Investment is the productive employment of savings to enhance the wealth of investors in an inherently uncertain economic environment.

◆   Investors are assumed to be risk averse, meaning that investments deemed not to offer returns consistent with the scale of risk will be rejected.

◆   The amount of risk that individual investors are prepared to take is a product of both circumstances and subjective factors.

◆   Portfolio theory starts from the postulation that investment is essentially a trade-off between risk and expected return.

◆   The really important claim of portfolio theory is that investors can add assets with high expected returns to their portfolios without increasing the total risk of the portfolio.

◆   Important characteristics of a portfolio are: the extent of asset diversification, the individual asset risks, the degree of liquidity, the scale of financial leverage, the presence of structured investments and hedging.

◆   Portfolio management has become an increasingly institutionalised and specialised activity.

Chapter Two
Modern financial markets

List of topics

1   The new trading environment
2   OTC versus exchange trading
3   The security trading process

Introduction

The fundamental role of financial markets and institutions is to effect the movement of money from those with surpluses that they wish to hold in reserve for later use to those with shortages who wish to access additional funds now. Financial markets offer society a mechanism for managing this flow of funds efficiently. Some of the efficiency comes down to cost savings connected to the guardianship of reserves, recording of financial balances and transactions, standardisation of products, dissemination of information, trading procedures and enforcement of contractual obligations. It is easy to imagine how much more burdensome financial management would be in the absence of institutions with expertise in these various tasks.

Aside from operational cost benefits, financial institutions are generally able to make better decisions than individuals in isolation. This has nothing to do with any innate superiority of the persons involved. It is simply that financial institutions are better informed. For instance, systematic interaction with large numbers of clients means that banks are better placed to assess the creditworthiness of loan applicants than individual investors. They are also in a privileged position to identify where economic innovation is most pronounced because it is in these areas where shortages of capital are generally most pressing and demand for outside investment most intense. The upshot is that financial reserves ought, in general, to flow to those capable of using them most productively and profitably, to the benefit of society and investors as a whole.

Financial institutions are able to offer, at least within constraints imposed by broader market conditions, investment products tailored to specific preferences. Even in the case of something as basic as savings accounts, a casual perusal of a comparison website shows that there are scores of products with different trade-offs between interest rates, interest payment schedules and withdrawal notice periods. In 2010 the London Stock Exchange (LSE) launched a new trading platform in **retail bonds** that allows small investors to trade directly in a range of UK government and corporate bonds, something previously the preserve of institutional investors. Such initiatives, in theory, stimulate investment that might otherwise not occur and therefore provide an additional stimulus to wealth creation.

Of course the recent banking crisis, and earlier debacles such as the collapse of many so-called dot.com companies around the turn of the new millennium, demonstrates that the performance of financial institutions in managing investors' wealth is sometimes woeful. Much of the evidence even suggests that these crises were to some extent caused by financial institutions' adoption of irresponsible investment and trading practices that were always destined to cost many investors dear.

These events raise important issues about how markets and institutions ought to be structured and managed. But they do not invalidate the importance of financial markets to the pursuit of economic growth and wealth enhancement. There isn't scope to engage at length in a wide-ranging debate on these matters, though we will come across elements of it on numerous occasions. The main purpose of this chapter is to outline some important characteristics of the contemporary trading environment and the procedures involved.

1. The new trading environment

In 1965, 3.78 million **secondary market** security deals took place under the auspices of the LSE. By 2011 the figure had grown to over 178 million – a 47-fold increase. Most of the growth took place after 1990, with the number of transactions in 1990 still below 10 million. The values involved have increased by even more staggering proportions. In 1965 the value of the securities traded was £19.5 billion. By 2011, it was over £8.6 trillion – in the region of a 440-fold increase.

In 1971 the Chicago Mercantile Exchange (CME) added **futures contracts** on currency transactions to its existing list of mainly livestock-related futures contracts (pork bellies, cattle, hogs). By 2011 more than 3 billion futures and **options contracts** were being traded annually on the CME covering interest rates, currencies, equities, energy, metals and other commodities.

The LSE and CME typify one of the most significant developments in financial markets over the last 20 years or so – the vast increase in the intensity of security *trading*, in terms of both the numbers of deals and the values dealt. This trend is true of all securities exchanges. Furthermore, economic liberalisation and the broadening scope of economic development mean that there are now many more securities exchanges operating around the globe.

Aside from exchange-based dealing, there is also **over-the-counter** (OTC) dealing to consider. OTC transactions, many of which involve similar financial arrangements to those available on organised derivatives exchanges, are privately negotiated between counterparties (typically a bank and a client) rather

retail bond
The retail bond market is an electronic trading system launched by the London Stock Exchange in 2010. It is designed to facilitate trading in both corporate and government bonds in denominations small enough to appeal to retail investors.

secondary market
A market for trading already existing financial securities, in contrast to the primary market where new issues take place.

futures contract
An agreement to transact a specified amount of an asset at a predetermined price on a specific date in the future.

option contract
A right to transact a specified amount of an asset at a predetermined price on a specific date in the future.

over-the-counter
A generic term for financial market transactions undertaken directly between willing parties rather than on securities exchanges such as the London Stock Exchange.

than being effected through an exchange. The volume of OTC transactions is difficult to quantify because private agreements are not registered with exchanges that publish trading information. Nevertheless, data compiled by the Bank of International Settlements (BIS) on the value of OTC trade shows that deals operate on a mammoth scale. The market value of outstanding OTC arrangements at the end of 2011 was $27.3 trillion, a value equal to around half of world gross domestic product (GDP) that year.

The exponential growth of security trading is a cause of controversy. For some it is a benign consequence of investors exercising opportunities to rapidly create and adapt asset portfolios in accordance with changing circumstances. Aided by powerful information and deal-processing technologies, investors are able to adjust asset holdings and risk exposures almost instantaneously. The increased scale of dealing in the modern era reflects technical advances in asset management.

For others, the rise of a 'deal culture' in finance is a cause for consternation, symptomatic of the spread of an illusory faith in the notion that dealing pure and simple offers the prospect of systematic gains. Critics suggest that the proper economic function of financial markets, that of encouraging the movement of capital towards dynamic business ventures, is being compromised. In its place is a corrupted vision of financial markets as combat arenas where traders compete in games of chance that produce winners and losers, victors and vanquished.

Whatever the truth behind the seismic increases in trading activity, it is a development associated with major changes in the character of financial markets.

derivatives
A general term describing financial arrangements whose values derive from some underlying asset. A futures contract is an example of a derivative.

Stock exchange trading of corporate equities and financial **derivatives** has increased in intensity. In fact, the entire increase in trading on the LSE is equity related. More than 177 million of the 178 million trades on the LSE in 2011 (around 99.6% of the total) were equity trades. By contrast, the 730,000 transactions involving government and corporate bonds in 2011 were unexceptional by historical standards.

Equity trading has also increased in its global scope with the emergence and growth of new exchanges, especially in countries where economic growth has been most pronounced. A striking example is that of the Shanghai Stock Exchange (SSE) which didn't open until 1990. By the end of 2011 there were 931 companies quoted on the SSE with a market capitalisation of nearly $2.35 trillion (based on a renminbi/dollar exchange rate of ¥6.325:$1).

The expansion of derivatives trading has seen institutions such as the Chicago Mercantile Exchange, the London International Financial Futures and Options Exchange (which via a complex series of mergers and takeovers is now part of IntercontinentalExchange) and Eurex grow from modest localised operations to global trading platforms. These exchanges trade a range of contracts related to commodity prices, the values of equities and equity indices, government bond prices, interest rates and currency rates. More recently they have broadened the product range to include contracts on energy prices, property prices and weather-related risks. A more detailed examination of how derivatives work is provided in Chapter 9.

Debt securities are traded far less frequently than equities. But in terms of the values involved things have changed dramatically. Those 730,000 deals accounted for £6 trillion of the £8.6 trillion worth of the securities traded on the LSE in 2011 (around 70% of the total). The average value transacted per deal has grown from around £44,000 in 1965 to over £8 million in 2011.

Stop and think 2.1

Bond prices tend to be less volatile than equity prices (the reasons are a subject for a later chapter). Try to work out why assets whose prices tend to be more stable over time are liable to be traded less frequently.

Some financial arrangements offered OTC are similar to securities traded on organised derivatives exchanges. For instance, forward exchange rates exhibit features in common with currency futures and forward rate agreements resemble interest rate futures in some respects. However, OTC markets also offer arrangements that are difficult or costly to replicate on an exchange. Swap agreements are a case in point. Of the $27.3 trillion of outstanding OTC arrangements recorded by the BIS at the end of 2011, nearly $21 trillion consisted of interest rate swaps, currency swaps and credit default swaps.

2. OTC versus exchange trading

While OTC and exchange dealing arrangements are similar in some aspects, they differ in the way that deals are structured. Two aspects are worth stressing:

◆   standardised versus tailored products; and
◆   margin requirements and counterparty risk.

2.1 Standardised versus tailored products

Securities traded on derivatives exchanges are standardised whereas corresponding OTC deals are more customised to specific requirements. A comparison of currency futures with forward exchange rates illustrates the point.

The CME operates a market in currency futures contracts offering dealers a mechanism for controlling risks associated with foreign exchange markets. Exchange rates are volatile and unpredictable. Currency futures enable dealers to establish rates of exchange in the present on currency transactions due to occur in the future. They therefore shield contract holders from the effects of changes in exchange rates.

The currency futures traded on the CME are standardised in terms of the cash sums involved. Take the example of a futures contract that facilitates the exchange of US dollars for British sterling. It specifies a contract size of £62,500.

A purchaser of a £/$ future effectively agrees to buy £62,500 for a fixed amount of US dollars at some point in the future.

The future currency delivery dates are also standardised. The £/$ currency futures market offers contracts with quarterly delivery dates on the third Wednesday in March, June, September and December. For instance, the purchase of a March 2013 contract amounts to a commitment to buy £62,500 on 20 March 2013, paying dollars in exchange.

The control over exchange rates offered by currency futures arises from the *futures price*, which in the case of the contract in question is the price of sterling quoted in dollars. The futures price is, in effect, a price available now at which sterling can be purchased in the future. If the futures price for the March 2013 contract was $1.6250 at the time of purchase, it means that the buyer agrees to pay $1.6250 per pound sterling on the delivery date in March, a total payment of $101,562.50 in return for £62,500. The result is that for the contract holder the exchange rate is fixed at £1/$1.6250; it is not affected by changes in the actual £/$ exchange rate during the period leading up to the delivery date.

Test yourself 2.1

An American company is due to pay £125,000 to a UK supplier in 30 days.

a) **Explain the character of the currency risk facing the American company.**

b) **How many £/$ futures contracts ought the company to buy if it wishes to protect itself from exchange rate risk?**

Protection against exchange rate uncertainty can also be acquired OTC by entering into a forward exchange with a bank. A forward currency exchange is an undertaking to trade a pair of currencies in the future at a rate agreed now. Like futures, forwards offer users the possibility of mitigating the effects of exchange rate uncertainty. But unlike futures the terms are not standardised. The sums involved and the delivery dates are agreed between the client and the dealer bank. Forward agreements are, therefore, more closely tailored to clients' needs.

The most common types of futures contracts and forward agreements relate to short-term interest rates and currency rates. Aside from exchange rates, businesses and investors are also sensitive to possible interest rate uncertainties. For instance, investors planning to hold forthcoming earnings in reserve might believe that interest rates are set to fall and, as a result, may choose to fix the future rate now by means of either futures or forwards.

marked to market
The practice of marking down profits and losses at the end of each trading day based on market prices.

2.2 Margin requirements and counterparty risk

Futures contracts are typically **marked to market**. This means that the futures price at the close of the market each day (actually a modified form of closing price known as the **settlement price**) is used as a basis for crediting and debiting gains and losses to and from contract dealers. Marking to market means that gains and losses are effectively cash settled immediately rather than carried forward. For instance, assume that the £/$ contract price rises from $1.6250 to $1.6300 – an increase of half a cent. The buyer of the contract makes a gain equivalent to the increase in the dollar cost of £62,500:

$$£62,500(1.6300-1.6250) = £312.50$$

The sum of £312.50 is credited to the buyer of the contract and debited from the seller of the contract.

The credits and debits flow into and out of accounts that investors are required to hold with brokers for the purpose of trading futures. They are known as **margin accounts**, accounts that allow investors to trade securities using funds borrowed from brokers. The 'margin' is the component of the total investment that must be funded from an investor's own wealth and constitutes collateral for the broker lending funds. Investors routinely supplement their own capital with funds borrowed from brokers to finance investment in a whole range of securities, not just exchange-traded derivatives. The amounts that investors are permitted to borrow are determined by brokers' margin requirements. For instance, if a broker is prepared to lend money on the basis of an **initial margin** of 50%, it means that an investor must finance at least 50% of any new investment from personal wealth.

settlement price
The 'market' price at the close of trade that is used to mark down profits and losses.

margin account
A dealing account in which a broker permits a client to trade on credit in return for the deposit of a margin.

initial margin
The proportion of a margin-based investment that must be financed from the investor's resources.

Worked example 2.1: Margin accounts

An investor wishes to purchase £20,000 of securities via a margin account held with a broker who operates on the basis of an initial margin of 50%. The investor would need to post the 50% margin of £10,000 to the account which, along with another £10,000 lent by the broker, is used to purchase the securities. The securities are held by the broker on behalf of the investor with half their total value being collateral for the loan.

Assume that the broker operates on the basis of a **maintenance margin** of 40%. This means that after the initial investment the collateral component must always be worth at least 40% of the total. Assume that the value of the securities falls to £16,000. The collateral falls to £6,000 because the investor still owes the broker £10,000. The margin falls to:

$$\frac{£6,000}{£16,000} \times 100 = 37.5\%$$

maintenance margin
A minimum level of collateral that an investor must maintain in a margin account.

The 37.5% margin is below the maintenance level and would result in the investor receiving a **margin call** from the broker. The investor has two options. The first is deposit additional cash in the account to bring the margin back up to the maintenance level. A deposit of approximately £700 would be required, raising the value of the collateral to £6,700 and the total value in the margin account to £16,700.

margin call
An instruction to deposit additional capital into a margin account that occurs when collateral falls below the maintenance level.

$$\frac{£6,700}{£16,700} \times 100 = 40.12\%$$

The second option is to sell some of the securities and use the proceeds to reduce the debt. The sale of £1,000 of securities cuts the debt to £9,000 and the amount deposited in the account to £15,000, while the collateral is still £6,000.

$$\frac{\pounds 6,000}{\pounds 15,000} \times 100 = 40\%$$

Trading futures is inherently leveraged. The purchase of a £/$ futures contract is an obligation to buy £62,500 with dollars on a specific date in the future at a pre-determined price without having to demonstrate ownership of sufficient dollars at the outset. At the time of writing, CME rules require that traders deposit an initial margin of $1,320 for each open £/$ futures contract traded. The $1,320 is collateral enabling dealers to trade the dollar value of £62,500. The CME also specifies a maintenance margin for the £/$ futures contract of $1,200 per contract. In the event of losses causing collateral to fall below $1,200, traders receive margin calls.

Test yourself 2.2

Assume that you purchased a £/$ futures contract when the futures price was $1.6250. The futures price has since fallen to $1.6150. The initial margin is $1,320 and the maintenance margin is $1,200.

a)   How much would be debited from your initial margin?

b)   How much would you need to deposit into the margin account to reach the maintenance level?

The main purpose of the margin system associated with trading futures and other securities is to minimise counterparty risk. The purchase of a futures contract represents a commitment to buy the underlying asset at a fixed price in the future. The sale of the contract is therefore a commitment to sell the underlying asset at a fixed price. If the price changes, one side must lose money. Hence there is, in principle, an ever-present incentive for losers to default. Margin arrangements offer counterparties some protection against default. In the case of futures, counterparty risk is, in a loose sense, limited to one day's worth of losses because failure to heed a margin call is liable to result in the guilty party's trading positions being closed.

In the case of OTC agreements such as forward exchange rates, counterparty risk is addressed by means of bilateral negotiation. Typically, agreements do not involve mark to market payments, meaning that gains and losses can accumulate. In theory this ought to make the incentive to default greater than is the case for marked to market securities. As a result, banks that act as counterparties to forward transactions often require that clients deposit funds with third parties as collateral. In the event of default, the bank can seize the funds.

The dilemma is that the setting aside of substantial amounts of capital reduces the incentive to enter forward agreements. Potential clients might be put off because they face forfeiting considerable amounts of interest on the funds over the term of the forward agreement. There are also the costs of compensating third parties to factor in. Another possibility is that a client might not have sufficient funds. Imagine an extreme situation where a US company needs to buy £500,000 with dollars in three months and a bank demands that it set aside the dollar equivalent today as a condition of agreeing a £/$ forward exchange rate. The company might as well use the dollars to buy sterling today outright at the prevailing **spot price**. A forward exchange offers no advantage.

The amount of collateral required by a bank will depend on the client's standing and reputation. It is liable to be affected by how much business the client already conducts with the bank. In many instances, arrangements similar to a mark to market system result from negotiations. A relatively small amount of capital is posted as collateral at the outset but is then subject to periodic adjustments in accordance with changes in the value of the underlying asset.

spot price
Refers to the prices of assets such as currencies and traded commodities involving immediate settlement. In practice immediate settlement normally means two to three business days.

3. The security trading process

Trading procedures in financial markets are highly formalised. Trades must be executed, the transfer and custody of securities effected, and payments settled. Trades must be booked and checked for errors. They must comply with external regulations and accord with internally developed risk management systems. They may necessitate the distribution of fees and commissions to salespeople and other parties. All are time- and resource-consuming procedures that have, to a considerable extent, evolved into specialised domains.

When investors trade securities, there are a number of aspects to the process. Some are specific to the type of security being traded or the market on which the trade takes place. Nevertheless, there are significant generic elements. For purposes of illustration we focus on the trading process characteristic of the London Stock Exchange.

Investors buy and sell securities via brokers with whom they will have trading accounts and to whom they are required to pay brokerage fees. The scale of payments depends first on whether an investor chooses full-service broking or an execution only service. The former provides investment advice and trade recommendations as well as trade execution and is, consequently, more expensive. The second factor affecting brokerage fees is, of course, the scale and frequency of trades undertaken. Nowadays brokerage services are readily available to small investors via the internet with single trade fees starting at around £10. Larger institutional investors will have more complex relations with brokers and will deal through a number of brokers rather than a single one.

The essence of the brokerage function is to act as an agent representing the interests of a client. In a basic sense, the broker should seek to obtain the highest possible price for those wishing to sell and the lowest for those wishing to buy.

Orders for company shares included in the FTSE All-Share Index, and for more liquid smaller company shares, are placed directly on to an electronic trading system known as SETS (there are alternative trading platforms for less liquid shares and other securities). SETS automatically matches and executes buy and sell orders, subject to terms stipulated by investors. An investor might want a simple 'at best' transaction which amounts to buying or selling at the best available price. A 'stop' order stipulates a particular price at which the investor is prepared to trade and can be parked on SETS for a period of time. If the stop price is met the order is executed, either entirely or partially. Any unfilled element or the order is eliminated. A 'limit' order specifies a 'no worse than' price and allows for the order to be filled gradually over a specified period of time. Hence a 'stop limit' order is one that starts off as a stop order and becomes a limit order once the stop price is reached.

An order includes a range of details. There is a company ticker symbol, which is the most common means of identifying the security in question. For example, the ticker symbol for Rio Tinto PLC shares traded on the New York Stock Exchange is RIO. For shares traded in London it is RIO.L, while for shares traded in Australia it is RIO.AX. As well as the ticker symbol, shares traded on the LSE also have a seven-digit SEDOL number (Stock Exchange Daily Official List) which identifies the security during the clearing process. For Rio Tinto the SEDOL number is 0718875.

Aside from the identity of the security being traded, an order also includes details such as the asset class, the status of the order, whether it is a buy or sell order, the number of securities traded and the price at which the bargain was struck.

Once a trade is undertaken, the clearing and settlement process starts. Clearing is integrated into the LSE's trading system. When a trade takes place it is actually two trades: one between the buyer and a central counterparty, and one between the seller and the central counterparty. The counterparty clears the trade for both sides, so that in the event of default by the buyer or seller, the other side is still able to complete the trade. In addition to reducing counterparty risk, clearing technology offers a centralised framework for transferring security ownership, crediting and debiting broker accounts, and maintaining records of trades. It therefore reduces the need to deliver securities in the form of certificates and move money through the writing of cheques and other time consuming transfer methods.

Normal practice on the LSE is for settlement to occur three days after a trade. The brokers for buyer and seller should have received payments from the buyer and titles of security ownership from the seller after three days. In practice, brokers often hold securities on behalf of a client in a **nominee account**, which is an account in the name of the broker but the contents of which are owned by the client. Nominee accounts offer advantages to clients in the form of the custody of securities, the keeping of records and transfer of securities arising from trades. They help effect the timely transfer of securities because there is no need to chase clients for ownership documentation.

nominee account
A security trading account where the nominated account holder (normally a broker) administers assets on behalf of clients defined as the beneficial owners.

Brokerages and institutional investors carry out a number of activities connected to security trading that are sometimes described as back office procedures.

◆ Trades occur in large volumes and involve sizeable sums. Confirming trades with counterparties and checking for errors in the recording of deals is therefore extremely important.

◆ The incorporation of new trades and their risks into broader portfolios of assets must be carried out. So must the impact of trades on the timing and character of future cash flows. Much of this work is computerised and automated, due to the high level of complexity and amounts of data involved.

◆ Innovations in financial products and trading strategies need to be tested to establish whether or not they are likely to work in practice in an efficient and cost-effective manner.

◆ There are compliance issues to consider. Securities exchanges, government-sponsored regulatory bodies and trade organisations enforce laws, design rules and promote codes of practice in relation to trading and investment. Institutions are responsible for ensuring that they comply with these strictures. Failure to do so can be costly. For instance, in recent years, banks and other lenders in the UK have been forced pay fines running into millions of pounds and have set aside many more millions to pay compensation claims after being found guilty of mis-selling **payment protection insurance**.

◆ Monitoring and ensuring the accountability of the front desk, of securities dealers and asset managers, is a critically important function of the back office. It is arguably the most difficult task as traders naturally tend not to appreciate directives from what many regard as mere support services. Traders are often at an advantage in the power plays that go on, being able to claim they are making the profits while the back office is pure expense.

payment protection insurance
A type of insurance designed to offer the policyholder some protection from the burden of loan repayments in the event of loss of income.

Chapter summary

◆ The fundamental economic role of financial markets and institutions is to facilitate an efficient movement of funds from those in possession of reserves to those in need of additional capital.

◆ Trading of financial securities has become has become a more prominent feature of financial market, suggesting a decline in the inclination to buy and hold over extended periods.

◆ Financial transactions and securities dealing take place on organised exchanges and via OTC arrangements.

◆ Exchange traded instruments tend to be highly standardised in terms of size, pricing procedures, maturity dates and settlement practices. OTC products exhibit more bespoke characteristics.

◆ Trading 'on margin' is routine practice. It means that it is common for investors and traders to employ leverage in an effort to bolster returns. It also suggests, however, that they are taking greater risks with their wealth.

◆ The growing scale of security trading has been accompanied by a proliferation of support functions. Some have been driven by the obvious need for close scrutiny and systematic error checking when huge volumes of transactions are involved. Others, such as risk assessment, have grown as a result of the increasing breadth and complexity of assets and asset portfolios being managed. There are also functions influenced by external pressures. Governments and central banks require adherence to rules covering disclosure of information, professional practice and consumer protection.

Part Two

The analysis of risk and return

Overview

Part Two focuses on the development of portfolio theory as an approach to interpreting the relationship between asset returns and how they connect to the business and economic uncertainties facing investors. Chapter 3 concentrates on the measurement of return and the effects of asset diversification on risk. Chapter 4 examines how earlier insights were developed into highly influential and tractable techniques that have aided investors in their decision-making about the trade-off between risk and return. Chapter 5 highlights some of the limitations of investment practices built on portfolio theory and how, according to some observers, it has caused considerable harm in the fields of investment and asset management.

Learning objectives

At the end of this part, students will be able to:

◆ demonstrate an understanding of how to calculate portfolio returns;

◆ demonstrate an understanding of how asset risk is measured;

◆ appreciate the impact of asset diversification on portfolio risk;

◆ tackle problems involving the measurement of the risk of a two-asset portfolio;

◆ tackle exercises based on the use of asset betas to determine expected portfolio returns;

◆ appreciate the implications of the view, put forward by efficient market hypothesis (EMH), that asset prices are primarily the product of objective, reasoned assessments by investors based on available information;

◆ articulate an explanation of the three levels of market efficiency as outlined by EMH; and

◆ demonstrate knowledge of the main arguments of prospect theory and behavioural finance, and their implications for the theory and practice of portfolio management.

Chapter Three
Portfolio risk and return

List of topics

1   The return on equity
2   The portfolio return
3   Security risk
4   The measurement of security risk
5   The measurement of portfolio risk

Introduction

In principle, anything that offers a reasonable prospect of yielding an income and/or appreciating in value can be incorporated into investment portfolios and treated as a capital asset. The tools, machines, materials and buildings deployed productively by businesses are obvious examples. So is the panoply of interest-yielding financial arrangements, company shares, public and private sector bonds, investment funds and so on that constitute the world of finance. The purchase of a home with the intention of letting means regarding residential property as a capital asset. But the issue is less clear cut in the case of buying a residential property for personal use, because both investment and consumption motives are at work. We can make a case for regarding works of art, jewellery, antiques and collectibles as capital assets despite the importance of non-pecuniary, aesthetic considerations motivating their acquisition.

Despite the vast array of things included in investment portfolios, much of the energy devoted to explaining how portfolios work has paradoxically focused on a very particular asset, namely company shares. In fact, the empirical foundations for most of the research are even narrower, being largely restricted to those company shares that are publicly traded on stock exchanges. What is routinely referred to as *modern portfolio theory* is, in the main, an investigation of the interaction between risk and return in the realm of exchange-traded corporate equities. Nevertheless, this does not automatically compromise the significance of its claims. Researchers across all fields have long appreciated that universally important insights often emerge from intensely concentrated investigations.

1. The return on equity

Philip Morris International Incorporated is a tobacco company listed on the New York Stock Exchange (NYSE). In 2011 it sold over 915 billion cigarettes worldwide, generating revenues in excess of $76 billion. In early September 2012 its ordinary share capital was valued at just over $150 billion, making it the thirteenth largest company included in the **S&P 500 index**. Johnson & Johnson is the world's largest healthcare products company and is also listed on the New York Stock Exchange. In 2011 its sales totalled just over $65 billion. In early September 2012 its ordinary share capital was valued at over $185 billion, making it the eighth largest company in the S&P 500 index.

S&P 500 index
A performance index based on the securities of 500 US companies publicly traded on either the New York or National Association of Securities Dealers Automated Quotations (NASDAQ) stock markets.

Imagine that you purchased shares in Philip Morris and Johnson & Johnson on 1 September 2009 and are in the process of reviewing the performance of your investments three years later on 31 August 2012. Table 3.1 shows the prices that you paid for the shares in 2009, what the shares were worth three years later and the total dividend per share that you would have received from each company over the three years.

Table 3.1 Share prices and dividend payments

	Philip Morris	**Johnson & Johnson**
Share price on 1 September 2009	$45.16	$59.94
Share price on 31 August 2012	$89.30	$67.43
Cumulative dividend per share 2009–12	$7.96	$6.64

Over the three years, your investments yielded rewards in the form of dividend payments and higher shares prices. In the case of Philip Morris the share price rose from $45.16 to $89.30 and you received dividends totalling $7.96 on each share. This represents a percentage return on your investment of:

$$\left[\frac{(89.30 + 7.96) - 45.16}{45.16}\right] \cong 1.154 \ (115.4\%)$$

In the case of Johnson & Johnson, the rate of return was approximately 23.6%.

Test yourself 3.1

Calculate the rate of return on the Johnson & Johnson investment and confirm the result cited in the text.

The rate of return on investments in company shares over a stated period of time is, therefore, a product of the change in the share price over the period and the dividends paid during the period. The procedure used to calculate the rates of return on Philip Morris and Johnson & Johnson can be expressed in the general form:

$$r_t = \left[\frac{(P_t + \Sigma_{i=1}^{n} d_i) - P_{t-1}}{P_{t-1}} \right]$$

Where:

◆ r_t = rate of return on the share over the investment period to time t;

◆ P_t = share price at time t;

◆ P_{t-1} = share price at the start of the investment period; and

◆ $\Sigma_{i=1}^{n} d_i$ = sum of the dividends over the investment term.

Stop and think 3.1

The usual procedure in financial calculations is to express percentages as portions of 1 rather than 100. Hence 1% appears as 0.01, 5% as 0.05, 50% as 0.5, 100% as 1.0 and so on. It is perfectly acceptable to employ the more familiar style when commenting on results.

Test yourself 3.2

a) **Assume that a company has just paid an annual dividend of 14 pence. Its share price on the dividend payment date was 540 pence. One year ago the share price stood at 485 pence. Calculate the annual return on equity.**

b) **Assume that another company has just paid an annual dividend of 22 pence. Its share price on the dividend payment date was 422 pence. One year ago the share price stood at 467 pence. Calculate the annual return on equity.**

c) **What is the significant factor causing a wide difference between the two rates of return?**

---

2. The portfolio return

Let's assume that back in September 2009 you acquired a portfolio consisting of 1000 shares in Philip Morris and 1000 shares in Johnson & Johnson. It would have cost you $105,100, as laid out below:

Philip Morris	1000 × $45.16 = $45,160
Johnson & Johnson	1000 × $59.94 = $59,940
Cost of investment	$105,100

Three years later those same shares were worth $156,730 and you would have received cash dividends from the two companies of $14,600. The value of your portfolio had risen to $171,330. In percentage terms the return on your portfolio grew by:

$$\left[\frac{(\$171,330 - 105,100)}{105,100}\right] = 0.63$$

The value of your portfolio rose by 63% over the three-year period.

We can arrive at the same result by a slightly different route. The initial investment of $105,100 is divided between two assets the significance of which we can express as weightings (w).

$$W_{PM}\left(\frac{45,160}{105,100}\right) = 0.4297$$

$$W_{JJ}\left(\frac{59,940}{105,100}\right) = 0.5703$$

Approximately 43% of the original funds were invested in Philip Morris shares, with the remaining 57% invested in Johnson & Johnson shares. Recall the rates of return on the two companies were 115.4% and 23.6% respectively. Multiplying these returns by the weightings and adding the result gives the portfolio return:

$$(0.4297 \times 1.154) + (0.5703 \times 0.236) = 0.63$$

It is the same result as before. The return on a portfolio is simply the sum of the individual returns that have each been multiplied by their proportional significance within the portfolio. More succinctly, the portfolio return is a weighted average of the individual security returns. Furthermore, this is true for portfolios consisting of any number of assets, so that:

$$r_{p,t} = \sum_{i=1}^{n} r_{i,t} w_i$$

Where:

◆ $r_{p,t}$ = portfolio rate of return over the investment period to t;

◆ $r_{i,t}$ = rate of return on each share in the portfolio over the investment period; and

◆ w_i = weighting of each constituent investment in the portfolio.

Test yourself 3.3

a) What if, instead of purchasing 1,000 shares in each company, you had bought 1,500 shares in Philip Morris and 500 shares in Johnson & Johnson? How would this have affected the size of your initial investment and your portfolio return over the subsequent three year period?

b) Alternatively, imagine that you originally bought only 500 shares in Philip Morris and 1,500 shares in Johnson & Johnson. Again work out the implications for the initial investment and the return.

c) Think about why the portfolio return changes with the weightings of the constituent investments.

3. Security risk

It is difficult to imagine many investment analysts in September 2009 anticipating that Philip Morris would be a double-your-money investment within three years. The US stock markets were picking up after a momentous collapse of share prices during 2008 and early 2009, but the pace of recovery was hardly encouraging. Most assessments of Philip Morris were muted with concerns expressed about its heavy reliance on sales in depressed European economies, the implications of anti-smoking legislation in many jurisdictions around the world and the potentially adverse impact of a rising US dollar exchange rate on a company that receives much of its sales revenues in other currencies.

Stop and think 3.2

Try to work out how an increase in the US dollar exchange rate could have an adverse effect on the profitability of a US company that receives a large portion of its revenues in other currencies.

Other analysts, far fewer in number, were more optimistic. They also focused on the distinctively international character of Philip Morris' business, arguing that its established presence in many emerging economies coupled with the aspirational status of the Marlboro brand offered the possibility of dynamic sales growth to offset possible stagnating demand in Europe and elsewhere. The optimists argued that Philip Morris' performance fundamentals (profit margins, earnings per share, earnings growth, etc) were markedly better than those of many similar companies. On both current performance and future potential, they believed Philip Morris to be undervalued and advised clients to invest.

These contrasting assessments highlight the predicament at the heart of investment and asset management. Investors would ideally like to know what is going to happen in the future. But they can't know. They can examine the available information for hints and insights into the prospects for different investment opportunities, form opinions and invest accordingly. Yet the fact remains that investors do not know at the outset how any given investment will perform. They are risking wealth because outcomes are unknowable until after the event.

Not surprisingly, investors take a keen interest in the degree to which they are risking their wealth. They want to know about the scale of risk associated with different investments. The analysts' assessments of Philip Morris, mentioned above, refer to a number of factors with uncertain implications; economic stagnation in Europe, anti-smoking agendas, exchange rate uncertainties and emerging market demand. Further investigation would furnish us with many more uncertainties to consider and through a painstaking process we can arrive at an overall risk-reward perspective on Philip Morris.

One problem with this narrative style of risk analysis is that it makes comparisons problematic. While two investments may share some risk factors, they will also face others of a more idiosyncratic character. Even in the case of the shared risk factors, the scale of exposure may differ. In many instances, it will be difficult to decide which of the two is the riskier investment overall. There is the additional problem that the qualitative analysis of risk is time-consuming and resource-demanding. Imagine, having satisfied yourself that the assessment of Philip Morris is complete, you then have to start on Johnson & Johnson, then a third company, a fourth and so on. There simply isn't enough time even to scratch the surface of all the investment options.

The identification and assessment of factors pertinent to appreciating the uncertainties inherent to investment will always be essential. But when decisions must be made about the structure of asset portfolios, especially large portfolios, it is seen by many in the profession as too cumbersome. Portfolio managers want to be able to sidestep the need to continually specify and review risk factors in detail. The solution is to adopt a quantitative approach to risk assessment.

4. The measurement of security risk

As mentioned earlier, Johnson & Johnson's share price grew from $59.94 to $67.43 over three years. But it didn't grow smoothly or evenly. Table 3.2 records the price changes for each month of the three-year period and reveals a much more chaotic-looking process than the start and finishing points might suggest.

Table 3.2 Johnson & Johnson monthly share price and return 2009–12

Date	Share price	Price change (%)
01/09/2009	$59.94	–
01/10/2009	$59.81	–0.22%
02/11/2009	$59.49	–0.54%
01/12/2009	$63.51	6.54%
31/12/2009	$64.41	1.41%
01/02/2010	$63.09	–2.07%
01/03/2010	$63.39	0.47%
01/04/2010	$65.77	3.69%
30/04/2010	$64.30	–2.26%
01/06/2010	$58.76	–9.01%
01/07/2010	$59.07	0.53%
02/08/2010	$58.72	–0.59%
01/09/2010	$58.29	–0.73%

Date	Share price	Price change (%)
01/10/2010	$61.75	5.77%
01/11/2010	$63.69	3.09%
01/12/2010	$62.42	–2.01%
31/12/2010	$61.85	–0.92%
01/02/2011	$60.63	–1.99%
01/03/2011	$60.70	0.12%
01/04/2011	$59.49	–2.01%
02/05/2011	$66.21	10.70%
01/06/2011	$66.48	0.41%
01/07/2011	$67.30	1.23%
01/08/2011	$64.41	–4.39%
01/09/2011	$65.33	1.42%
30/09/2011	$63.69	–2.54%
01/11/2011	$63.38	–0.49%
01/12/2011	$64.45	1.67%
03/01/2012	$65.88	2.19%
01/02/2012	$65.69	–0.29%
01/03/2012	$64.83	–1.32%
02/04/2012	$66.21	2.11%
01/05/2012	$65.22	–1.51%
01/06/2012	$61.78	–5.42%
02/07/2012	$68.00	9.59%
01/08/2012	$69.38	2.01%
31/08/2012	$67.43	–2.85%

The third column of table 3.2 shows the monthly (log-normal) percentage change in the share price. For instance, the price was $59.94 at the outset and fell to $59.81 by the end of the first month, representing a percentage price fall of just over two-tenths of 1%, i.e.:

$$ln\left(\frac{59.81}{59.94}\right) \times 100 = -0.22\%$$

The share price sometimes rose and sometimes fell. In some instances the percentage variation was significant and in others less so. Adding the percentage changes together and dividing by 36 (the number of months) gives the average monthly price change. In the case of Johnson & Johnson, its share price rose by 0.33% per month on average. Investors in Johnson & Johnson shares would have earned on average (ignoring dividend payments) nearly 0.33% per month from 1 September 2009 *if they persisted in holding them* until 31 August 2012. But would they have persisted?

The issued share capital of Johnson & Johnson consisted of just under 3.12 billion shares. Over the period in question, there were 758 stock market trading days. The average *daily* turnover of Johnson & Johnson shares was nearly 12.2 million. That adds up to transactions of over 9 billion Johnson & Johnson shares, equivalent to each share changing hands three times. Of course, some shares would have changed hands considerably more times, while others fewer times or not at all. It means that there is considerable scope for the returns accruing to individual investors to deviate from the average return. For example:

◆ After a year (September 2010) the share price had fallen $1.65 to $58.29. Some investors, maybe frustrated at the declining share price, might have decided to sell. Far from earning 0.33% a month, they would have lost money.

◆ Those who purchased shares at the September 2010 price would have a good chance of earning above the 0.33% monthly average.

◆ An investor who sold in July 2011, when the share price reached $67.30, would have earned more than the monthly average.

There are countless possible scenarios that point to the fact that most investors will not earn the average return over a specified period because they will not have held the investment for precisely that period. Individual actual returns are liable to differ from the average return. The critical point is that the scale of the divergence between actual and average returns provides a framework for quantitatively representing the uncertainty, or risk, associated with the average return.

One possibility is to measure the extent to which the best and worst returns deviate from the average. In the case of Johnson & Johnson the best monthly return was 10.70% and the worst was −9.01%, producing deviations of:

$$\text{Upside deviation} = 10.70 - 0.33 = 10.37\%$$
$$\text{Downside deviation} = -9.01 - 0.33 = -9.34\%$$

But this provides a limited insight into the risk, since it ignores everything except for the most extreme results. By definition, extreme changes occur sporadically. Investors also need a sense of the uncertainty that they can expect to face on a routine basis. In effect, alongside the average return investors want a measure of the average risk, a measure of the average amount by which the actual return is prone to deviate from the average return.

This loosely formulated notion of average risk can be given a more precise representation in the statistical concepts of *variance* and *standard deviation* or, more generally, mean-variance analysis. The framing of the investment risk-return relationship in terms of mean and variance is standard portfolio management practice.

The mean return is simply the average return that we have already encountered. In the case of Johnson & Johnson the mean monthly return is 0.33%. The variance and standard deviation are normally symbolised mathematically using the Greek letter σ (sigma) and can be calculated as follows:

$$\text{Variance} = \sigma r_i^2 = \frac{\Sigma(r_{i,t} - \bar{r}_i)^2}{N}$$

$$\text{Standard deviation} = \sigma r_i = \sqrt{\frac{\Sigma(r_{i,t} - \bar{r}_i)^2}{N}}$$

Where:

◆ σr_i^2 = Variance of returns on security i;

◆ σr_i = Standard deviation of returns on security i;

◆ $r_{i,t}$ = Rate of return on security i for each time period;

◆ $\bar{r}_i$ = Mean (average) rate of return on security i; and

◆ N = Number of observed t period returns.

Let's take an intuitive approach to these equations to understand how they measure risk.

◆ The expression $r_{i,t} - \bar{r}_i$ is the difference between each periodic return (in our example monthly) and the average return. It is, in effect, a measure of the deviation of the actual return from the mean return.

◆ The calculation of the variance consists of summing the squared values of all the deviations. Squaring makes all the $r_{i,t} - \bar{r}_i$ values positive, irrespective of whether the actual return was below the average (negative deviation) or above (positive deviation). The rationale is that in order to determine the average divergence from the mean we first need to establish the cumulative divergence. If negatives are preserved they would offset positive values, producing a smaller and misleading measure of the extent to which the pattern of actual returns fluctuates around the mean.

◆ Dividing the cumulative deviation by N (the number of months of returns in our example) gives the variance. The variance measures the average, periodic, divergence from the average return.

◆ The standard deviation is the square root of the variance and is useful because it scales the risk to the average return.

In the case of Johnson & Johnson the variance and standard deviation of the monthly returns are:

$$\sigma_{r_{jj}}^2 = \frac{(-0.22 - 0.33)^2 + \cdots + (-2.85 - 0.33)^2)}{36} = 13.79$$

$$\sigma_{r_{jj}}^2 = \sqrt{13.79} = 3.71$$

The average monthly return on Johnson & Johnson shares was 0.33% with a standard deviation of 3.71% (notice the scaling, with the standard deviation expressed in the same units as the mean). Returns in the range 0.33% ± 3.71% are within 1 standard deviation of the mean. In other words, monthly returns between -3.38% and 4.04% are within 1 standard deviation.

Figure 3.1 shows that 29 of Johnson & Johnson's 36 monthly returns were within ±1 standard deviation. The remaining 7 were further from the mean return. For instance, on two occasions the return exceeded 7.75%, equivalent to 2 standard deviations to the right of the mean.

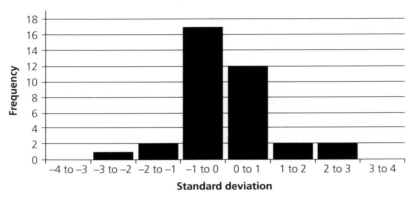

Figure 3.1 Johnson & Johnson share price deviation

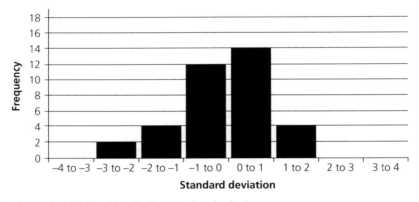

Figure 3.2 Philip Morris share price deviation

The average monthly return for Philip Morris of 1.89% compares favourably with that of Johnson & Johnson. However, the monthly standard deviation of 5.78% was higher, indicating that Philip Morris was a more risky investment.

The higher risk is evident from a comparison of Figures 3.1 and 3.2. In the case of Philip Morris, 26 of the 36 monthly returns were within ±1 standard deviation of the average return, compared to 29 for Johnson & Johnson. Hence more of the monthly returns lie further from the mean return. Philip Morris' pattern of monthly returns is characterised by both a higher standard deviation and a greater propensity for the monthly returns to stray beyond 1 standard deviation. The monthly returns are more volatile, more widely dispersed around the mean. Hence, the investment is riskier.

Test yourself 3.4

The table below presents monthly returns for two companies over the six months.

Table 3.3 Monthly returns for companies A and B

Month	Company A monthly return (%)	Company B monthly return (%)
1	−7.0	16.3
2	−12.0	5.0
3	28.5	−4.1
4	14.0	2.5
5	6.2	6.2
6	3.9	−2.1

a)   **Calculate the average monthly return for each company.**

b)   **Calculate the standard deviation of returns for each company.**

---

5. The measurement of portfolio risk

5.1 Specific risk and shared risk

The selection of Philip Morris and Johnson & Johnson to illustrate some basic techniques for risk and return on company shares was, to some extent, deliberate. Philip Morris is one of the world's largest tobacco producers while Johnson & Johnson is one of the world's leading suppliers of healthcare products. They invoke contrasting images. Philip Morris is one of a group of businesses whose shares have been nicknamed 'sin-stocks' by market professionals (the term embraces predominantly alcohol, tobacco and gambling companies and should not require explanation). The pharmaceutical industry, while not free from censure by some surrounding its standards of ethics, has a more positive public image.

In principle, the contrast between the two companies ought to be good for investors and portfolio managers.

Philip Morris operates against the backdrop of increasing restrictions, both informal and officially sanctioned, on the consumption of tobacco products in many countries. Tolerance of smoking is on the wane in many societies, potentially jeopardising the longer-term prospects for tobacco companies. Yet the anti-smoking mood is also part of an increasingly influential, broadly articulated, 'healthy lifestyle' narrative. Shifts in social attitudes and behaviour in this direction could stimulate increased consumption of healthcare products and greater profits for companies in the industry.

The storyline can be spun in other ways depending on one's reading of economic and social conditions. But the main point is that what could be bad for Philip Morris might potentially be good for Johnson & Johnson, and vice versa. Or, to express it in more technical terms, we might reasonably expect to witness a strong tendency for the returns on the two companies to evolve independently rather than in harmony.

It is plausible to suggest, therefore, that a portfolio containing both Philip Morris and Johnson & Johnson will be *less risky than their individual risks might suggest*. An investment in Johnson & Johnson ought, in theory, to be a quite effective buffer against some of the particular risks associated with Philip Morris. If so, it follows that Philip Morris can likewise offer investors some safeguards against risks peculiar to Johnson & Johnson. We would not expect this to be the case, at least not to the same extent, if we had chosen a portfolio coupling Johnson & Johnson with Pfizer, the next largest US healthcare producer.

Risk determines return. Some risk factors have widespread effects and cause investment returns to move in similar ways. Other risks are more specific. Their effects are confined to individual or small numbers of investments and stimulate shifts in returns that are independent of what happens to other assets. Specific risks are, by definition, dissimilar (otherwise they would form part of the shared risk) and produce compensating rather than comparable outcomes. The overall performance of an individual asset emerges out of the interaction of general and specific risk factors. The key point is that the precise terms of the interaction will not be the same for any two assets. Hence there will be at least some element of independence in the return structure of each asset and where there is independence, there is risk reduction via asset diversification.

This suggests that the greater the breadth of assets contained in a portfolio, the less investors should fret about specific risks; they should instead focus their anxieties on the shared risk. The positive twist to the tale is that bigger combinations of assets ought to reduce overall risk without having to sacrifice return. This conundrum is the very essence of portfolio analysis.

5.2 Covariance

In portfolio theory, the risk that is common to the constituent parts of a portfolio is represented by the concept of *covariance*. Therefore, portfolio risk embodies two elements:

1 the variance of return of each constituent asset; and

2 the degree to which the returns on individual assets move in step with one another. This aspect of portfolio risk is embodied in the concept of the *covariance* of returns.

The covariance should not be understood as an element of risk on top of the individual risks of the constituent assets. Instead, the covariance replaces a portion of the individual risks because some of the latter is neutralised by asset diversification. Furthermore, the size of the covariance will be smaller than the elements of individual risk that it replaces, leading to a portfolio risk that is less than the average of the individual risks of the constituent assets. The scale of this difference depends on the extent of the independence of the returns on those assets. The greater the independence of individual returns, the lower is the covariance of portfolio returns.

The argument leads logically to the conclusion that the importance of individual asset risk to portfolio return becomes progressively weaker the greater the number of assets incorporated. As more assets are added to a portfolio, the prospects of compensating independent outcomes grows. Increasingly, the only risk remaining is that identified with shared uncertainties: those factors that cause different assets to perform in similar ways rather than independent ways.

Given that the covariance between two assets measures the extent to which their return profiles match, a moment's reflection ought to make it clear that the desirable outcome is to *maximise the mismatch*. Imagine if the returns on Johnson & Johnson and Philip Morris always moved in harmony, sometimes exceeding expectations to the same degree and other times underperforming to the same extent. There would be no reduction of risk; the covariance would be as great as the individual risk that it replaced. But no two investments systematically perform in this manner. In practice, portfolio risk is less than the average of its constituent risks. The question is, by how much? Recall the formula for individual security variance:

$$\sigma r_i^2 = \frac{\Sigma(r_{i,t} - \bar{r}_i)^2}{N}$$

The expression (σr_i^2) is the variance of returns for an individual asset and measures the average amount by which actual returns deviate from the average return. A simple adaptation provides a representation of the variance of returns on a portfolio:

$$\sigma r_p^2 = E(r_p - \bar{r}_p)^2$$

Portfolio return (r_p) has replaced individual security return. Secondly the variance has been refashioned as being equal to the *expected* (E) difference between the portfolio actual and portfolio average returns. This modification does not alter the content of the equation; the main purpose is to make the expression easier to work with mathematically. For a two-asset portfolio, the variance of returns is:

$$\sigma r_p^2 = w_1^2 \sigma_1^2 + w_2^2 \sigma_2^2 + 2w_1 w_2 \sigma_{12}$$

The w terms represent the weight of each asset in the portfolio. The term σ_{12} is the covariance of returns between the two assets and is equal to:

$$\sigma_{1,2} = E(r_1 - \bar{r}_1)(r_2 - \bar{r}_2)$$

Notice that in contrast to the calculation of variance, the covariance does not involve squaring values, and hence does not involve adding up deviations from the mean. In fact, it entails the opposite: independent return variations on one asset are allowed to counteract independent return variations on the other. The greater the mutual independence of the two assets' returns, the lower is the covariance between them. The covariance is, therefore, a residual amount of risk; it is a measure of the risk the two assets share. Hence, the greater the 'mismatch' between two assets, the lower the covariance and the lower the portfolio risk.

Stop and think 3.3

You might be wondering how we arrived at the formula for the variance of a two-asset portfolio from the initial expression $\sigma_{r_p}^2 = E(r_p - \bar{r}_p)^2$. The first step is to specify the two assets explicitly.

$$\sigma_{r_p}^2 = E[w_1(r_1 - \bar{r}_1) + w_2(r_2 - \bar{r}_2)]^2$$

The right-hand side is a version of the general form $(x + y)^2$ which expands to $x^2 + y^2 + 2xy$. In the formula for portfolio risk:

$$x^2 = w_1^2(r_1 - \bar{r}_1)^2$$
$$y^2 = w_2^2(r_2 - \bar{r}_2)^2$$
$$2xy = 2w_1 w_2(r_1 - \bar{r}_1)(r_2 - \bar{r}_2)$$

And because $(r - \bar{r})^2 = \sigma_r^2$, and $(r_1 - \bar{r}_1)(r_2 - \bar{r}_2)$ is the covariance σ_{12}, we have:

$$\sigma_{r_p}^2 = w_1^2 \sigma_1^2 + w_2^2 \sigma_2^2 + 2w_1 w_2 \sigma_{12}$$

5.3 The risk reduction effect

Table 3.4 cites the monthly risk and return data for the Philip Morris and Johnson & Johnson.

Table 3.4 Return and risk for Johnson & Johnson and Philip Morris

	Philip Morris	**Johnson & Johnson**
Average monthly return	1.89%	0.33%
Monthly standard deviation	5.78%	3.71%

Assume that we invested half of our money in Johnson & Johnson shares and half in Philip Morris shares. The average monthly return on the portfolio is:

$$(\bar{r}_p) = 0.5(1.89) + 0.5(0.33) = 1.11$$

The covariance of returns is 10.24 (this is based on the monthly share price data for the two companies covering the three years to 31 August 2012) and the monthly portfolio variance is:

$$= 0.5^2 (5.78^2) + 0.5^2 (3.71^2) + 2(0.5)(0.5)(10.24) = 16.91$$

This converts to a portfolio standard deviation of 4.11% (the square root of 16.91).

Let's clarify the scale of the risk reduction. The equally weighted average of their variances is $0.5^2 (5.78^2) + 0.5^2 (3.71^2) = 23.59$, equivalent to a standard deviation of 4.86%. But the standard deviation of the portfolio is actually less, at 4.11%. The monthly standard deviation of the portfolio is 0.75 percentage points lower, meaning that it is a less risky investment than the individual standard deviations suggest.

5.4 The correlation coefficient

The covariance can seem a rather odd quantity. What, for instance, does the covariance between Johnson & Johnson and Philip Morris of 10.24 signify? Does it indicate a large degree of risk reduction? It's difficult to say because the covariance doesn't obviously lend itself to being compared against an objective yardstick. A clearer picture emerges if we divide the covariance by the product of the two standard deviations to produce a value known as the *correlation coefficient*, symbolised by the Greek letter ρ (rho).

$$\rho_{1,2} = \frac{\sigma_{12}}{\sigma_1 \sigma_2}$$

The correlation coefficient standardises the potency of the risk reduction force, making it easier to gauge and compare. It measures covariance using a scaled method, with the possible value ranging from −1 to +1.

◆ A value of +1 is *perfect positive* correlation. If, over a given period of time, the returns on two assets are perfectly positively correlated, it means that the patterns of positive and negative returns correspond to such a high degree that they effectively behave as though they were a single asset. If this is the case there is no reduction of risk associated with the portfolio.

◆ A value of −1 is *perfect negative* correlation. If, over a given period of time, the returns on two assets are perfectly negatively correlated it means that the patterns of positive and negative returns offset one another to such a degree that it becomes possible to construct a portfolio of the two assets offering a positive return for no risk at all.

Plus one is hell for investors, minus one is heaven. The real world is in between, but on the plus side. Think of the fact that market economies develop in cycles, shifting from periods of growth to periods of recession. In the growth phase most businesses expand output, increase investment and enjoy rising profits. In the recession phase most curtail output, cut investment and experience falling profits. In both cases the predominant correlation is positive, with asset returns generally growing in a boom and declining during a slump. The correlation of returns will not be perfectly positive – far from it. Nor will positive correlation hold for all portfolios all of the time. However, a portfolio that systematically exhibits a significant degree of negative correlation would be a recession-proof investment. If it existed, wouldn't everybody have long ago bought it?

The correlation coefficient for the portfolio consisting of Johnson & Johnson and Philip Morris is:

$$\rho_{JJ,PM} = \frac{10.24}{5.78 \times 3.71} = 0.48$$

A correlation of 0.48 indicates that over the period analysed, there was a quite notable degree of positive correlation between the returns on the two companies. This is evident even from a more cursory assessment. After all, over the period as a whole, both share prices rose and both generated positive returns. A closer inspection reveals that in 23 of the 36 months, the share prices of both companies shifted in the same direction, providing further confirmation of positive correlation.

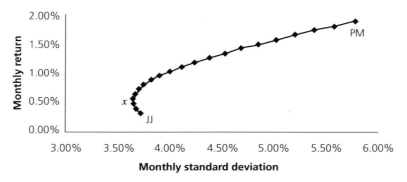

Figure 3.3 Portfolio return and standard deviation

Figure 3.3 depicts the relation between risk and return for a portfolio consisting of various weightings of Johnson & Johnson and Philip Morris. One extreme (JJ) specifies the risk and return on an investment consisting solely of Johnson & Johnson, while the other extreme (PM) specifies the same for Philip Morris. Each point along the schedule represents a shift of 5% in the portfolio weightings, i.e. 95%JJ:5%PM, 90%JJ:10%PM and so on. Some striking insights emerge:

◆   It makes no sense to invest exclusively in Johnson & Johnson. Initially, the schedule shifts upwards and leftward, indicating that diversification into Philip Morris offers the prospect of a higher return *for less* risk.

◆   A minimum risk portfolio lies at point *x*. Any mix of the two companies corresponding to points below *x* should be rejected because they offer a lower return for higher risk. Looking at Figure 3.3 suggests that the minimum risk portfolio is approximately 85% Johnson & Johnson and 15% Philip Morris. More precise weightings of the minimum risk portfolio can be obtained using the following formula:

$$w_1 = \frac{\sigma_2^2 - \sigma_{12}}{\sigma_1^2 + \sigma_2^2 - 2\sigma_{12}} = \frac{5.78^2 - 10.24}{3.71^2 + 5.78^2 - 2(10.24)} = 0.868$$

The minimum risk portfolio consists of Johnson & Johnson shares equivalent to 86.8% of the total investment and Philip Morris shares equivalent to 13.2% of the total.

◆ Investors seeking a return above that corresponding to portfolio *x* must increase the proportion invested in Philip Morris. Note in Figure 3.3 that the gaps between the 5% shifts in weightings get progressively wider. This indicates that each increment of expected return involves a larger addition to the total risk than the previous. Put another way, there is a declining incremental return to risk even though the aggregate expected return grows.

Test yourself 3.5

Assume that you invest 86.8% of your money in Johnson & Johnson and 13.2% in Philip Morris (equivalent to the minimum risk portfolio in Figure 3.3). Calculate the expected return and the standard deviation of the return for this portfolio.

5.5 Annualising risk and return

The analysis of the two-asset portfolio has focused on the *monthly* risk and return. We could have chosen daily returns or weekly returns. We could have extended or shortened the observation period. We could have used prices recorded in the middle of each month rather than those at the start. There are numerous issues to consider when deciding on suitable data on which to base an investigation. Statistically trained analysts can provide compelling arguments about why particular methods of framing data offer superior diagnostic outcomes.

Nevertheless, there is invariably a need to articulate the results in annual terms for the simple reason that it is what the majority of investors most readily understand.

The average annual return is a simple multiple of the average monthly return. For instance, we saw earlier that the equally-weighted portfolio generated an average monthly return of 1.11%. This translates into an annual return of 1.11% × 12 = 13.32%.

The annual risk is obtained by multiplying the monthly variance by 12 and then converting to the standard deviation. In the case of the equally weighted portfolio the monthly variance is 16.91, giving an annual variance of 16.91 × 12 = 202.92. This corresponds to a standard deviation of 14.24. Alternatively, multiply the monthly standard deviation by the square root of 12, i.e. 4.11 × $\sqrt{12}$ = 14.24%.

Making it work 3.1: Checking the annual return

As mentioned earlier, Philip Morris' share price on 1 September 2009 was $45.16 and ended up at $89.30 three years later. The average monthly return was 1.89%, which translates to an annual return of 22.68%. If we allow the share price to grow by this rate for three years the price will be:

$$45.16e^{0.2268 \times 3} = \$89.18$$

This is the same as Philip Morris' actual share price three years (in fact, it is 12 cents less, but this is solely due to effects of rounding the monthly growth rate to two decimal places). The example shows one reason why investment analysts typically model investment returns in their log-normal form: it generates average return values (weekly, monthly, annual, whatever) that are consistent with the whole period return. Incidentally, e is the base of natural logarithms and is equal to 2.71828.

A simpler alternative would be to divide the total return by the number of years to obtain an arithmetic average. In the case of Philip Morris the share price grew by:

$$\left(\frac{89.30 - 45.16}{45.16}\right) \times 100 = 97.74\%$$

This is equal to a simple annual average of 97.74/3 = 32.58%. This is a reasonable enough assessment if we understand it to mean that the share price grows by the equivalent of 32.58% of the initial price each year, rather than grows by 32.58% each year. If the latter is the case, we would end up with a share price of:

$$45.16(1.3258)^3 = \$105.24$$

This is clearly a significant over-assessment of the actual performance of the investment, which was actually worth $89.30 after three years.

Chapter summary

◆ The holding period return on a company share is the sum of the price change and the dividend payments expressed as a ratio of the initial share price.

◆ Any holding period perspective can be adopted. However, normal practice is to express returns in annual form.

◆ Portfolio returns are simply weighted averages of the returns of the individual constituent assets.

◆ Many investment analysts undertake detailed investigations of asset risks, focusing on qualitative aspects that cause uncertainty. Nevertheless, the sheer scale of the information that requires assessment does encourage the adoption of methods of risk analysis based on the processing of market data.

◆ Individual security risk is measured as the standard deviation of returns from the average return, based on past asset price data.

◆ At the core of portfolio theory is the statement that portfolio risk is less than the weighted average risk of the constituent assets.

◆ The risk reduction effect of asset diversification arises because the independent causes of returns are liable to offset one another to some degree.

◆ The uncertainties shared by different investments are not diversifiable and can be measured as covariances between asset pairs.

◆ The degree of covariance can be scaled by calculating correlation coefficients.

◆ The lower the covariance/correlation, the greater the scale of risk reduction.

Chapter Four
Risk, return and capital markets

List of topics

Introduction

The relevance to investors of a model of the risk-return interplay between two assets is not immediately obvious. They make investment decisions against the backdrop of vast markets functioning on a global scale, offering a bewildering array of financial securities. Not surprisingly, many favour methods of analysis that are suitable for processing masses of information from various sources about assorted investments, yet still able to offer timely insights into opportunities and risks. From this vantage point, pondering the variance of returns on a pair of assets seems thoroughly pedestrian. Yet it was precisely this exercise that inspired a far-reaching transformation in beliefs and assumptions about the forces driving asset prices, the functioning of capital markets and the ideal approach to managing investments. This chapter looks at how the framework provided by portfolio theory evolved into a comprehensive system of procedures that is of enormous significance for investment analysts and asset managers to this day.

1. Beyond two assets

The two-asset model of portfolio risk and return already contains the seeds of a solution to the analysis of more complex portfolios. First of all, the calculation of the expected return on a portfolio of any size presents no new problems. As before, the expected return is simply a weighted average of the expected returns for each constituent asset. All that changes is the number of assets considered.

Worked example 4.1: The return on a four-asset portfolio

You own a portfolio consisting of investments in Philip Morris, Johnson & Johnson, AT&T and HJ Heinz. The expected annual returns are:

Philip Morris	26.68%
Johnson & Johnson	3.96%
AT&T	11.11%
HJ Heinz	11.60%

The portfolio is equally weighted between the four assets, meaning that you invested 25% of funds in each company. The expected return on the portfolio is:

$$E(r_p) = 0.25(26.68) + 0.25(3.96) + 0.25(11.11) + 0.25(11.60) = 13.34\%$$

Test yourself 4.1

Take the expected returns for the four companies listed in Worked example 4.1 and assume that instead of equally weighted investments you spent 15% of the total on Philip Morris shares, 40% on Johnson & Johnson, 35% on AT&T and the remaining 10% on HJ Heinz.

a) Calculate the expected return for the portfolio and compare it to the expected return for the equally weighted portfolio.

b) Comment on the reasons for the difference between the two expected returns.

So what about portfolio risk? Recall that for a two-asset portfolio, risk consists of two elements.

1. the risk specific to each asset, expressed as the degree of variance from its own expected return; and

2. the risk that the assets share, expressed as the degree of variance of one asset's return from that of the other asset – their covariance.

The solution to the measurement of risk for larger portfolios is to regard them as amalgams of pairs of assets. For instance, the risk of a three-asset portfolio is the sum of three individual variances and three covariance pairings (1 with 2, 1 with 3, 2 with 3), all weighted according to the portions of the total investment directed to each asset. The process can be applied to portfolios containing any number of assets.

A critically important feature of portfolio risk emerges as we increase the number of assets in a portfolio. *The significance of the individual asset risks declines.* Portfolio risk is increasingly dependent on the covariance of returns. In order to demonstrate this point, refer to the formula for the variance of a two-asset portfolio:

$$\sigma_{r_p}^2 = w_1^2\, \sigma_1^2 + w_2^2\, \sigma_2^2 + 2w_1 w_2\, \sigma_{12}$$

In the case of an equally weighted two-asset portfolio, where both w_1 and w_2 are 0.5, 25% (i.e. 0.5^2) of the variance of asset 1 is included in the portfolio risk. The same is the case for the individual risk of asset 2. In addition, 50% of the covariance is factored into the total risk (i.e. $2w_1 w_2 = 2 \times 0.5 \times 0.5 = 0.5$, or 50%).

Now think of an equally weighted three-asset portfolio with each asset accounting for 33.33% of the total investment. Only 11.11% (0.3333^2) of the risk of each individual asset is counted in the total risk. Two-thirds of the aggregate covariance, based on the three pairs of assets, enters into the portfolio risk (i.e. $3[2 \times 0.333 \times 0.333] = 0.6666$, or 66.66%). When we reach a ten-asset equally weighted portfolio, only 10% ($0.1^2 = 0.1$) of each of the ten individual variances finds its way into the measure of portfolio risk, while 90% of the aggregate covariance is included.

Stop and think 4.1

Take care when reflecting upon the amount of a portfolio's risk that is due to the individual asset variances and to the covariance relations. In the case of an equally weighted two-asset portfolio, for instance, the fact that 25% of each individual risk is included in the portfolio risk *does not mean that it accounts for 25% of the portfolio risk*. Individual risks are liable to be greater in absolute terms than the covariance values (at least for portfolios of few assets), meaning that a significant portion of the total risk can remain dependent on the individual risk factors, despite the shifting weights.

Of course, as the number of assets in a portfolio increases, the decline of the individual risk weightings takes its toll and portfolio risk becomes increasingly identified with the measure of covariance.

Calculating the risk of larger portfolios, therefore, seems almost as straightforward as measuring the expected return of larger portfolios; it is an uncomplicated multiplication of the two-asset case. However, it generates somewhat paradoxical results.

On the one hand, the number of individual variance calculations grows with the number of assets. Yet the more diverse the portfolio, the less important are the individual risk factors to the determination of the aggregate risk, making the need to consider them less compelling. On the other hand, what remains is the shared risk which, paradoxically, occurs as multiple covariance calculations. Figure 4.1 provides a sense of the scale of the computational task, using the example of a ten-asset portfolio. It lists the ten assets horizontally and vertically. Each square represents a covariance between two assets, of which there are 100 (10^2).

Asset	1	2	3	4	5	6	7	8	9	10
1		σ_{12}								
2	σ_{21}									
3								σ_{38}		
4							σ_{47}			
5										
6										
7				σ_{74}					σ_{79}	
8			σ_{83}							
9							σ_{97}			
10										

Figure 4.1 Covariance calculations for ten assets

The ten black squares represent the covariance of each asset with itself which is, by definition, perfect and so doesn't require computing. That leaves 90 covariance calculations. The covariance for each pair occurs twice (as can be seen from those squares where the covariance values have been explicitly included). But as they must equal one another, they only require calculating once. That still leaves 45 calculations to determine the impact of covariance on the risk of a ten-asset portfolio. For 50 assets it's 1,225 calculations and for 100 assets it's 4,950.

There is a further factor to consider. In the case of a two-asset portfolio the portion invested in one asset automatically defines the portion invested in the other. All possible mixes of the two assets can be plotted as a risk return schedule (such as that presented in Figure 3.3) from which conclusions about which combinations are acceptable investment opportunities, 'efficient portfolios' in the language of portfolio theory, can be drawn.

In the case of a three-asset portfolio, matters are more complicated. Specifying the portion invested in any one asset doesn't determine the individual portions invested in the other two. The dilemma recurs with every change in the portion invested in one asset. Thus, the number of potential asset combinations grows enormously. Furthermore it is possible, probable even, for two different combinations of three assets to have the same expected return but a different risk – or the same risk but a different return. Both of these factors become even more compelling the greater the number of assets incorporated into a portfolio.

One consequence is that the visual representation of risk-return trade-offs when there are more than two assets to choose from no longer appears as a line function in the manner of Figure 3.3. Instead the risk-return combinations are dispersed across an area like that portrayed by Figure 4.2.

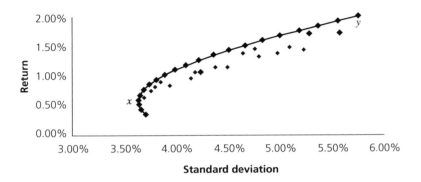

Figure 4.2 Portfolio return and standard deviation

Two important observations stem from Figure 4.2:

◆ 'Superior' portfolios are those whose risk-return trade-offs lie along the upper boundary between *x* and *y*. They are superior because it is neither possible to improve on the expected return without accepting more risk, nor to reduce the risk without accepting a lower return. In the language of portfolio theory the line from *x* to *y* is an 'efficient frontier' and consists of those portfolios that ought to be preferred by risk-averse, wealth-maximising investors.

◆ Points below the efficient frontier are examples of 'inferior' portfolios. They are inferior because there are alternatives offering either a better return for the same risk or an equal return for less risk. Being inferior portfolios, they should be rejected by investors.

Nowadays it is possible to produce efficient frontier models that incorporate large numbers of assets on a personal computer. With ample share price data on hundreds of companies readily available, you need decent quality data analysis software and a working knowledge of statistical methods. An efficient frontier model based on randomly generated weighted combinations of the constituent companies can be programmed to adjust automatically to changes in asset prices over time. The resulting image of the efficient frontier 'in action' can be used to aid investment management by suggesting which portfolios, or types of portfolios, tend to remain at or close to the efficient frontier and which have a propensity to drift into the inferior region.

The pioneers of portfolio theory were not so fortunate in having the technology to generate efficient portfolios instantaneously in real-time and were driven to find other ways of making the theory more directly relevant to investment decision-making.

2. Risk-free assets and the market portfolio

A significant innovation in the progress of portfolio theory seems at first quite facile. It is the idea that aside from risky assets, investors can acquire assets offering a certain return – assets that are risk-free. Figure 4.3 is the outcome.

Figure 4.3 adds an investment offering a risk-free rate of return, denoted by the expression r_f. The risk-free return lies on the vertical axis as this corresponds to a standard deviation of zero. Investors can choose to put all their money in risk-free assets and accept a return equivalent to r_f. Alternatively they can aim for higher returns by constructing portfolios combining both risk-free and risky assets.

Given the assumption that investors look to maximise the risk-return trade-off, the set of feasible options is a given by drawing a line extending from the risk-free return and which is tangent to the efficient frontier at point M. Let's assess the range of investment choices in more detail.

◆ An investor can choose to avoid all risk and earn a certain return equivalent to r_f. This effectively consists of lending funds at the risk-free rate.

◆ An investor can choose risky assets only. In this case, a risk-return trade-off corresponding to that of asset M is the best option.

◆ An investor can choose a combination of risk-free assets and risky asset M, such as portfolio 1.

◆ An investor can choose to borrow (the model assumes at the risk-free rate) to invest in asset M. This corresponds to a risk-return trade-off beyond M, such as that situated at point 2. It is riskier than investing just personal wealth in M because of financial leverage; the obligation to service the debt in addition to facing the risk of asset M.

If we join all these options together we get an ascending straight line, as depicted in Figure 4.3. This line is known as the Capital Market Line (CML). The CML suggests that portfolio decisions come down to a simple choice between risk-free assets and asset M. We're back to a two-asset portfolio, but with a twist – one of the assets, being risk-free, has a variance and standard deviation of zero. Incorporating this modification into the standard two-asset portfolio variance equation generates the following result:

$$\sigma_{r_p}^2 = w_{r_f}^2 \, 0 + w_M^2 \sigma_M^2 + 2 w_M w_{r_f} \, 0 = w_M^2 \sigma_M^2$$

and

$$\sigma_{r_p} = w_M \sigma_M$$

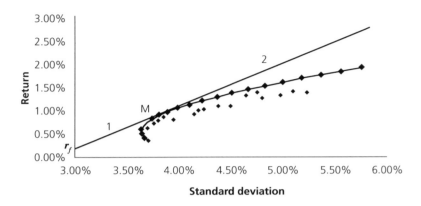

Figure 4.3 Capital Market Line

Portfolio risk is now identified with the risk of asset *M*, because both the variance of the risk-free asset and its covariance with *M* must be zero. The issue of how to measure the risk-return trade-off appears simplified. In fact, it looks simpler than is the case for the original two-asset model. Worked example 4.2 illustrates this point.

Worked example 4.2: Portfolio risk and return with risk-free assets

Assume that the annual return on a risk-free investment is 2% and that the expected annual return for the risky asset *M* is 8%, with a standard deviation of 5%. The return and risk calculations below are for portfolios involving successive 20 percentage point shifts in the weights, starting from an investment made up entirely of risk-free assets.

Table 4.1 Return and risk calculations

Portfolio weighting	Expected return	Risk
	$w_{r_f}(r_f) + w_M (E[r_M]) = E[r_p]$	$w_M \sigma_M = \sigma_{r_p}$
100% risk-free: 0% *M*	1.0(2.0%) + 0.0(8.0%) = 2.0%	0.0(5.0%) = 0.0%
80% risk-free: 20% *M*	0.8(2.0%) + 0.2(8.0%) = 3.2%	0.2(5.0%) = 1.0%
60% risk-free: 40% *M*	0.6(2.0%) + 0.4(8.0%) = 4.4%	0.4(5.0%) = 2.0%
40% risk-free: 60% *M*	0.4(2.0%) + 0.6(8.0%) = 5.6%	0.6(5.0%) = 3.0%
20% risk-free: 80% *M*	0.2(2.0%) + 0.8(8.0%) = 6.8%	0.8(5.0%) = 4.0%
0% risk-free: 100% *M*	0.0(2.0%) + 1.0(8.0%) = 8.0%	1.0(5.0%) = 5.0%
−20% risk-free: 120% *M*	−0.2(2.0%) + 1.2(8.0%) = 9.2%	1.2(5.0%) = 6.0%

The portfolio expected return grows by equal increments (in this example 1.2 percentage points) for each 20 percentage point change in the weights. This is nothing new; it merely reiterates the point already made on numerous occasions that the expected return is simply a weighted average of individual returns.

However, note that the portfolio risk is also growing by equal increments (1 percentage point) as the weights change. This differs from the earlier analysis of two-asset portfolios, which indicated that portfolio risk is less than a simple weighted average of the two risks. The reason for the change is that now one of the risk values is zero, meaning that portfolio risk can only be a weighted value of the other.

The last portfolio in the list involves an investor borrowing funds equivalent to 20% of personal capital and investing them in *M*. It is a financially leveraged portfolio, which is riskier still. But note that it also offers a higher expected return.

The upshot is that the expected return grows at a constant rate relative to the risk – it appears as a straight, ascending line, known as the Capital Market Line.

The CML is an important step in the development of portfolio analysis for a number of reasons. It introduces the possibility of lending and borrowing funds at a risk-free rate. This is in and of itself important, because it means that in one respect at least the model of portfolio choice is more realistic.

A more significant legacy is the identification of the risky asset denoted by *M*. The CML suggests that for any given set of market conditions, there exists only one truly efficient risky asset, and that portfolio management is fundamentally about how much of this asset to hold. Low-risk investors favour lending funds at the risk-free rate and limit their exposure to the risky asset. High-risk investors are prepared to borrow money to access the potential rewards offered by the risky asset. But all of these decisions are made with respect to the same risky asset, *M*. So what is *M*?

The CML tells us that the scale of portfolio risk is wholly determined by the weight of *M* in the portfolio. The fact that risk is a simple weighted value means that there is no further risk reduction to be had from widening the range of assets included in a portfolio. Investors can modify portfolio risk by altering the ratio of risk-free assets to asset *M*. Risk-free assets operate as a kind of lever, enabling investors to adjust portfolio risk to the preferred level; more risk-free means less portfolio risk and vice versa. But the resulting portfolio risk is always just a weighted amount of the risk of asset *M*.

The exhaustion of the risk reduction effects of asset diversification suggests that *M* must be a fully diversified asset. It must be, in the vernacular of portfolio theory, the *market portfolio*: a uniquely efficient combination of all risky assets in the market.

There is much to criticise about the CML as a method of portfolio analysis. For instance, risk-taking borrowers cannot borrow at the rate r_f. Who, after all, would lend money at rates of interest deemed appropriate for assets considered risk-free to someone intending to invest it in obviously risky assets like company shares? It is not a risk-free investment for lenders as they could lose if borrowers' investments are unsuccessful. In practice, risk-free lending is normally identified with the purchase of short-term government securities (treasury bills). Borrowing rates are almost always higher than lending rates.

Another issue is the implausibility of investing in the 'market' portfolio. The number of assets involved is huge. Then there's the daunting task of combining them in proportions suitable for ensuring that all the risk that can be neutralised is neutralised. It's practically impossible. Ultimately, the CML fails to offer what we need: a workable framework for assessing individual assets with a view to effective portfolio construction.

Nevertheless, the ideas of risk-free rate of return, market portfolio and the linear relation between risk and return lead very directly to what is, in many ways, the pinnacle achievement of portfolio theory – the Capital Asset Pricing Model (CAPM). CML analysis includes ideas critical to the CAPM, notably the *market risk premium* and *market price of risk*.

$$\text{Market risk premium} = E(r_M) - r_f$$

The market risk premium is the difference between the expected return on the market portfolio and the risk-free return. It is the reward investors expect for risk taking; a premium component of the total return, over and above the risk-free rate, that provides the incentive to take risks.

The expected return on any portfolio, therefore, consists of a risk-free element plus a risk premium. The scale of the risk premium for a particular portfolio depends on how much an investor is willing to devote to the market portfolio relative the amount spent purchasing risk-free assets. The portion is equivalent to σ_{r_p} / σ_M (because $\sigma_{r_p} = w_M \sigma_M$) and the expected return on a portfolio is, therefore:

$$E(r_p) = r_f + [E(r_M) - r_f]\left(\frac{\sigma_{r_p}}{\sigma_M}\right)$$

Refer back to Worked example 4.2, where the risk-free return was 2% and the return on the market portfolio was 8%, giving a market risk premium of 6%. Take the case where 80% of funds are placed in the risk-free asset and 20% in the market portfolio. The portfolio risk, σ_{r_p}, is 1% (i.e. $w_M \sigma_M = 0.2 \times 5\% = 1\%$). Therefore, the expected return is:

$$E(r_p) = 2\% + [8\% - 2\%]\left(\frac{1\%}{5\%}\right) = 3.2\%$$

The return of 3.2% is 1.2 percentage points more than the risk-free rate, and one-fifth of the 6% market risk premium. The portfolio offers a risk premium one-fifth of the market risk premium because one-fifth of the portfolio is market risk.

With a market risk premium of 6% and market risk (σ_M) of 5%, each percentage point of risk offers 1.2 percentage points expected return, i.e. 6/5 = 1.2. This is known as the market price of risk. It is the extra return offered by the market portfolio per unit of market risk.

$$Market\ price\ of\ risk = \frac{[E(r_M) - r_f]}{\sigma_M}$$

Investors can decide how many units of market risk they wish to accept and calculate the expected return by multiplying the market price of risk by the chosen number of units. Take the case from Worked example 4.2, where 40% of funds are place in the risk-free asset and 60% in the market portfolio. This is equivalent to three units of market risk (3%). Hence:

$$E(r_p) = 2\% + \frac{[8\% - 2\%]}{(5\%)} \times 3\% = 5.6\%$$

This is the same outcome as before and is so for all the other cases.

Test yourself 4.2

Use the risk premium version of the expected return formula to calculate the expected returns on each of the weighted portfolios presented in Worked example 4.2. Compare the outcomes.

Changes in the market price of risk can be useful in portfolio management. For instance, if the market risk premium is high by historical standards, it might encourage a belief that asset values are set to rise in general over the forthcoming period, because the high premium ought to encourage investors to accept risks. By contrast, if the market risk premium is low, it might fuel a growing sense of gloom about asset values. After all, a low-risk premium suggests that risky investments are not expected to offer much more than risk-free investments, a factor that would tend to make investing in risk-free assets more appealing.

Test yourself 4.3

The annual return on UK government treasury bills on 10 October 2012 was 0.34%. At the same time, the expected annual return on the FTSE All-Share index was 7.4% with an annual standard deviation of 13.8%. Assume that the returns on treasury bills yield and the FTSE All-Share Index are representative of the risk-free and expected market returns respectively.

a) **Calculate the expected returns for portfolios with the following weightings.**

   i.   **100% treasury bills: 0% FTSE All-Share Index**

   ii. **75% treasury bills: 25% FTSE All-Share Index**

iii. **50% treasury bills: 50% FTSE All-Share Index**

iv. **25% treasury bills: 75% FTSE All-Share Index**

v. **0% treasury bills: 100% FTSE All-Share Index**

vi. **Borrow funds, at the treasury bill rate, to increase the investment in the FTSE All-Share Index by another 25%.**

b) **Calculate the market risk premium and the market price of risk.**

3. The Capital Asset Pricing Model

Portfolio theory suggests that the broader the range of securities that an investor owns, the less important the individual security risks. Portfolio risk increasingly revolves around factors that cause individual investments to perform in similar rather than independent ways; risk factors that continue to impact irrespective of the scale of asset diversification. The CML portrays this as risk attached to a fully diversified investment which, by inference, is the market portfolio.

The Capital Asset Pricing Model (CAPM) takes the reasoning a step further by hypothesising that investors view assets not in isolation, but purely as components of diversified portfolios. The dissipation of idiosyncratic risks is more than a logical outcome of a theory; it is an integral aspect of the investor mindset. Investors disregard singular characteristics because they have a negligible impact on portfolio returns and are interested only in the market risk of individual securities and how it will affect portfolio risk. The portfolio is the primary object of the decision-making process.

A fundamentally important implication is that particular risk factors have no impact on asset prices. If all investors view all assets exclusively in terms of their 'market' risk, then all else is irrelevant to judgements about what assets are worth. This is precisely the claim of the CAPM; that the prices of *individual securities* are determined by market risk alone, sometimes described as *systematic risk* as distinct from the non-systematic (diversifiable) risk. If the market risk can be measured in a judicious manner, it offers the prospect of a system of asset evaluation that can be applied to individual securities. It offers the possibility of portfolio analysis achieving a practical relevance that had previously proved elusive.

In portfolio theory, shared risk is measured by covariance. The CAPM echoes this by measuring the covariance between the return on an individual asset and the return on the market portfolio. To facilitate this, CAPM replaces the 'theoretical' market portfolio of the CML with a proxy, in the form of a suitably broad-based market index such as the FTSE All-Share Index in the case of equities quoted on the London stock market or the S&P 500 for shares trading on the New York stock market. This is not simply for convenience. If investors do behave according to the assumptions of the CAPM, then asset values ought to generate broad-based indices that are good, robust approximations of a market portfolio.

The covariance between security and market returns is calculated in the same way as the covariance between two security returns (you might wish to remind yourself by referring back to section 5.2 of chapter 3). The CAPM then divides the covariance by the variance of returns on the market portfolio to produce an asset *beta* value:

$$\frac{Covariance_{iM}}{Market\ Portfolio\ Variance} = \frac{\sigma_i \sigma_M \rho_{iM}}{\sigma_M^2} = \beta_i$$

Beta (symbolised by β) is a coefficient that expresses an individual asset's covariance with the market portfolio as a ratio of the market portfolio's risk (in the form of its variance). If the covariance is greater than the market variance, it produces a beta value above 1. This should be interpreted as meaning that the asset in question is among the riskier constituents of the market portfolio. A covariance value less than the market variance produces a beta value below 1, signifying an asset among the less risky constituents.

The beta value of the market portfolio is always 1. Think about it this way: the market portfolio's covariance with itself must always, by definition, be the same as its variance, meaning that for the market portfolio the equation for beta must come to 1. All of those assets for whom the beta exceeds 1 are therefore classified as being of higher than average risk; they exhibit more market risk than assets on average. The rationale behind this notion is that securities with betas above 1 (we'll refer to them as high beta securities) amplify movements in the market return. When the market index rises, the values of high beta shares tend to rise by a greater degree. When the market index falls, high beta share prices tend to fall to a greater degree. In effect, the prices of high beta securities are more volatile than the market on average, which suggests that returns are less certain, thereby justifying their being considered riskier.

It follows that 'low' beta securities are those whose prices are generally less volatile than the market index, suggesting a more stable pattern of returns, which implies less risk. Allying beta to the CML risk-premium framework gives:

$$E(r_i) = r_f + \beta_i [E(r_M) - r_f]$$

This *is* the CAPM. It modifies the CML by replacing the term σ_{r_p} / σ_M with a beta coefficient. The modification has profound implications. The CAPM can be employed to construct portfolios from individual securities, whereas the CML offers the implausible scenario of investors managing risk by varying the scale of their investments in a market portfolio. It should be clear that the former is far more workable.

A further and equally significant feature of this system is that the market risk of a portfolio is a function of a weighted average of the betas of the constituent securities. Hence, once the betas have been calculated, the task of addressing the risk-expected trade-off for any portfolio becomes relatively simple and routine. The CAPM is one of the single most influential statements produced in the field of financial analysis. An important reason for this is the sheer tractability of the method: the ease with which it can be applied to all manner of investment decisions.

Making it work 4.1: Security betas and expected return

Listed below, in ascending order, are the beta values for a sample of five companies listed on the London Stock Exchange.

Sainsbury	0.60
Experian	0.94
ARM Holdings	1.00
Burberry Group	1.29
Xstrata	1.71

The annual return on UK government treasury bills is 0.34% and the expected return on the FTSE All-Share Index is 6.50%. Let's start by calculating the expected return for each security.

$$E(r_{Sainsbury}) = 0.34\% + 0.60[6.5\% - 0.34\%] = 4.04\%$$

$$E(r_{Experian}) = 0.34\% + 0.94[6.5\% - 0.34\%] = 6.13\%$$

$$E(r_{ARM}) = 0.34\% + 1.00[6.5\% - 0.34\%] = 6.50\%$$

$$E(r_{Burberry}) = 0.34\% + 1.29[6.5\% - 0.34\%] = 8.29\%$$

$$E(r_{Xstrata}) = 0.34\% + 1.71[6.5\% - 0.34\%] = 10.87\%$$

The beta and expected return for an equally weighted portfolio of the five securities are:

$$\beta_{portfolio} = 0.2(0.60 + 0.94 + 1.00 + 1.29 + 1.71) = 1.11$$

$$E(r_{portfolio}) = 0.34\% + 1.11[6.5\% - 0.34\%] = 7.18\%$$

The simplicity of the exercise is striking. Estimates of the expected return for both individual assets and portfolios of assets require the alteration of only one element, namely the beta value. Furthermore, the beta for a portfolio of assets is a straightforward weighted combination of individual beta values.

Test yourself 4.4

Listed below, in ascending order, are the beta values for a sample of five companies listed on the London Stock Exchange.

BSkyB Group	0.40
Pearson	0.70
Kingfisher	1.00
Aviva	1.29
Barclays	1.71

The annual return on UK government treasury bills is 0.34% and the expected return on the FTSE All-Share Index is 6.50%.

a)   Calculate the expected return for each security.

b)   Calculate the beta and expected return for a portfolio that includes equal weightings of the five assets.

4. Uses of the CAPM

The CAPM has had an enormous impact on professional practice related to finance and investment. Three areas are worth stressing as follows.

The CAPM is employed as a method of managing portfolios – the function it is designed for. It is used to review and interpret the past performance of individual assets. Review results are used to inform estimates about future performance. The estimates can be compared retrospectively to actual outcomes to see whether a portfolio under- or outperformed initial expectations.

The CAPM has influenced the evolution of financial assets themselves. The CAPM – in fact, portfolio theory more broadly – associates the principle of asset diversification with sound investment practice; diversified investments are connected to positive-sounding terms such as 'efficient' and 'optimal'. It also provokes cynicism from some quarters towards investment styles that claim success by concentrating on discovering future winners and avoiding (or shorting) future losers. One example of the influence of this outlook is the growth in popularity of index tracking investment funds – investments structured to replicate the performance of an index such as the FTSE 100 or S&P 500. They operate according to the maxim that more discriminatory styles of choosing securities rarely 'beat the market' and so an index-tracking approach is better, especially as they enjoy the additional benefit of being easier and cheaper to manage. In fact, according to some observers, the significance of index tracking is more pervasive than the data suggests as many so-called **actively managed funds** are little more than 'closet trackers', maintaining a pretence of independent judgement largely to justify charging high management fees.

actively managed funds
Investment funds that involve managers adopting trading and investment strategies that aim to exceed the performance of predetermined benchmarks as opposed to merely achieving the benchmark outcome.

Many industrial and commercial enterprises use the CAPM for capital budgeting purposes. Senior management is responsible for the strategic planning of capital investment. Decisions about the maintenance, expansion or shrinkage of current projects, about investment on new projects or about the acquisition of another business are all areas where the CAPM can help. It offers a framework for establishing appropriate rates of return for different investment initiatives. For instance, management could apply a CAPM-based expected return to the relevant cash flow estimates for a new investment proposal to establish whether or not it is expected to generate a competitive return.

Chapter summary

◆   Increasing the number of assets in a portfolio means that the significance of independent risk factors tends to decline, so that portfolio risk is increasingly dependent on risk factors that assets share.

◆ The introduction of risk-free investing into portfolio theory leads to the notion that risk-taking depends on an investor's exposure to the risk of a 'market portfolio'.

◆ The capital market line measures the market risk premium: the incremental return that the market portfolio offers for each unit of risk-taking.

◆ The Capital Asset Pricing Model (CAPM) suggests that asset prices are a function of systematic risk.

◆ CAPM scales the exposure of individual assets to market risk by reference to beta values, which measure asset return volatility relative to market portfolio return volatility.

◆ Assets with beta values in excess of 1 exhibit more systematic risk than the market portfolio, while those with betas below 1 exhibit less systematic risk than on average.

Chapter Five
Portfolio analysis: doubts and dilemmas

List of topics

Introduction

The Capital Asset Pricing Model (CAPM) is a hypothesis that states that all of the uncertainty surrounding asset prices on capital markets is due to systematic risk. It is founded on a specific characterisation of investor behaviour within a precisely defined capital market environment. It assumes that all investors seek to maximise wealth within the constraints imposed by their subjective attitudes to risk-taking. Furthermore, all investors are presumed to hold assets only as components of well-diversified portfolios and, as a result, identify the economic uncertainties connected to their investments with systematic risk alone.

The capital market in which investors operate is assumed to be a competitive market devoid of barriers to trading and price setting. Neither individuals nor consortia are large enough to influence prices. No one has privileged access to valuable information about investments. There are no constraints on lending and borrowing at the risk-free rate. And there are no taxes or brokerage fees to pay.

For anyone minded to be critical of portfolio theory and CAPM, there are two strikingly obvious targets: the idealised portrait of the investor and the idealised portrait of the capital market. However, the would-be critic should be aware, before rushing to censure, that the architects of portfolio theory were well aware that the assumptions were 'unreal'. But they defended the theory on the basis that it offered important and informative guidelines for the practice of investment management. To this day, a host of both academic and professional practitioners of finance remain broadly sympathetic to the understanding of risk and return rooted in portfolio theory.

A systematic analysis of each and every reservation concerning portfolio theory and their influence of the evolution of investment analysis and asset management practices is beyond the remit of this text. We confine the examination to some of the more pertinent observations and those that have most influence on current thinking and practice.

1. Information and capital markets

Investment is a future-oriented activity. Success or failure depends on what happens in the future. The perennial problem is that individuals can't know the future when they invest, and for this reason investment is risky. Asset values and income streams change in ways that weren't predicted at the outset; predictions made at the outset turn out to be wrong. But this does not imply that investors are helpless in the face of an uncertain future. They know at the outset that values and cash flows will change in ways that they didn't expect. Furthermore, they are able to assess the implications of unforeseen events when they do occur and adjust their investment portfolios accordingly.

According to the CAPM, individual investors are clear-headed beings with an unsentimental outlook on to the world of wealth-enhancing opportunities. They trust that prevailing asset prices arise from cogent reflection upon the available information by persons disinclined to impulsive actions based on far-fetched speculation. Asset prices are a product of wealth-maximising investors examining the relevant information equipped with tools that encourage rational, clear-sighted, rapid assessment and discourage capricious behaviour. The resulting prices are, therefore, fair or 'efficient' prices, the outcome of judicious decision-making by securities traders and investors.

Making it work 5.1: BP's share price and the Deepwater Horizon disaster

On 22 April 2010, the Deepwater Horizon offshore drilling rig sank in the Gulf of Mexico following an explosion a few days earlier. It was bad news for BP PLC, the oil company operating the rig. Between 22 April and 25 June 2010 BP's share price fell from £6.65 to £3.05 on the London Stock Exchange, a decline of over 53%. By comparison, the share price for Royal Dutch Shell PLC, another major global oil and gas company, fell a relatively modest 13.5%, while the FTSE 100 index fell 12.8%.

Nobody could have foretold the Deepwater Horizon disaster. But as the incident unfolded over many weeks, financial analysts and fund managers set about the task of assessing the implications for BP as an investment. It wasn't easy. There was genuine uncertainty about the scale of the incident, at least in the initial stages. Much of the information emanated from commentators with partisan agendas attempting either to downplay its seriousness or to whip up emotions. Estimating the direct effects in terms of lost resources, dislocation of the local economy and environmental damage was highly complex and, to a degree, speculative.

There was also the issue of claims for compensation against BP, as well as the longer-term damage to its commercial reputation to consider.

It is no surprise that BP's share price fell as the event unfolded. Investors and traders inevitably took the view that it would have an adverse effect on the company's reputation, earnings and dividend payments, and so downgraded their valuations accordingly. But was a halving of the value of BP in two months, knocking around £66 billion from its market value, a fair assessment of the financial significance of the event? Portfolio theory suggests that the answer ought to be yes.

This characterisation of capital market valuation is deeply ingrained in much of the theory and practice of asset analysis and management. It has a title, the efficient market hypothesis (EMH). Most financial market professionals are well versed in the arguments of the EMH. Its pivotal position in financial analysis means that it merits closer attention. Be aware, however, that what follows merely touches on what is a theme enormous in scope and a focus of controversy among financial academics and professionals.

2. Market efficiency and information

Are capital market prices efficient? The question is typically framed in terms of three levels of price efficiency, distinguished by the scope of the information set considered. They are described as weak form, semi-strong form and strong form efficiency. The research objective is to establish the extent to which actual markets support the hypothesis.

2.1 Weak form efficiency

The concept of weak form market efficiency is so-called because the information considered is confined to the past price and trading data associated with securities and markets. It asks: is it possible to gain valuable insights about the course of future asset prices by analysing historical price data? If it is, then investors with access to these insights will earn superior returns. A more precise formulation is that they will systematically earn a rate of return in excess of that which is explained by the level of systematic risk.

However, if a market is weak-form efficient, then *current prices* already fully incorporate the value of all insights discernible from any examination of the past; otherwise it would not be an efficient market. Any analysis of price data produces only what is already known and, therefore, already reflected in current prices. The EMH argues, in effect, that security trading based on such information does not enable traders to 'beat the market'.

Tests for weak-form market efficiency fall into two broad categories. The first focuses on market data itself. A basic example might involve taking a list of daily closing share prices for a company over one year and calculating the daily percentage returns. The EMH suggests that there ought to be no evidence that the return on a given day is influenced by the return on any previous day. In mathematical terminology, the daily returns are independent, random events. The returns data can be tested for serial autocorrelation, a technique for determining whether there is evidence of self-dependence of the returns on a particular security. According to the EMH, the scale of correlation ought to be no greater than what is liable to occur by chance. If this is the case, then past prices do not offer a valuable guide to the future and the market is weak-form efficient. By contrast, if the correlation of returns is higher than the level to be expected from a random process then analysing past data is a potentially lucrative activity.

Stop and think 5.1

The suggestion of the EMH that periodic returns on assets are random events does not imply that actual returns have no logical explanation. After all, the EMH stresses that asset prices result from the actions of rational investors responding to new information. The EMH is saying that events unfold in a random manner. Investors are very capable of assessing the implications of different developments. But what they can never truly know beforehand, despite their best efforts, is what the actual developments will be.

The second type of test of weak-form market efficiency focuses on the performance of security trading schemes rooted in technical analysis. Technical analysis is a catch-all term for a wide variety of trading techniques reliant on the examination of prices and other trading data. A belief in the efficacy of technical analysis as a method for consistent profit generation is the antithesis of the EMH because it requires that prices series exhibit patterns of dependence strong enough and frequently enough for technical traders to profit. If a market is weak-form efficient, then technical analysis ought to be a waste of time and money.

Stop and think 5.2

If one were to represent the development of an asset's price in chart form, it would typically exhibit phase-like or pattern-like characteristics. This could seduce an observer into believing that prices exhibit some serial dependence and are therefore, to an extent, foreseeable. One problem with this outlook is that similar-looking charts are liable to emerge from, say, repeatedly tossing a coin and recording the heads and tails results. The exercise will generate 'runs'. Yet no one would conclude that looking at such charts raises the probability of calling the next result correctly above – in this case, 50%. Every event is independent of the previous results; it is a random outcome.

The coin-tossing analogy does not prove that analysing past security price data is of no value. It does, however, indicate that the presence of patterns and trends, of whatever character, is not in itself sufficient proof that the past is worthy of attention.

2.2 Semi-strong form efficiency

Semi-strong market efficiency broadens the information set to include all publicly available information. It poses the question: does the prevailing asset price fully reflect the implications of all the information in the public domain? This includes price data but extends to other company information (published accounts, strategic plans, media commentary, etc). It also includes consideration of issues such as competition, regulation and the overall macroeconomic climate. If security prices are semi-strong efficient, then no amount of careful appraisal of the information can reliably produce above average returns.

Semi-strong efficiency is, by a long distance, the most exhaustively researched version of the hypothesis. The investigations typically take the form of corporate event studies involving the analysis of large samples of a particular sort of event. Common examples are mergers and acquisitions, dividend announcements, corporate borrowing, new equity issues and the release of audited accounts. In each case a hypothesis consistent with market efficiency is formulated and the sample evidence assessed against this standard, with the view of establishing whether a market may be regarded as efficient.

Making it work 5.2: Semi-strong efficiency

On 25 October 2012, the board of directors of ABC PLC decided at its monthly meeting to launch a takeover bid for XYZ PLC. Details of the two companies' equity capital are contained in Table 5.1.

Table 5.1 ABC PLC's and XYZ PLC's equity capital

Company	Issued share capital	Share price	Market value of equity
ABC PLC	100 million	£4.50	£450 million
XYZ PLC	40 million	£2.50	£100 million

ABC intended to make a cash offer of £3.00 per XYZ share. The board of ABC believed that the merged company would be more efficient and that improved profitability would result in the merged company being worth £100 million more than the two companies operating as separate entities.

Assume that the board's decision remained private on 25 October. According to the semi-strong version of market efficiency, nothing would happen to the share price of either company, as none of the information was in the public domain.

On 30 October ABC publicly announced the terms of the takeover bid, but remained tight-lipped on the issues of improved profitability and increased market value of the merged company. XYZ's share price should immediately rise to £3.00, the offer price publicly declared by ABC. What about ABC's share price? ABC's offer amounted to £120 million (40 million shares x £3.00) for a company that was worth £100 million. In effect, rational investors would see ABC gaining assets worth £100 million but paying £120 million, a net reduction in the company's value of £20 million to £430 million. Therefore, according to semi-strong efficiency, ABC's share price falls to £4.30.

On 5 November ABC revealed to the public its views on improved profitability and market value. A semi-strong efficient market would value a merger at £530 million (£430 million plus £100 million) and the share price would rise to £5.30.

At each step prices adjust immediately upon the information becoming public. Furthermore, prices adjust not in an arbitrary way but in accordance with the judgements of rational investors.

2.3 Strong form efficiency

Strong form efficiency suggests that asset prices reflect the impact of *all* information so that even investors with privileged access to information would not earn an excess return. Few observers maintain that capital markets are efficient in the strongest sense. And anyway, it is difficult to test as insider trading is a criminal offence in most financial jurisdictions, meaning that obtaining the information on which to conduct the tests can be rather difficult.

Test yourself 5.1

An equities dealer uses a trading rule which states that in the long run the market can be beaten by purchasing shares whose prices reach a 52-week low. The rationale is that there is empirical evidence to suggest that such shares have a tendency to rebound strongly and, thereby, outperform the market.

a) Which 'level' of market efficiency do you think the dealer's trading rule most directly questions?

b) How might an advocate of efficient market theory articulate doubts about the efficacy of this trading rule as a mechanism for earning risk-adjusted excess returns?

3. Are markets efficient?

The EMH argues that the actions of rational investors produce security prices that are efficient reflections of all the pertinent information. Add to this the idea that markets are also operationally efficient, and the result is that it is very difficult for individual investors to repeatedly outperform their peers. Operational efficiency refers to the technical aspects of market processes such as how long it takes for agreed transactions to be executed, the volume of deals that can be executed and how instantaneously asset prices adjust in the intense trading environment. In 2011 the London Stock Exchange switched to a new trading platform called Millennium Exchange which, according to its designers, can handle 3,500 incoming orders per second and process 40,000 price quotes per second with order time delays under 50 milliseconds.

Twenty-first century financial markets are operationally more efficient than ever. When thousands of investment decisions can be processed more or less simultaneously and instantaneously, prices are liable to adjust to levels that reflect the thinking behind those decisions extremely quickly, making the idea of outperforming the crowd a daunting challenge.

Making it work 5.3: News and market prices

Just after 7.00am (UK time) on 1 November 2012, Reuters news agency posted details of BT Group PLC's just released quarterly financial statement which revealed, among many other things, a 7% increase in pre-tax profit and a 15% increase in the planned **interim dividend** payment. When the London Stock Exchange began trading at 8.00am, BT's share price opened at 217 pence, having closed 212.5 pence the previous day. By 8.30am it reached 224 pence and eventually closed for the day on 227 pence. In total BT's share price rose 6.8% on the previous day's closing price. The fact that the FTSE 100 Index rose by a relatively modest 1.37% on the day indicates that the increase in BT's share price largely reflected a positive response to the news of improved profits and dividends.

interim dividend
A dividend payment paid prior to a company's end-of-year financial statements and, technically, paid from past years' earnings. It is distinct from the 'final' dividend, which is declared in conjunction with the full year financial statements.

Let's accept for the moment that the increase in BT's share price was a fair reflection of the information disclosed on the morning of 1 November. What is interesting is that most of the increase occurred in the first half hour of trading. Investors had to act quickly if they hoped to profit from the information. Some no doubt did. But the main beneficiaries would have been the existing owners of BT shares who, according to the EMH, are merely lucky.

The EMH can understandably be interpreted as inferring that efforts to absorb and interpret information in the belief that it improves investment decision-making are wasted efforts because they are unlikely to yield extraordinary returns. But this is a mistaken inference. The EMH states that markets are efficient *because* investors only trade on an informed basis. It is difficult, verging on impossible, for particular investors to systematically outperform the rest because capital markets are largely populated by assiduous, calmly calculating, well-informed investors. According to the EMH, this is a highly desirable characteristic of capital markets because it implies that the resulting assets prices ensure that capital is directed towards the most profitable enterprises, thereby maximising the aggregate level of wealth creation to the benefit of investors in general.

None of this proves one way or the other whether capital markets really are efficient in the sense meant by the hypothesis. In fact, the debate about market efficiency is broad and intense, with many subtleties and nuances that lie beyond the scope of this text. Nevertheless, the EMH is clearly of great significance to the theory and practice of portfolio management and, therefore, some of the reservations merit elaboration.

4. Are investors rational?

Before reading on, take a few moments to engage with the Stop and think 5.3 exercise.

Stop and think 5.3

Assume that you *intend to* invest £100 and must choose between two outcomes:

> **Outcome 1: You are certain to get back £150.**
>
> **Outcome 2: You have a 50% chance of getting back £200 and a 50% chance of getting back £100.**

Note down your preference.

Now assume that you *have invested* £200 and must choose between two outcomes:

> **Outcome 1: You are certain to get back £150.**
> **Outcome 2: You have a 50% chance of getting back £200 and a 50% chance of getting back £100.**

Note down your preference.

In the case of the investment offering the prospect of a gain, many studies based on asking similar questions suggest that most people would choose Outcome 1. This corresponds to the notion that investors are risk-averse, meaning that they will not undertake investments that fail to offer the prospect of compensation for risk in the form of greater expected returns. The expected return for Outcome 2 is:

$$(£200 \times 0.5) + (£100 \times 0.5) = £150$$

This is equal to the certain return on 1 and, therefore, Outcome 2 offers no reward for risk-taking. You might obtain £200, but that would be due to luck rather than risk-taking driven by rational assessment. Survey evidence indicates that most respondents to this type of questioning make the 'rational' choice.

But when confronted with the prospect of a loss on an existing investment, research indicates that most people choose Outcome 2. This is the risk-embracing rather than the risk-averse option, i.e. the option about which the actual outcome is unknown beforehand. You might get lucky and get back £200, thereby losing nothing. But you might be unlucky and lose £100. The key point is that you cannot *expect* to be better off by opting for the risky choice. The expected loss on the £200 investment is £50, equal to the loss associated with certainty. The behaviour of most respondents appears 'irrational', with risks being taken without the expectation of a more favourable outcome. How did you choose?

Note that for all scenarios the expected outcome is £150 of wealth. But the prospect of wealth increasing from £100 to £150 is associated with risk-averse behaviour, while the prospect of a decrease from £200 to £150 is associated with risk-intense behaviour. In a more practical context, it suggests that investors may be too keen to bank gains *fearing* a reversal of performance, while also being overly inclined to carry losses *hoping for* a reversal of performance. They are prepared to take bigger risks to avoid losses than to make gains. Investors value financial gains differently to financial losses of the same magnitude.

This interpretation of investor behaviour is known as prospect theory (the character of the behaviour depends on whether the investor is facing the prospect of a loss or a gain). It suggests that the so-called risk-averse, 'rational' investor of portfolio theory is, at best, a description relevant to understanding behaviour under highly contingent conditions and is not inherent to behaviour in all circumstances. The implication is that asset prices do not, therefore, reflect the actions of rational, wealth-maximising, efficient portfolio constructing individuals.

The observations of prospect theory form part of a grouping of arguments that appear under the heading behavioural finance. There are various strands, not necessarily supportive of one another. They share an emphasis on demonstrating that much of the behaviour of investors, even of those who are undeniably skilled and well informed, is 'irrational' if judged by the standards of the EMH and portfolio theory. Let's outline a few of the arguments to be found under the rubric of behavioural finance:

◆ Investors have preconceived notions about different assets and asset classes. Also they place undue importance on first impressions. The upshot is a tendency for investors to filter information for elements that support preconceptions and initial impressions, rather than to examine all the information systematically and dispassionately. This behavioural characteristic is known as confirmation bias. It results in asset prices being biased towards confirming what investors believe in the first place.

◆ Investors exhibit a propensity to latch on to fashionable trends. In the years immediately prior to the new millennium, 'dot.com' companies (new operations connected to the commercialisation of the internet) were all the rage. The huge sums invested drove up the values of businesses, most of which had still to demonstrate serious earnings potential. Investors were under pressure to climb aboard the dot.com bandwagon for fear of missing out on profits from the rapidly rising share prices. Interestingly, even those who believed that values were irrationally inflated could argue that it was still wise to join in, justifying their actions on the basis of the 'greater fool theory' – the idea that so long you're confident that there's a bigger fool prepared to pay even more, there's money to be made playing the fool. As a result, entire classes of assets can become prey to herd behaviour that drives prices well away from any reasoned measure of fair value. And these trends can persist for long periods before eventually blowing up.

◆ Investors tend to oversimplify the causes of past events to the point of suggesting that they could have been easily foreseen. Numerous bankers, analysts, fund managers, traders and regulators are on record stating that they recognised the seeds of the 2007 banking crisis well before it occurred. Unfortunately, the majority are on record making this point after 2007, not before. They could be guilty of hindsight bias, a tendency to convert explanations articulated after an event into before-the-event consciousness. It implies a distorted impression of the prevailing mindset during a past event and encourages an overly optimistic view of one's powers of foresight. If true, hindsight bias generates a tendency among investors to misprice assets because they will underestimate the scale of what is unknown.

Behavioural finance provides much food for thought for anyone looking to gain more insight into asset valuation and investment management. It has an intuitive appeal because many of us, probably all of us, recognise in ourselves and others who we know at least some of the behavioural traits that it identifies. Advocates of technical analysis tend to be sympathetic to many of its observations because they provide a basis for the argument that prices are sufficiently 'irrational' often enough for technical traders to profit. It makes it harder for the efficient market school to mock technical analysis as the application of astrology to financial markets.

Behavioural finance also offers a plausible explanation for what is arguably the Achilles' heel of the portfolio theory-efficient market axis – its discomfort over the frequency of severe, abrupt, market-wide disruptions to supposedly rationally formed systems of prices. Portfolio theory is uneasy with capital market crashes and asset price bubbles, because the theory suggests that they should hardly ever occur. In fact some critics argue that even the routine, everyday price volatility in asset markets exceeds levels that can be explained on the basis of supposedly efficient markets. The response of many who broadly concur with the efficient market model has been a rather lame and vague suggestion that markets are efficient 'most of the time'. By contrast, behavioural finance, with its stress on herd action and 'cognitive biases', is more at ease explaining systemic crises.

Nevertheless, behavioural finance remains some way from dislodging the rational market orthodoxy as the dominant perspective in finance. It is an intriguing but still rather *ad hoc* grouping of ideas. Its most receptive audience is among technical traders and stock-picking investors, who welcome suggestions of excess returns rooted in asset price anomalies and irrational behaviour by others. It also appeals to many of those looking to make sense of the many and varied capital market crises of recent times.

Test yourself 5.2

One of many apparent financial market anomalies is that small companies listed on stock markets tend to offer investors higher returns than larger listed companies after adjusting for risk. One way of thinking about this is that two companies, one large one small, with the same beta values ought to offer the same return. But more often than not, the smaller company outperforms the larger.

a)   **If investors are aware of this anomaly, how would you expect them to respond?**

b)   **If asset markets really are efficient, explain why anomalies of this kind ought not to persist.**

---

5. Should investors be rational?

A glance through contemporary textbooks on investment shows that belief in the notion of risk as something to be managed primarily via asset diversification and in security prices reflecting reasoned expectations are powerful influences on education and practice in finance. Arguably, they have had too much influence. Or perhaps it is fairer to suggest that simplistic and dogmatic renderings of these arguments have helped encourage bad habits in the world of investment management. A July 2012 report on UK equity markets, commissioned by the UK government and chaired by Professor John Kay of the London School of Economics, suggested that some market practitioners 'displayed an almost mystical faith in market efficiency, expressed in simple maxims such as "you can't buck the market" ' (The Kay Review of UK Equity Markets and Long-Term Decision Making). The report went on to indicate that palpable evidence of systematic mispricing of numerous asset classes over many years had done little to dent the faith in market efficiency.

One symptom of this faith has been the spread of asset management styles exemplified by the practice of index tracking. Nowadays fund managers promote a range of investment funds explicitly designed to track the performance of a specified market index. In the UK common examples track the FTSE 100 Index or the FTSE All-Share Index. They offer investors the prospects of returns corresponding to those achieved by the market index, plus or minus a small **tracking error**.

tracking error
A measure of the difference between the actual return on an investment fund and the return on a benchmark. In the case of funds set up to track a market index, the tracking error ought to be negligible.

It is easy to understand the appeal of tracker funds to investors and fund managers conversant in contemporary asset pricing theory.

◆ They resemble investing in a 'market' portfolio, which is something that portfolio theory suggests is beneficial since it offers the fullest dissolution of unrewarded specific risk.

◆ It is an operationally economic method of managing investments because funds merely need to be periodically rebalanced in accordance with the changing relative values of the constituent securities in the index. There's no need for time-consuming and costly investigations of the minutiae of individual assets. And this is doubly welcome because the EMH appears to suggest to many that such efforts are of no value anyway.

It's no surprise that advocates of index tracking cite portfolio theory and efficient markets to justify their arguments. But a more significant development is that the index tracking ethos informs asset management practice well beyond the boundaries of actual tracker funds. While fund managers like to encourage an impression of diligently searching for companies with strong prospects and being discerning in security selection, the reality is that many are managing broadly focused portfolios that look and perform much like index trackers.

According to some authoritative voices (including contributors to the aforementioned Kay Review), this development is symptomatic of problems in the operation of capital markets that require urgent remedies. Too many professionals in the asset management business are, to use the colourful vernacular of the critics, 'closet trackers' and 'index huggers'. They point to:

◆ an unwarranted degree of replication in the investment decisions undertaken by fund managers and the structure of the portfolios that they administer. Despite the enormous range of funds offered by large numbers of institutional providers, the preponderance of investment philosophies emphasising the desirability of broadly spread portfolios means that ostensibly distinct funds are often very similar;

◆ a shift away from investment decision-making rooted in the analysis of corporate fundamentals in favour of a style based on staying attuned to evolving market trends and sentiments, analysing the trading behaviour of other participants and reverse-engineering the trading strategies of successful performers in the hope of discovering their 'secrets';

◆ a shift of performance criteria from absolute measures (such as, to put it a little crudely, making money or losing money) towards relative measures. Nowadays the performance of fund managers is typically assessed against benchmarks such as a market index or the results achieved by other fund managers. Critics suggest that this inculcates an inherently conservative attitude to investment because asset managers are less interested being among the best performers than avoiding being among the worst;

◆ a tendency to generate levels of asset price volatility disconnected from actual shifts in the underlying economic and commercial outlook. Why? Because institutions holding broadly spread, but not dissimilar portfolios have a propensity to adjust and restructure them at similar times. For instance, tracker funds are liable to exhibit high levels of coordinated trading activity because of the need to maintain a predetermined and shared relation to the index in question. This results in bouts of generalised, price-destabilising security trading for largely technical reasons, due primarily to dependence on a particular portfolio management philosophy; and

◆ a tendency for large, established funds to invest almost exclusively in large, established companies that feature prominently on stock markets. As the amounts of client wealth being managed grow, funds tend to become less prepared to invest in smaller companies because of the complexities of managing enormous numbers of different securities. The upshot, according to critics, is that administrative convenience rather than asset returns drives many investment and trading decisions. A further by-product is that it exacerbates the obstacles that younger, more entrepreneurially driven companies typically experience in gaining access to capital. In effect, the increasingly institutionalised character of asset management encourages a misallocation of capital: precisely the opposite of what the EMH claims.

Making it work 5.4: Are funds too big for our good?

Imagine the case of an UK investment fund managing a portfolio of securities with an aggregate market value of £2 billion. This is a large fund but not unusual by UK standards. The management takes the view that it does not wish to hold more than 50 different securities in the portfolio, because the task of administering the portfolio in line with the fund objectives would become too complex. Furthermore, it does not wish to own more than 5% of the shares of any individual company. The average investment per company would be £40 million:

$$\frac{£2,000,000,000}{50} = £40,000,000$$

If ownership of any one company is capped at 5%, it means that the average company in which the fund invests will have a market value of £800 million:

$$\frac{£40,000,000}{0.05} = £800,000,000$$

The **median** value of companies listed on the **FTSE 250 Index** stood at around £720 million at the end of October 2012, which suggests that the normal investment habitat for a fund of this size would be the largest 200 or so UK companies. It does not mean that the fund would not invest in smaller companies. But there are compelling practical reasons why the fund's managers are liable to concentrate on shares in larger companies.

median
The middle value in a sample as distinct from the mean, which is the average of a sample.

FTSE 250 Index
A stock market index that expresses developments in the value of the 250 companies below the FTSE 100 constituents by market capitalisation.

In making decisions about risking wealth on uncertain ventures, it is obvious that investors ought to be as well informed as possible and adopt a reasoned attitude to assessing the prospects and pitfalls. It's the rational and sensible thing to do. But whether this can be comprehensively represented in a theory and codified as a set of guidelines is extremely doubtful. Eminent critics of the EMH have highlighted an internal contradiction. If asset prices reflect the reasoning of well-informed investors to the extent that investors cannot expect to gain an advantage from their knowledge, then why would they bother to become well informed? The rational act would be to not bother with the task of becoming informed, with the result that asset prices reflect nothing in particular at any time. This is absurd.

Let's finish the chapter by revisiting Philip Morris. Recall that this company's share price effectively doubled over the three years to September 2012. Over the same period the S&P 500 index rose by 40%. Hence the increase in Philip Morris' share price was part of a broader process encompassing the shares of most large US companies.

The connection between the performance of individual investments and broader market trends is a fundamental concern of portfolio management. But we need to be careful about how we articulate the connection. A general rise in the stock market does not explain what happened to Philip Morris' or any other company. It does not constitute an answer to the question why; it merely rephrases the question in terms of why did the market index rise? Secondly, it is just as reasonable to suggest that variations in market indices reflect rather than cause changes in the share prices of the constituent companies. Incidentally Philip Morris' beta value for the period, based on the three years of monthly returns, was approximately zero. Thus, according to the CAPM, Philip Morris' exposure to systematic risk ought to have resulted in a return comparable to the risk-free return, which during this period was under 1% a year.

share-buyback
The use of liquid reserves by a company to buy, and effectively retire, a portion of its issued share capital.

In a sense the CAPM result – that the return on Philip Morris shares had little to do with the market – might be instructive. Over the period in question Philip Morris was undertaking a large-scale **share-buyback** programme. Between the start of the scheme in May 2008 and June 2012 the company spent $24.4 billion retiring 449.9 million shares – equivalent to 21.3% of its issued share capital of 2008. In August 2012 Philip Morris revealed plans for a further $18 billion worth of share buybacks.

Spending tens of billions of dollars retiring more than one-fifth of a company's equity is without doubt of enormous import to investors. However, establishing how it will impact on the company's share price is not straightforward. There is no reason why a buyback scheme should automatically have a positive impact on the price of the remaining shares. In fact, the opposite is just as plausible. Paying shareholders cash for shares reduces the number of shares outstanding but also reduces the assets of the company (it has less money). Indeed should a company, as an inducement, offer a buyback price above the prevailing market price, then logic suggests that the price of the remaining shares ought to fall, for the simple reason that the assets of the company decline by a greater amount than the share capital.

So why did the share price rise? There isn't scope here to undertake a systematic analysis of how the actions of Philip Morris affected its share price. We would need to examine its sales and earnings performance, its debt and dividend policies, the characteristics of its shareholders, the evolution of the market environment and many other factors. Even then, there would be plenty of room for disagreement. For the record, here's my take on events.

Philip Morris is a classic **cash cow** business. It has low production costs and a stable (some might say addicted) customer base. Competition is muted but there are limited prospects for the market to grow. The upshot is that annual earnings are healthy and reliable but there is little purpose reinvesting them in the same line of business, due to the limited growth prospects. Such companies have essentially two options. They can use the surpluses to effect diversification into other more dynamic markets, or they can become cash cows consistently channelling most of the earnings to the shareholders as dividends and share buybacks. In addition to the buyback programme, Philip Morris also raised dividend payments significantly over the period.

cash cow
A business that consistently produces earnings well in excess of those needed to grow the business to its maximum potential.

Now put this in the context of the aftermath of the 2007–8 banking crisis with yields on savings below 1%. To investors in these conditions, cash-rich companies like Philip Morris might look like stable and reliable payers of income over the medium term. In other words, they might well regard Philip Morris shares as being, in a sense, low-risk, interest-bearing assets.

In 2012 Philip Morris paid a dividend of $3.08 per share, representing a yield of 3.45% on the share price of $89.30. While modest, this compares very favourably to yields on savings accounts and government bonds. A yield in excess of 3% on a 'reliable' investment suddenly looks attractive and $89 a share doesn't seem inordinately expensive. In effect, the primary drivers of Philip Morris' share price over the period in question may have been its idiosyncrasies rather than market developments. Of course, the real skill would be to have anticipated this back in 2009.

The point is not whether the interpretation is correct (it's certainly well short of being complete). It is that investment analysis involves judgements and interpretations, many aspects of which only make sense in context. Contexts change and demand reappraisal. Furthermore, part of change is innovation: the emergence of genuinely novel investment possibilities. Attempting to understand and anticipate changes in the investment environment is a daunting task. Too many rely on portfolio theory as a substitute, believing that it offers a set of procedures which, if applied in a systematic fashion to investment, ought to work. Critics have convincingly demonstrated this to be a fallacy – worse still, one that can have unintended and unfortunate consequences. Portfolio theory is an important tool for providing insights into the exposure of particular investments to broader market risk factors. By inference, it can also help specify and quantify specific risk factors. But it is less useful for measuring the ebb and flow and scale of market risk itself.

Test yourself 5.3

American professor of economics Burton Malkiel has suggested that a blindfolded chimpanzee throwing darts at the *Wall Street Journal* listing of companies is likely to produce a portfolio that performs as well as that of the average fund manager. Explain whether this constitutes an argument for or against the claims of EMH.

Chapter summary

◆ EMH suggests that asset prices in well-developed markets are 'fair' in the sense that markets exhibit a tendency neither to systematically overvalue nor to systematically undervalue assets.

◆ Highly developed levels of operational efficiency in financial markets mean that prices ought to adjust very rapidly to new information, suggesting few technical impediments in the way of prices adjusting to fair values.

◆ A key implication of EMH is that it is very unlikely that individual investors can systematically earn excess returns through the application of either technical trading techniques or via decision-making based on fundamental analysis.

◆ The investigation into efficient markets stresses three characteristic levels of efficiency: weak, semi-strong and strong form efficiency.

◆ Behavioural finance points to evidence provided by choice experiments conducted under controlled conditions and high levels of asset price volatility to argue that the assumptions of EMH are flawed.

◆ EMH and portfolio theory, intentionally or otherwise, have helped to legitimise investment practices (such as index tracking) that some commentators insist do damage in the long run.

Part Three

Asset valuation, risk and risk management

Overview

Part three focuses on the interaction between financial asset prices, returns and risk. Chapter 6 concentrates on money markets where relatively straightforward products offering single cash returns are traded. It is generally assumed to be an arena of low risk, where the primary motives are to hold funds in reserve for short periods and access working capital for operational purposes. Chapter 7 shifts the spotlight onto the market for longer term credit provision and examines the growth of securitised debt arrangements. Chapter 8 highlights important features of the markets for equity capital. Investors in both debt and equity assets are effectively supplying capital to productive enterprises and are therefore, to varying degrees, risking wealth with some expectation that it will be enhanced.

Chapter 9 argues that some risks arising from economic processes ought to be nullified since they do not hold out the prospect of systematic gains. In particular, uncertainties connected to interest rates and currency rates can damage fundamentally successful investment performance. Chapter 9 outlines how derivatives can be employed to hedge against these uncertainties. It also indicates how they can be used to facilitate leveraged risk-taking.

Learning objectives

At the end of this part, students will be able to:

◆ demonstrate competence in the use of some basic security valuation techniques relating to assets traded on the money and capital markets;

◆ understand the scale of risk typically associated with different types of financial assets;

◆ demonstrate knowledge of the institutional context in which different classes of assets are created, valued and traded;

◆ distinguish those factors that are known and highly predictable from those which are difficult to measure with any certainty when examining the risks and returns on financial securities;

◆ appreciate that exposure to some uncertainties that arise during the course of investing bears a closer comparison to gambling than the risk-taking connected to productive investment;

◆ articulate the case for hedging those risks that are extraneous to the core process of investment;

◆ tackle basic problems concerning the relationship between spot and forward asset prices, and the application of derivatives to hedge interest rate and currency risks; and

◆ articulate an understanding of the paradox that financial derivatives offering the possibility of hedging against certain risks also facilitate leveraged speculation related to those very same risk factors.

Chapter Six
Money markets and short-term securities

List of topics

1   Money markets
2   Treasury bills
3   Commercial paper
4   Banker's acceptances
5   Sale and repurchase agreements (repos)

Introduction

In the conduct of business, companies (financial and non-financial), not-for-profit organisations and public bodies find themselves periodically in possession of temporary cash surpluses. At other times they experience temporary shortfalls of liquidity and so require access to funding. Such occurrences have long been a normal part of the ebb and flow of commerce and are managed via the money markets.

1. Money markets

The term 'money markets' summarises a range of financial practices that, broadly speaking, involve decisions to invest or borrow funds for short periods of time. It is normal practice to regard short-term as referring to investments and loans with less than a year to maturity. While a loosely accurate description, this notion doesn't properly specify what distinguishes the money markets from capital markets; the difference is more than a simple issue of the maturity of assets.

◆   A key motivation behind money market investment is the need or desire to hold money in reserve for future purposes. The aim is not to risk capital on uncertain ventures but to store it for limited periods until it is needed. Of course, investors could hoard funds privately. But the money markets offer a better solution – a range of financial products that offer a return over short periods. These products ought to be 'safe' given that the objective is to hold wealth in reserve for future risk taking, not to risk capital in the present.

◆   The driving force behind money market borrowing is the need to manage temporary deficits that occur as a normal feature of corporate activity. Borrowers do not want to take out long-term loans when funds are only required for short periods. Money markets offer methods of borrowing funds for short periods. Naturally, therefore, money market borrowers are generally regarded as being very highly creditworthy.

The definition of money markets as revolving around financial arrangements that mature within one year is practically relevant because the terms to maturity of an asset is itself a component of risk in the sense that the longer the period, the more time there is for things to go wrong. A variety of financial securities issued and traded on money markets may be described as short-term. The following sections focus on the most significant examples.

2. Treasury bills

The single most significant class of security on the money markets is treasury bills, the generic term for securities issued by central governments that have maturities of less than one year. Treasury bills represent short-term borrowing on the part of the issuing government.

The usual method of issuing treasury bills is via weekly auction. In chapter 1 it was mentioned that the US government sold $124 billion of bills at the end of July 2012. In the UK the process is administered by the Debt Management Office (DMO) which offers treasury bills with one-month, three-month, six-month and twelve-month maturities (although since taking over the role in April 2000 the DMO has yet to issue any twelve-month bills). A UK treasury bill is a promise, made by Her Majesty's Treasury, to pay the investor a fixed sum of £100 on the maturity date. This fixed sum has a variety of names: face value, par value, nominal value, maturity value, redemption value. The question is: how much will an investor be willing to pay for the bill at the outset?

Table 6.1 Treasury bill returns and prices

Term to maturity	Annual return	Market price (per £100)
1 month	2.00%	
3 months	2.50%	£97.087
6 months	2.80%	
12 months	3.00%	£97.087

Table 6.1 lists the annual rates of return and market prices for treasury bills with differing periods to maturity. In each case, investors are being offered a cash sum of £100 at a specified point in the future. The prices that they are prepared to pay at the outset must be such that they offer annual returns equivalent of those listed. In finance, these prices are known as the present values or discounted values of the future cash flows. The rates of return are also known

as discount yields. In the case of treasury bills there is only a single cash flow, £100. Hence prices are the discounted values of £100.

To illustrate the principle of market price as a present value, let's start with the twelve-month treasury bill. Investors are being offered a cash sum of £100 a year from now and require a rate of return of 3%. The price of the bill can be determined using the following formula:

$$P_0 = \frac{100}{(1 + r)}$$

Where:

P_0 = the current market price of the treasury bill;

100 = the maturity value of the bill; and

r = the annual rate of return.

The price is:

$$P_0 = \frac{100}{(1.03)} = £97.087$$

An investor buys the bill for £97.087 today and receives £100 a year from now, representing a monetary gain of £2.913. The sum of £2.913 is equivalent to an annual return of 3% on the investment of £97.087.

What about, say, the bill with three months to maturity? It is normal practice to express rates of return on securities as annualised rates, so that the returns on securities in the same asset class but with different maturities can be easily compared. Investors in the three-month bill require a return equivalent to 2.5% on an annual basis. But since they are only investing for three months (a quarter of the year) the annual rate must be divided accordingly in order to determine the price of the bill. The modified pricing formula is:

$$P_0 = \frac{100}{\left(1 + \dfrac{r}{365/n}\right)}$$

Where:

n = the number of days to the maturity of the treasury bill.

$$P_0 = \frac{100}{\left(1 + \dfrac{0.025}{365/91}\right)} = £99.381$$

An investor buys the bill for £99.381 today and receives £100 in 91 days. The gain is £0.619, which translates into an annual return of 2.5% on the investment of £99.381.

Test yourself 6.1

Assume that the one-month bill matures in 30 days and the six-month bill in 182 days. Calculate their prices and monetary gains based on the annualised returns in Table 6.1.

zero coupon
Term that describes
financial securities that
offer a single payment on
maturity, with no interim
reward. Also known as pure
discount.

pure discount
See **Zero coupon**.

coupon payment
A term that is often used to
describe interest payments
on bonds.

Treasury bills exemplify a widespread feature of financial securities traded on money markets, namely that they trade as **zero coupon** or **pure discount** securities. Investors receive just a single cash payment, equivalent to the face value of the security, on the maturity date. There are no interim cash flows in the form of interest payments (or **coupon payments**). Hence, the financial gain is entirely dependent on the securities trading at prices below face values (they trade at discounts to face values). Investors earn a return because as time passes, the market values of these securities edge closer and closer to their face values. On the maturity date, prices will equal face values.

Treasury bills also provide a clear demonstration of another important characteristic of security prices. Security prices are equivalent to the discounted value (or present value) of the future cash flows being offered. Thus in the examples above where the £100 received is divided by 1 plus the discount rate in decimals, the resulting security price is a discounted or present value of the future cash flow. The notion of security prices as the present value of future cash flows reoccurs constantly in the context of asset valuation.

At the weekly auction on 16 November 2012, the DMO sold £2.5 billion of treasury bills. The results, as reported by the DMO, are presented in Table 6.2.

Table 6.2 Treasury bill tender results for the week ending 16 November 2012

Maturity	Amount borrowed	Average yield	Average price (per £100)
1 month	£500 million	0.20534%	£99.98425
3 months	£500 million	0.22627%	£99.94362
6 months	£1,500 million	0.30315%	£99.84907

The bills are sold initially to 'primary participants', which currently consists of 28 banks. Investors wishing to bid for the latest issue must go through a primary participant. The minimum bid size at auction is for £500,000 face value. Alternatively, previously issued treasury bills can be bought on the secondary market.

Let's focus on the one-month bill. The auction took place on Friday 16 November and successful bidders were required to pay for the securities on the next business day, Monday 19 November (known as the **settlement date**). In return they were paid £100 on the maturity date of 17 December. The investment period was, therefore, 28 days. What *rate of return* did investors receive?

settlement date
The day on which the terms
of a trade are completed
with cash and assets being
credited to and debited
from participants' accounts.

An investor paying the average price would have spent £99.98425 and received £100 after 28 days; a cash gain of £0.01575. Dividing this by the price paid for the bill gives the percentage rate of return. The *annual* rate of return can be calculated using the following formula:

$$r = \frac{100 - P_0}{P_0}\left(\frac{365}{n}\right)$$

The annual return on the 28-day bill is:

$$r = \frac{100 - 99.98425}{99.98425}\left(\frac{365}{28}\right) = 0.0020534 \ (0.20534\%)$$

Note that this is the same as the return quoted in Table 6.2.

Worked example 6.1: Pricing the three-month treasury bill

The maturity date for the three-month bill is 18 February 2013. From the settlement date of 19 November 2012 it is 91 days. The average sale price was £99.94362, giving an investor a cash gain of £0.05638. The annualised return was:

$$r = \frac{100 - 99.94362}{99.94362}\left(\frac{365}{91}\right) = 0.0022627 \ (0.22627\%)$$

Note that the return once again corresponds to the rate given in Table 6.2.

Test yourself 6.2

The six-month bill matures on 20 May 2013. Work out the number of days from the settlement date to the maturity date and, based on the treasury bill price in Table 6.2, calculate the cash gain and the annualised yield.

Investors buy treasury bills primarily because they offer a safe medium for holding cash reserves. The enhancement of wealth is not a key motivation. Indeed, it may not have escaped your notice that UK treasury bills offered barely any wealth enhancement at the end of 2012. One-month bills sold on 16 November offered a return of little more than 1.5 pence on an investment of nearly £100. A perusal of treasury bills issued by the governments of most of the world's major economies would reveal a similar pattern of negligible rates of return in recent years. It is in marked contrast to the era before the global banking crisis when yields on treasury bills, though among the lowest available, were at least of a meaningful size. For instance, between 2004 and 2007, UK treasury bills offered annual returns in the region of 4.5–5.5%, which was 20 or more times higher than the returns of late 2012!

Why are investors prepared to buy treasury bills offering returns close to zero? The vast majority of investors are large institutions such as investment and pension funds, banks and sovereign states. In the case of sovereign states, the most important example being China, there are significant economic and strategic considerations informing the willingness to buy what are primarily US treasury bills. Funds and banks hold large amounts of bills but they form only small components of the entire assets that they manage. Treasury bills are not bought for the contribution they might make to portfolio returns, but for their status as the safest method of holding reserves. Even so, it says much about the fear running through the financial system that institutional investors are prepared to accept virtually zero returns for the protection of reserves.

3. Commercial paper

Commercial paper refers to securities issued by financial and non-financial corporations with short-term maturities. It is effectively a private sector form of treasury bills. Typical reasons for issuing commercial paper are: to address temporary cash flow shortages arising from variations in working capital needs or seasonal factors; provide bridging finance while longer-term funding is organised, and for use in the structuring of **interest rate swaps**. In fact, many corporations operate ongoing commercial paper programmes designed to provide funding for 'general company purposes'. The programmes are managed flexibly with the scale of new security issues dictated by the needs of the moment.

interest rate swaps
An OTC agreement between two parties to swap streams of interest payments. The most common type involves swapping a stream of fixed rate payments for variable rate payments.

Commercial paper offers investors a fixed payment on maturity. Terms to maturity are short: as little as a single day and, usually, up to one year. In the US, maturities rarely exceed 270 days as they otherwise have to be registered with the Securities and Exchange Commission, thereby incurring additional issue expenses. According to the US Federal Reserve, the average terms to maturity of commercial paper issued in the US was around 50 days in late 2012. The face values of commercial paper are large. In the case of dollar-denominated paper, typical values are $100,000 and $500,000.

At the end of October 2012, the total amount of dollar-denominated commercial paper debt outstanding in the USA was $946 billion. Even this enormous figure does not accurately reflect the scale of dealing. The paper is short-term, much of it very short-term, with many companies operating rollover programmes whereby new issues fund the repayment of maturing issues. So even if the aggregate outstanding debt is unchanged, the new issues business remains active.

Commercial paper, like treasury bills, is issued on a pure discount basis. Discount yields are calculated in the same way as those for treasury bills. Yields are higher than for treasury bills because commercial paper, despite the fact that most of it is assessed as high grade by ratings agencies such as Moody's and Standard & Poor, still entails greater risk than placing funds with central government. Table 6.3 compares yields on commercial paper and treasury bills recorded by the US Federal Reserve on 16 November 2012.

Table 6.3 Yields on US money market securities 16 November 2012

	Term to maturity	
	1 month	**3 months**
Treasury bills	0.12%	0.09%
Commercial paper AA (non-financial)	0.15%	0.21%
Commercial paper A2/P2 (non-financial)	0.45%	0.42%
Commercial paper AA (financial)	0.16%	0.22%
Asset-backed commercial paper	0.27%	0.30%

The highest rated commercial paper, accorded AA status by the Federal Reserve, offered very small premiums over treasury bill yields. The one-month yield on AA rated commercial paper issued by non-financial companies was just 3 **basis points** over the treasury bill rate, while the three-month yield was 12 basis points higher. A2/P2 is a lower credit rating for commercial paper, as defined by the ratings systems of Standard & Poor (A2) and Moody's (P2 or Prime 2). It is still a high grade classification; securities with an A2/P2 rating are included in the category of **investment grade** assets. Table 6.3 shows that A2/P2 paper was offering a premium in the region of 30 basis points above the treasury bill rate.

basis point
In finance a basis point is equal to one hundredth of 1% and is a widely used method for quoting interest rate changes and differences.

investment grade
A term that applies to debt securities deemed by ratings agencies to be of high quality and low risk.

Making it work 6.1: Network Rail commercial paper programme

Network Rail Infrastructure Ltd is responsible for the maintenance and development of Britain's rail tracks. Its borrowing requirements are undertaken by a **special purpose vehicle** known as Network Rail Infrastructure Finance Plc (NRIF), which is a company legally independent of Network Rail. In effect, investors lend to NRIF, which then lends to Network Rail.

NRIF is authorised to issue commercial paper up to a maximum of £4 billion under two programmes: a US and a Euro programme. The paper is offered on a pure discount basis and can be issued in a wide variety of currencies, but may not exceed the equivalent of £4 billion. The standard issue denominations are $500,000, €500,000 and £100,000, with maximum maturities of 364 days.

special purpose vehicle
A subsidiary operation set up for a specific financial undertaking. In some cases the aim is to reduce tax payments by registering the SPV in a tax haven. They also offer mechanisms for removing liabilities from sponsors' balance sheets.

The paper issued by NRIF is indemnified by the UK government. As a result it is assigned the highest credit ratings: Moody's P1, Standard & Poor A1, Fitch F1+. NRIF has appointed a number of banks to act as dealers for its commercial paper, effectively making them responsible for disseminating relevant information to existing and potential investors.

Asset-backed commercial paper (ABCP) is a type of commercial paper that is used to fund investment in other financial assets. A typical example involves a bank setting up a special purpose vehicle (SPV), which sells commercial paper in its own name. The resulting funds are used to buy assets, typically securities created from income streams connected to corporate sales, credit card debts, car loans, equipment leases, mortgages, student loans, etc. Often these income streams are assets of the sponsoring bank.

An SPV is normally set up to be 'bankruptcy remote' from the originating organisation, meaning that should it become insolvent, it has no direct financial impact on the parent body. For a sponsoring bank, an SPV initiative provides a means of turning gradually maturing assets such as mortgage and credit card repayments into cash. The attraction of asset-backed commercial paper for investors is the prospect of competitive yields on short-term assets.

ABCP can appear a very safe investment even if individual components of the supporting collateral are risky. The underlying collateral usually consists of diverse and varied assets. By applying 'portfolio' assumptions to the collateral, it is tempting to assume that the prospect of losing money is remote because only a small percentage of the underlying assets are liable to default. This was, in fact, the attitude of credit rating agencies before 2007 about schemes by banks to securitise various credit-related income streams and sell them to SPVs using commercial paper and other short-term borrowing devices. The low default estimations proved to be wildly optimistic and values of collateral assets collapsed.

Commercial paper can be traded. In practice, the market is not very active. One reason for this is that many issuing companies deal directly with institutional investors and can, therefore, take into account the maturity preferences of the investors when structuring new issues.

Making it work 6.2: Cantor Fitzgerald's asset-backed commercial paper

In May 2012 the global financial services company Cantor Fitzgerald (one of 21 authorised primary dealers of US government securities) announced a new ABCP programme. Cantor Fitzgerald set up a bankruptcy remote SPV called Institutional Secured Funding Ltd (ISF) in Jersey, which is authorised to issue up to $20 billion of commercial paper.

ISF uses the proceeds from the sale of ABCP to finance sale and repurchase arrangements (see below) with banks. ISF effectively buys securities from banks who commit to repurchase them at predetermined prices. It amounts to ISF lending money to banks on a short-term basis, for which it will charge interest (known as a repo rate). This, in turn, is the source of the returns on ISF's commercial paper.

Test yourself 6.3

Identify three reasons why companies might wish to issue commercial paper.

4. Banker's acceptances

Banker's acceptances are financial securities that originate in short-term corporate borrowing, especially borrowing to finance international trade transactions. Assume that a UK company must pay $1 million for imports from the US but wishes to pay in two months' time. By contrast, the US company wants immediate payment. The UK company approaches a bank (probably one it normally deals with for other corporate banking services) which agrees to lend the money needed to pay the US company. In return the company issues a security to the bank: a promise to pay the face value to the bank in two months. This is a banker's acceptance.

Assume that the face value is $1,006,000, i.e. the company agrees to pay the bank an additional £6,000 over the amount lent. This is equivalent to an annualised return on the acceptance note of:

$$r = \frac{1,006,000 - 1,000,000}{1,000,000} \left(\frac{365}{60}\right) = 0.0365 \ (3.65\%)$$

Banks can, in turn, sell these acceptance notes prior to maturity. They are not very intensely traded, mainly due to the lack of standardisation. After all, each commercial transaction on which an acceptance is based is unique in terms of the company, amount and maturity involved. Nevertheless, there are investment funds that specialise in managing portfolios of short-term securities and banker's acceptances form one of the core assets classes in these portfolios.

5. Sale and repurchase agreements (repos)

According to the International Capital Market Association's (ICMA) semi-annual survey of repo markets in June 2012, the total value of outstanding repos on the books of the institutions responding to the survey stood at $5,647 billion (or $5.647 trillion). Technically, repos are not themselves securities since they are not traded. Nevertheless, they constitute a very important mechanism by which traders and fund managers can hold funds on reserve for short periods as well as offering opportunities to leverage investments in other securities. For these reasons, repos are worth examining.

A repo, short for 'sale and repurchase agreement', involves one party selling securities to another while simultaneously agreeing to repurchase those securities at an agreed price on a specified date in the future. From the standpoint of the party selling securities, the repurchase commitment means that a repo is really a method of borrowing funds short-term rather than a genuine sale of assets. The recipient of securities effectively makes funds available to the seller, i.e. lends funds secured by assets that exist as collateral supporting the loan.

From the perspective of the lender the transaction is known as a reverse-repo: a purchase of securities coupled with an agreement to sell them back to the counterparty at the predetermined price on an agreed date. In money markets, banks and brokerages have institutionalised the counterparty function, acting as the reverse-repo party for clients wanting repo arrangements and as the repo party to clients wanting reverse repos. Since reverse repos are merely the same as repos, but from the opposite vantage point, there is no need to address both separately.

Repos are based on a wide variety of financial obligations. However, the largest component of the market is repos on government-issued securities. According to the ICMA June 2012 survey, 41.6% of outstanding repos referred to government securities, with a further 12.2% constituted by repos on securities issued by municipal and supranational public bodies. A further 19% referred to corporate bonds and 14.7% to corporate equities.

What attracts money market participants to repos?

◆   Traders in fixed interest assets, such as corporate and government bonds, sell repos to obtain cheap finance for the acquisition of securities. It is a flexible method of financing because repos can be arranged quickly and arrangements readily extended or shortened. Traders also use reverse repos to hedge short positions in securities or speculate on falling prices.

◆   Buyers of repos, such as money market funds, obtain returns on assets that are invariably low risk given the collateral provided by sellers. Another attraction is that repos offer flexible lending periods, making them useful tools in fund management. Repos can also be a convenient, cost-effective, method of acquiring assets needed to settle other trades.

Repo terms are mostly very short, with maturities of one month or less being the most common. Again, data from the ICMA survey indicates that 49.9% of repos have maturities of less than one month. Indeed, 17.5% are 'overnight' with a sale followed by repurchase the next day (it's worth stressing that much of the overnight business is subject to rollover, with repo arrangements being renewed daily). Only 13.3% of outstanding repos in June 2012 had maturities in excess of one year with this being a record figure.

In order to illustrate how a repo deal is structured, assume that a bond trader wishes to buy government bonds but does not have access to the necessary funds, and therefore acquires the bonds via a repo arrangement.

1.   The bond trader purchases bonds and simultaneously enters into a repo with a brokerage company. The repo involves selling the bonds to the broker and agreeing to buy them back for a fixed price on a predetermined date in the future.

2.   The broker charges the bond trader a rate of interest, known as the repo rate.

3.   The broker may not be willing to lend the bond trader the full market value of the bonds. The most likely reason is concern that the bond trader might not deliver on the promise to repurchase, thereby leaving the broker holding bonds that could have fallen in value (a decline in the value of the collateral provides an incentive to avoid repurchase). The broker may, therefore, only lend a portion of the value of the collateral. The difference is known as a **haircut**.

4.   On the repurchase date the bond trader repays the money advanced together with the interest charge and receives the bonds in return. In principle, this could be done by entering into another repo so that newly borrowed funds are used to pay what is owed on the previous repo.

haircut
The difference between the market value of an asset and the value assigned by a broker lending a client funds to purchase the asset.

Worked example 6.2: Repos and leverage

Imagine that the UK government has just issued bonds with the interest rate fixed at 0.75% of the face value. Since the face value is £100, the annual interest is £0.75. Let's further assume that the market price is £100 (they are trading at face value), meaning that the bonds offer investors an annual rate of return of 0.75%.

A bond trader wishes to buy £10 million of these bonds and has decided that a one-month repo offers the most cost-effective method. The annual rate of interest on one-month repos is 0.45% and a broker charges a haircut of 2% on UK government bond repos. The trader pays £10 million for the bonds and at the same time enters into a repo. The broker charges a haircut of 2% and, therefore, lends the trader:

$$\frac{£10,000,000}{1.02} = £9,803,900$$

The sum £9,803,900 implies a haircut of £196,100, which is equivalent to the 2% of £9,803,900. The bond trader, in effect, contributes £196,100 to purchase the £10 million of bonds.

Assume that after one month (30 days) the bond's price has risen to £100.06 and that this is due to 30 days' worth of accrued interest. Given the annual interest payment of £0.75 per bond, the accrued interest is:

$$\frac{£0.75}{365} \times 30 = £0.06$$

Accrued interest causes the bond price to rise by 6 pence, meaning that the total value of the bonds is £10,006,000.

After 30 days the repo is due for termination. The bond trader has to repay the broker £9,803,900 plus interest:

$$£9,803,900 \left(1 + \frac{0.0045}{365/30}\right) = £9,807,526$$

With bonds worth £10,006,000 and a repayment of £9,807,526 the bond trader is left with £198,474. The trader's investment of £196,100 has grown to £198,474 over one month, equivalent to an annual return of:

$$\frac{£198,474 - £196,100}{£196,100} \times \frac{365}{30} = 0.147 \ (14.7\%)$$

The trader achieves a rate of return of 14.7% on UK government bonds that are themselves yielding only 0.75%. The additional return is due to the fact that the majority of the capital to purchase the bonds was borrowed using a repo that charged just 0.45%.

Test yourself 6.4

Worked example 6.2 suggests that repos can be used to increase returns significantly due to the leverage potential. Assume that after one month the bond price was unchanged at £100. Calculate the bond trader's return and comment on the impact of leverage.

Chapter summary

◆   Money markets provide mechanisms for corporations, governments, public bodies and other institutions to hold temporary surpluses in reserve and borrow funds for short periods.

◆   Money market transactions are conventionally defined as those with maturities of one year or less.

◆   A prominent feature of money market activity is the issue of pure discount securities, primarily treasury bills and commercial paper.

◆   Financial security prices correspond to the present value of future cash flows. Pure discount security prices are relatively simple to calculate because there is only a single cash flow to consider.

◆   Whatever the term to maturity of an asset, yields are normally expressed as annual yields. Hence when examining the interaction between asset yields and prices, adjustments must be made to account for the actual term to maturity.

◆   Banker's acceptances involve banks being prepared to provide trade credit that helps facilitate commercial transactions.

◆   Sale and repurchase agreements offer a particularly flexible method for gaining access to short-term finance, because arrangements can be created quickly and can be shortened or extended in accordance with circumstances.

Chapter Seven
Fixed interest markets and bonds

List of topics

1   The market for securitised debt
2   Plain vanilla bonds
3   Risk and fixed interest securities
4   Variations on plain vanilla
5   Fixed interest securities and portfolio management

Introduction

The arrangement of short-term credit is the characteristic feature of money market transactions. Those seeking to borrow for longer terms look for finance in the capital markets. The difference between the money markets and capital markets is mainly one of purpose. In general, borrowers seek funding in money markets to manage routine and temporary cash flow imbalances, whereas borrowers in capital markets seek funding for longer-term commitments such as new investment projects that invariably entail a greater degree of uncertainty.

Capital market lenders effectively hand over use of funds to others for extended periods of time. It means that the motive of holding money on reserve is much less likely to be primary. Rates of return as rewards for risk figure more prominently in lenders' calculations; lending longer-term implies investment in the fuller sense of earning rewards commensurate with the risks taken.

Credit occurs in non-securitised and securitised forms. Individuals agree personal and mortgage-related loans with banks and other financial institutions. Corporations also make use of credit offered by the banking system. But along with governments and other public bodies, many corporations borrow funds by selling securities rather than applying to banks for loans. These securities, known as bonds, are similar in key respects to bank loans. The indebted party, in return for access to funding, agrees to make interest payments and to repay the principle amount in accordance with the terms of the agreement. However, bonds also differ in important ways, especially when viewed from the vantage point of investors in bonds.

1. The market for securitised debt

Term loans entail borrowing from financial institutions, primarily banks. The banks function as intermediaries, converting the deposits from savers into loans forwarded to borrowers. By contrast, the sale of bonds (to pension funds, insurance companies, mutual funds, investment trusts, hedge funds and other investors) means approaching investors directly.

The practice of central governments borrowing money via the issue of bonds goes back centuries. But nowadays it is commonplace for large corporate borrowers to do likewise, bypassing banks and borrowing money by offering bonds directly to investors. This development is known as financial **disintermediation**, a process whereby the status of banks in mediating the flow of savings to corporate borrowers has declined. Table 7.1 indicates the scale of bond issues by corporations (Eurobonds) and the UK government over the decade to 2011.

disintermediation

Financial disintermediation describes a growing tendency for large corporations to bypass banks and borrow money directly from investors by selling bonds to them. It constitutes an erosion of the traditional intermediary position of banks between savers and borrowers.

Table 7.1 Bond Issues on the London Stock Exchange 2002–11

Year	Eurobond issues		UK government bonds
	Number of issues	Gross amount raised (£bn)	Gross amount raised (£bn)
2002	1,824	159.94	22.19
2003	2,077	213.41	52.53
2004	2,939	217.69	48.34
2005	2,550	269.39	71.94
2006	3,159	414.29	56.29
2007	4,325	375.89	59.75
2008	3,735	585.93	114.05
2009	3,121	459.73	216.93
2010	3,585	408.62	143.87
2011	3,593	416.57	167.15

Disintermediation is largely restricted to the borrowing arrangements of large, well-established companies. For smaller companies, banks continue to be the primary source of credit. However, even in relation to borrowing by larger bodies, banking institutions continue to play a key role. Instead of lending funds from their own accounts, banks act as agents helping corporate clients to arrange bond issues. It is one of many corporate client services that banks offer. The process of administering a bond issue embraces:

◆ advice on how to structure the issue in terms of maturity, interest payments, currency denomination, etc;

◆ obtaining credit ratings;

◆ negotiating with relevant regulatory and listing bodies;

◆ promoting the issue to potential investors; and

◆ underwriting the bond issue.

In schematic terms, a typical bond issue involves a lead bank being mandated to act as the 'arranger' whose first task is to organise a syndicate of other banks willing to participate in the issue. Each bank in the syndicate agrees to subscribe to a portion of the issue and in the meantime seeks to register customers prepared to buy the bonds. By the time the banks are required to pay for the bonds, they aim to have persuaded sufficient numbers of investors to take up the allotted amount. In general, banks do not wish to hold bonds themselves beyond what might be required for trading purposes.

The lead bank is paid a management fee by the borrower and shares it out among the syndicate members. The fee covers the expenses incurred by the banks administering the bond issue as well as incorporating a premium paid for underwriting the bonds. Furthermore, the bonds are priced so that the banks can expect to sell them to clients at a modest premium. According to one survey of 255 corporate bond issues, when all factors are considered the average issue cost averaged just 0.37% of the funds raised.[1] This compares very favourably with the costs of equity capital issues of a similar size. It is also possible for companies to raise funds quickly – in as little as six weeks after mandating the lead bank, according to issuing guidelines available from the London Stock Exchange. Given that the amounts of money being raised often run to many hundreds of millions (of dollars, euros, pounds, etc), this is very quick.

Table 7.1 refers to the non-government bonds issued via the London Stock Exchange as 'Eurobonds'. The term can cause confusion. Its origins lie in the growth of a US dollar-denominated capital market in Europe – a process that stretches back to the 1960s and which was initially stimulated by tax reforms in the US that made borrowing dollars in New York expensive. Today, the Eurobond market is best understood as an internationally oriented capital market that operates with minimal interference from the financial regulatory frameworks of national jurisdictions. Eurobonds are offered to investors internationally and can be denominated in any currency that is internationally tradable. The Eurobond market differs in important respects to domestic bond and foreign bond markets, as follows.

◆ Domestic bonds are issued in a particular country by an agency domiciled in that country and denominated in the currency of that country. It does not imply that only investors domiciled in the country can buy the bonds. Central government bond issues generally form the most important component of the domestic bond market.

◆ Foreign bonds are issued in a particular country, denominated in that country's currency, but undertaken by foreign agencies. A typical example might be a South Korean company seeking to finance an investment in France and choosing to do so by issuing euro-denominated bonds in Paris.

◆ Eurobond issues are internationally focused and usually involve issuers selling bonds denominated in currencies other than their own.

Test yourself 7.1

Which of the following should be classified as a domestic bond issue, a foreign bond issue and a Eurobond issue?

a) **A Singaporean company issues bonds in New York, denominated in US dollars.**

b) **A Russian company issues bonds in London denominated in Japanese yen.**

c) **The German central bank (the Deutsche Bundesbank) auctions government bonds to authorised dealers in Germany.**

The Eurobond market is a self-regulated market. The regulatory apparatus operates under the auspices of the International Capital Market Association (ICMA), formed in 2005 through an amalgamation of the International Securities Market Association (ISMA) and the International Primary Market Association (IPMA). It is an association of over 400 institutions central to the operation of money and capital markets, including banks, asset management companies, security exchanges, securities dealers and professional support services. The ICMA is essentially an industry association that seeks to develop and enforce codes of practice regarded as essential to the proper functioning of capital markets. It also represents investment banking and asset management interests in deliberations with sovereign legislators and regulators over reform proposals.

The self-regulated status of the Eurobond market is one reason why it has become the main medium for corporate bond issues. According to the ICMA, outstanding issues on the international capital market amounted to $18 trillion in 2011. Table 7.1 shows that new Eurobond issues going through the London market, which according to the London Stock Exchange accounts for 75% of all deals, stood at nearly £417 billion in 2011. This compares to just £17.8 billion raised via new equity issues under the auspices of the London Stock Exchange in 2011. Eurobond issues raised more than 23 times the capital generated by new equity sales.

2. Plain vanilla bonds

The basic and most common form of securitised debt is sometimes referred to as a 'plain vanilla' bond. The characteristics of a plain vanilla bond are as follows.

◆ The issuer borrows capital for a fixed period, starting from the issue date and ending on a specified redemption or maturity date.

◆ The bond specifies a repayment value, an amount paid to the owner of the bond on the maturity date. This is known by various names: par value, face value, nominal value, principal value, redemption value.

◆ The bond offers a fixed rate of interest expressed as a percentage of the face value. The rate is also known as a coupon rate, with the payments being called coupon payments.

The market value of a plain vanilla bond is a function of four factors: the par value, the term to maturity, the interest rate and the yield to maturity.

◆ The par value is the amount that the borrower pays the owner of the security on the maturity date. Par values vary but are normally standardised. For instance, US government bonds are offered with a par value of $1,000. The par value for an individual UK government bond is £100. For Japanese government bonds it is Y50,000 or Y100,000, while bonds issued by member states of the Euro currency area have a par value of €100. Despite these different sizes, it is normal practice to value bonds as though the par is 100 and the coupon payment is 100 multiplied by the coupon rate.

◆ The term to maturity is a straightforward reference to the time remaining until the bond matures.

◆ The interest rate on a bond is expressed as a percentage of the par value. The calculation of interest payments is therefore straightforward. A UK government bond with a coupon rate of 5% offers £5 interest per year. Interest rates and payments on bonds are routinely called coupon rates and coupon payments. This is a legacy of a now increasingly redundant practice of issuing paper bond certificates with detachable coupons that are presented to the borrower in exchange for the interest payment on the relevant date. Nowadays it is normal for interest payments to be made via electronic transfers. Nevertheless, the language of coupon rates and coupon payments survives.

◆ The yield to maturity is a measure of the rate of return that an investor receives on a bond if it is held until the maturity date.

2.1 Valuing a plain vanilla bond

The section on money market securities demonstrated that the market price of a treasury bill is equivalent to the discounted value of the future cash flow. It is the same for coupon paying bonds, except that there is more than one cash flow to consider. There is a stream of coupon payments occurring at regular intervals together with the redemption payment on the maturity date. Consider a bond with five years to maturity and offering an annual coupon of 4% and a redemption payment of £100. The cash flows are outlined in Table 7.2.

Table 7.2 Cash flows on a five-year bond

	Year 1	Year 2	Year 3	Year 4	Year 5
Cash flow	£4	£4	£4	£4	£4 + £100

Assume that investors require a yield to maturity (shortened to 'yield' from now on) of 4%, i.e. equal to the coupon rate. What price would they be willing to pay?

$$P_0 = \frac{4}{(1.04)} + \frac{4}{(1.04)^2} + \frac{4}{(1.04)^3} + \frac{4}{(1.04)^4} + \frac{4}{(1.04)^5} + \frac{100}{(1.04)^5} = £100$$

The calculation is, in essence, the same as for a single cash-flow pure-discount security. Each cash flow is discounted by the required rate of return to produce a present value for each. The security's market value is the sum of these present values. Discounting the cash flows by the required rate of return produces the price that should be paid for the security. Note the following points.

◆ The discount rate is the same for all cash flows but the power applied to the discount increases with time. This reflects something that is, in fact, intuitively quite obvious. The further into the future that a cash flow occurs, the less valuable it is in today's terms. In the case of the calculation above, £4 due to be received in one year is of greater worth than £4 due in two years, in three years and so on. Hence each payment should be discounted to an intensity that corresponds to its timing.

◆ The market value of £100 corresponds to its par value. This is because the required return is the same as the coupon rate. If these two numbers correspond, then so do the par and market values.

The latter point is important. While the cash flows on plain vanilla bonds are fixed, yields can (in fact, almost certainly will) alter. As circumstances in capital markets change so do interest rates generally. For instance, if the central bank cuts its own lending rate it is liable to encourage lower interest rates across the money and capital markets. Indeed, this is exactly what the central bank would be hoping for by reducing its lending rate. Assume that the yield on the five-year bond falls to 3%. The bond price will be:

$$P_0 = \frac{4}{(1.03)} + \frac{4}{(1.03)^2} + \frac{4}{(1.03)^3} + \frac{4}{(1.03)^4} + \frac{4}{(1.03)^5} + \frac{100}{(1.03)^5} = £104.58$$

The price of the bond rises to £104.58. Investors still receive £4 per year for five years plus a £100 redemption payment in five years. But this is now equivalent to a 3% annual return on the investment of £104.58. The upshot is that the bond trades at a price that is at a *premium* to its par value. There is, in other words, no reason to expect that bonds will trade at par values. Given the fixed cash payments that are characteristic of plain vanilla bonds, market prices vary in accordance with changes in yields.

Test yourself 7.2

Imagine that the central bank decides to increase its lending rate due to concerns that rapid economic growth is causing inflationary pressures to intensify. The central bank hopes that a rise in its lending rate will force up the general cost of borrowing and, thereby, reduce demand for credit. The upshot is that the yield on the five-year bond paying an annual coupon of £4 rises to 5%.

Calculate the new price of the bond and comment on its relationship to the bond's par value.

The method of pricing a bond outlined above is somewhat inconvenient. Imagine a bond with a maturity of 20 years paying interest every six months. That's 40 coupon payments that require discounting – very tedious. However, the coupon payments on a plain vanilla bond constitute an annuity-type cash flow.

Annuity is a term that can be applied to cash flow streams where the payments are of equal size, occur at regular intervals and are for a finite period. Many financial arrangements exhibit annuity-like features, such as mortgage repayments, personal pension payments, insurance premiums, regular savings schemes, etc. Indeed, in the UK savings accumulated in pension funds are used to buy products called 'life annuities' for the funds' beneficiaries upon retirement. There is a more economic method of determining the present value of an annuity than calculating the present value of each cash flow separately:

$$PV_A = C\left[\frac{1-[1+r]^{-n}}{r}\right]$$

Hence the price of a bond can be determined using the following formula:

$$P_0 = C\left[\frac{1-[1+y]^{-n}}{y}\right] + \frac{100}{(1+y)^n}$$

It still states that the price is the present value of the future cash flows, but the coupon payments (C) have been collected together and treated as an annuity. Note in addition that y has been substituted for r, to stress the fact that the relevant rate of return is the yield to maturity.

Test yourself 7.3

Take the five-year bond paying an annual coupon of £4 and a £100 redemption payment, and calculate the price using the annuity approach. Try it using yields of 3%, 4% and 5%. You ought to obtain prices that are the same as previously.

2.2 Plain vanilla bonds and coupon payments

It is standard practice to quote coupon rates and bond yields as annual rates. However, this does not necessarily mean that coupons are paid annually. For instance, some bonds offer semi-annual payments. A case in point is UK government bonds (known as 'gilts'), which divide the annual coupon payment into two six-monthly instalments. Take the case of a gilt with five years to maturity, paying an annual coupon of £4 and offering an annual yield of 2%. Its price is:

$$P_0 = 2 \left[\frac{1- [1.01]^{-10}}{0.01} \right] + \frac{100}{(1.01)^{10}} = £109.47$$

The bond offers ten payments of £2 rather than five payments of £4. Hence the present value of the coupon payments is a function of ten six-month periods. As a result the discount rate is cut in half – from 2% to 1% in this example – to account for the half-yearly cycle of payments. The reason for making this modification is in order to allow for the fact that that a bond paying £2 every six months for five years will be worth slightly more than one paying £4 once a year for five years. Why? Because in the former case the coupon payments can be reinvested, and therefore themselves earn interest, from six months onwards rather than from one year. It means that the bond paying a coupon after six months generates more 'interest-on-interest' and hence will have a higher market value.

Test yourself 7.4

Take a seven-year gilt paying an annual coupon of 5% and offering an annual yield of 3%.

a) Calculate the price of the gilt assuming that the coupons are paid annually and recalculate the price based on semi-annual coupon payments.

b) Specify the reasons for the different prices.

2.3 Clean and dirty bond prices

Bonds are tradable securities. When sold, the seller is entitled to part of the next coupon payment with the amount depending on the time elapsed since the last payment relative to the time remaining until the next. This affects the price at which the bond is sold.

Assume that a trader sells a bond that has nine and a half years to maturity, pays a coupon of £3 annually and offers an annual yield of 6%. Its price will be:

$$P_0 = 3 \left[\frac{1- [1.06]^{-9.5}}{0.06} \right] + \frac{100}{(1.06)^{9.5}} = £78.75$$

The price of £78.75 is the bond's *clean* price. However, the bond sells for its *dirty* price, which includes a component of accrued interest. A maturity of nine and a half years implies that the last coupon payment was six months ago, with the next being in six months' time. As a result, the seller has invested in the bond for half of the year and is therefore entitled to half of the next coupon payment. The bond should sell for the clean price plus accrued interest: a dirty price of £78.75 + £1.50 = £80.25.

Table 7.3 Accrued interest on a UK government bond

Semi-annual coupon	£1.000
Accrued interest	£0.712
Number of days since the previous coupon payment	131 days
Number of days to the next payment	53 days
Number of days in the payment cycle	184 days

Normally, accrued interest is calculated on a daily basis. The data in Table 7.3 refers to a UK government bond paying a semi-annual coupon of £1.00. On the day in question the Debt Management Office, the agency responsible for managing UK government bond issues, listed accrued interest as £0.712. This was 131 days after the previous coupon payments and 53 days to the next payment – a total of 184 days between coupon payments. The accrued interest after 131 days was:

$$£1.00 \times \frac{131}{184} = £0.712$$

This corresponds to the accrued interest stated by the DMO.

3. Risk and fixed interest securities

3.1 Credit risk

Government bonds (at least those of major economies) are normally deemed free of credit risk, meaning that the prospect of default is regarded as negligible. Corporate debt, the debt of governments outside of the small (and, as of 2012, dwindling) 'risk-free' group, and municipal government bond issues are not free of credit risk. Investors take a keen interest in the creditworthiness of these borrowers.

A key method of gauging the creditworthiness of corporate borrowers is to consult the opinions of credit rating agencies. In the US there are ten ratings agencies registered with the Securities and Exchange Commission, the main regulatory body overseeing securities markets in the USA, as Nationally Recognized Statistical Rating Organizations. Three dominate the industry: Moody's Investors Service, Standard & Poor's Ratings Service and Fitch. They rate bond issues and other credit arrangements, monitor the creditworthiness of issuers, place them on watch lists if they feel there is cause for concern, and declare upgrades or downgrades when they consider it necessary. Table 7.4 provides a condensed version of the grading systems employed by the agencies for bonds and other long-term debt.

Table 7.4 Credit ratings

Ratings agencies			
Moody's	**Standard & Poor's**	**Fitch**	Investment grade
Aaa	AAA	AAA	
Baa3	BBB–	BBB–	
B2	B	B	High yield
Caa	CCC	CCC	
C	D	D	

Debt securities with ratings of BBB– or above (Baa3 in the case of Moody's) are known as investment grade securities. These are bonds whose issuers are regarded as being well able to fulfil repayment obligations and are, therefore, very unlikely to default. The data on past default rates indicates that it is extremely rare for companies with investment grade ratings to default. It should be stressed that this does not take into account borrowers who started off being highly rated but were later downgraded and eventually defaulted. In other words, the sporadic nature of investment grade defaults understates the risk, because high-rated defaulters tend to be downgraded before they default.

Ratings below investment grade are generically described as high yield debt, meaning that default rates are higher and investment is hence riskier. High yield should not be understood to imply a bad investment, one to be avoided. Many investors specialise in high yield debt, attracted by the prospect of high yields.

The investment grade label is important because banks and many institutional investors are legally allowed, or choose, to hold only investment grade securities. An investment grade rating is also important to borrowers because it means that there is a broader potential demand for the bonds and borrowing costs will be lower.

Credit ratings have a decisive impact on bond yields. A common method of assessing the return associated with credit risk is to take the yield on government bonds as a risk-free benchmark and measure the additional yield offered by corporate bonds. This is known as the credit spread or yield spread.

Table 7.5 Credit spreads on dollar-denominated corporate bonds 2006 and 2012

	2006		2012	
	Aaa	**Baa**	**Aaa**	**Baa**
Annual yield	5.27%	6.15%	3.58%	4.56%
Less five-year US Treasury	−4.55%	−4.55%	−0.70%	−0.70%
Credit spread	**0.72%**	**1.60%**	**2.88%**	**3.86%**

Table 7.5 compares the credit spreads for dollar-denominated, investment-grade, corporate bonds in late 2012 with those six years earlier, before the onset of the banking crisis. It shows that yields in general were significantly lower in 2012, which is not surprising, given that central banks cut their lending rates to unprecedentedly low levels in an effort to help refinance ailing banks.

The second striking characteristic of the data in Table 7.5 is the increase in the credit spreads for both Aaa- and Baa- rated bonds. In 2012, investors demanded much higher credit spreads. In the case of Aaa-rated corporate bonds, the average spread of 2.88% was four times the spread in 2006. It suggests that in recent times, borrowers have had to offer significantly larger spreads over risk-free rates to persuade lenders to lend. Nevertheless, the yields in 2012 were still significantly lower in absolute terms than in 2006. And judging by the scale of new Eurobond issues in recent years (see Table 7.1), there has been no shortage of borrowers willing to pay the higher spreads.

3.2 Market risk

Plain vanilla bonds offer fixed streams of income. But yields change. Given the fixed character of the cash flows, yields can only vary as a result of changes in market prices. Yields variation therefore exposes investors in bonds to uncertainty regarding the market values of their investments; they have an exposure to market risk.

Three bonds all offer a coupon of £3.00 per annum. Their maturities are one year, five years and 20 years, with yields to maturity of 3%, 4% and 5% respectively. The market price of each bond is.

$$P_0 = \frac{3}{(1.03)^1} + \frac{100}{(1.03)^1} = £100.00$$

$$P_0 = 3\left[\frac{1-[1.04]^{-5}}{0.04}\right] + \frac{100}{(1.04)^5} = £95.55$$

$$P_0 = 3\left[\frac{1-[1.05]^{-20}}{0.05}\right] + \frac{100}{(1.0)^{-20}} = £75.08$$

Assume that the yields for all three bonds rise by one percentage point to 4%, 5% and 6%. The new prices, together with the percentage changes are listed in Table 7.6.

Table 7.6 New bond prices

	1-year bond	5-year bond	20-year bond
New price	£99.04	£91.34	£65.59
Price change	£0.96	−£4.21	−£9.49
Percentage price change	−0.96%	−4.41%	−12.64%

For all three bonds the one percentage point rise in yields leads to a fall in price. But whereas the bond with one year to maturity falls by less than 1%, the value of the 20-year bond falls by 12.64%. Investors in 20-year bonds would lose a much greater portion of their wealth than investors in one-year bonds. Longer-term bond prices generally are more volatile than bonds with short-term maturities. Their prices are subject to greater uncertainty. In effect, market risk is greater the longer the term to maturity. For this reason, longer-term bonds tend to offer higher yields; the additional element is compensation for the greater exposure to market risk.

The significance of market risk for individual investors depends on whether they intend to trade the bonds or hold them to maturity. If the intention is to trade, market risk is an important consideration because it means that traders are exposed to the possibility of capital loss. On the other hand, there is also the possibility of significant capital gains in the event of yields falling. For investors intending to hold bonds to maturity, market risk is less of an issue because investors receive all of the remaining coupon payments and the redemption payment. What happens to the market price in the interim is of little importance.

Test yourself 7.5

Check the prices and percentage price changes provided in Table 7.6.

3.3 Reinvestment risk

The method used to value plain vanilla bonds assumes that the interim coupon payments are reinvested at current yield. Take the earlier example of a five-year bond.

$$P_0 = 3\left[\frac{1-[1.04]^{-5}}{0.04}\right] + \frac{100}{(1.04)^{-5}} = £95.55$$

Investors receive £3 interest per year for five years and a £100 redemption payment. The market price of £95.55 is based on an annual yield to maturity of 4%. There is, implicit with the valuation model, an assumption that each £3 coupon is reinvested at 4%. So in coming to the price of £95.55, the £3 received in one year is presumed to be reinvested at 4% for the remaining four years of the bond's life, the £3 received in two years reinvested for three years and so on.

In practice, of course, investors do not know what yields will be when the interim cash flows accrue. They could in practice be higher or lower. There is, therefore, reinvestment risk to consider when assessing the return on coupon-paying bonds.

3.4 Inflation risk

Inflation means that the rate of return in monetary terms and the return in 'real' terms differ. Imagine that the yield on a bond is 5% and that the annual rate of inflation is expected to be 2%. The expected real rate of return is:

$$E(r^*) = \frac{1 + y}{1 + E(i)} - 1 = \frac{1.05}{1.02} - 1 = 0.0294 \ (2.94\%)$$

where:

$E(r^*)$ = expected real rate of return;

y = yield; and

$E(i)$ = expected rate of inflation.

In this example, investors' wealth grows by 5% in nominal or monetary terms. But over the same period, prices in general rise by 2%. The result is that investors are 2.94% better off in real terms; the expanded wealth buys 2.94% more goods and services than a year ago.

Inflation in itself is not the risk. Investors routinely factor in expectations concerning future inflation rates when calculating expected returns. The risk is that actual inflation might differ from expectations. What if, for instance, inflation turns out to be 6% instead of 2%?

$$\frac{1.05}{1.06} - 1 = -0.0094 \ (-0.94\%)$$

Investors end up being nearly 1% worse off in real terms.

Uncertainty about future inflation rates tends to be a more significant facet of the risk associated with bonds than with money market securities and company shares. The maturities of money market instruments tend to be too short for inflation to erode purchasing power dramatically. In the case of company shares, dividend payments are variable and might themselves exhibit inflationary trends that cause share prices to rise as well. But bonds, with fixed income streams and long maturities, are less inflation proof.

4. Variations on plain vanilla

Companies and other bodies issues bonds with characteristics that differ from the standard plain vanilla form. There are many variations, mostly relating to the structure of the coupon payments or the term to maturity.

4.1 Variable coupon payments

A common alternative to the fixed coupon rate is a variable or floating rate. These bonds, generally referred to as **floating rate notes** or FRNs, cite coupon rates as premiums above a specified reference rate, usually Libor (London Interbank Offered Rate). Hence if Libor rates change, so do the coupon rates on FRNs.

floating rate note
A bond whose periodic interest payments vary in line with changes in a specified benchmark rate such as Libor.

Rate changes do not occur continually. Instead they are adjusted on regularly occurring 'reset' days in accordance with the prevailing Libor rate. Assume that a FRN is issued with reset dates every six months. On each reset date the Libor rate for six-month borrowing is taken and used to set the coupon rate on the FRN for the next six-month period. For instance, if the Euribor (Euro Interbank Offered Rate) is 2% on the reset day and a FRN offers a premium of 1%, the coupon rate is set to 3%. If six months later Euribor has risen to 3%, the coupon rate on the FRN rises to 4%.

Test yourself 7.6

Table 7.7 lists the (annualised) six-month Libor rates for five currencies, the premiums being charged on a loan denominated in each currency and the size of each loan.

Table 7.7 Six-month Libor rates for five currencies

Currency	Six-month Libor rate	Annual premium	Loan
Euro	0.358%	1.0%	2,000,000
Dollar	0.636%	1.2%	5,800,000
Sterling	0.840%	0.5%	25,000,000
Canadian dollar	1.546%	2.5%	16,400,000
Swiss franc	0.158%	0.6%	7,750,000

Assume that today is the half-yearly coupon rate reset date for each loan. Calculate the coupon rate and the amount of interest payable on each loan in six months.

index-linked bond
A bond whose coupon and principal payments vary in line with changes in a specified index of inflation.

Some bonds, known as **index-linked bonds**, offer coupon payments that are adjusted for inflation and deflation. In recent years, the UK government has issued large amounts of index-linked gilts – much of them with very long terms to maturity, up to 50 years.

Index-linked bonds quote fixed coupon rates but the actual coupon payments incorporate an adjustment in line with a specified index of consumer prices. Inflation causes the index value to rise, leading to an increase in the coupon payment. Deflation, on the other hand, causes the index and the resulting coupon payment to decline. In order to illustrate how index-linked coupon payments evolve, assume:

◆ a bond offering a coupon rate of 4% on a par value of £100, payable annually; and

◆ an inflation index of 100 at the outset and a rate of inflation for the first year of 2%.

Since consumer prices rise by 2%, it means that after one year the inflation index will be 102. The coupon payment will be:

$$4 \times \frac{102}{100} = £4.08$$

If the index reaches 105 after two years, the coupon payment will be:

$$4 \times \frac{105}{100} = £4.20$$

Indexation may also apply to the redemption payment. If the above bond were to mature after two years, the redemption payment would be:

$$100 \times \frac{105}{100} = £105$$

The investor would be repaid £105 rather than the original par value of £100. Note that the coupon of £4.20 paid at the end of the second year is equivalent to 4% of the redemption value of £105; the coupon *rate* remains fixed.

Test yourself 7.7

An index-linked bond offers a coupon rate of 2% on a par value of £100, payable annually. The inflation index falls from 100 to 98 after one year, to 96 after two years before rising to 103 after three years. Work out the coupon payments for years 1, 2 and 3, and the redemption value, assuming that the bond matures at the end of year 3.

FRNs neutralise a large element of the market risk associated with bonds. Recall that for plain vanilla bonds, rising interest rates cause bond prices to fall, leading to potential capital losses for investors. With FRNs, however, coupon payments are liable to increase in an environment of rising interest rates, thereby providing support for market prices. In a similar manner, index-linked bonds neutralise much of the exposure to inflation risk. It should be stressed, however, that this protection comes at a cost: both FRNs and index-linked bonds will be more expensive than plain vanilla bonds with similar credit risks, coupons and maturities. In other words, they offer lower returns.

There are other, less common, modifications to the system of coupon payments. Bonds may be offered with coupons deferred for a specified initial period. Others pay coupons in the form of more bonds (so-called payment-in-kind bonds), effectively deferring the entire cash reward to the maturity date. There are 'inverse floaters' whose coupon rates vary in the opposite direction to reference rates. Other bonds cap coupon rates to a maximum, or place floors under coupon rates, effectively promising a certain minimum rate. Others might offer both a cap and a floor, known as a collar coupon rate.

4.2 Variable maturity dates

Many bonds, especially Eurobonds, are issued with a provision permitting the borrower to repay the debt prior to the maturity date. They are known as **callable bonds**. The terms of the 'call option' are stipulated at the outset. Among the most significant are:

callable bond
A bond that entitles the issuer to repay the debt earlier than the specified redemption date.

♦   the length of the call protection period (the initial term during which the bond may not be called) compared to the term to maturity;

♦   the structure of the call option (can it be exercised at any time during the call period or only on certain dates?); and

♦   the terms of repayment. It is customary to offer the par value plus a premium in return for the right to exercise the option, with the premium equivalent to the annual coupon payment being common. This is known as the exercise price.

Borrowers have an incentive to exercise call options if interest rates fall. They can undertake new bond issues offering lower interest rates and use the proceeds to call in the existing bonds. The net effect is to reduce the cost of borrowing.

From the standpoint of investors, call options constitute additional risk: call risk. As interest rates fall, bond holders might normally expect to see bond prices rise. But with callable bonds, the greater the fall in interest rates, the greater the probability that the call option will be exercised, at the exercise price. The implication is that when interest rates fall significantly, the exercise price acts as a ceiling on developments in market price. The precise impact depends on the specifics of the call option feature in each instance.

Given the additional risk that callable bonds entail for investors, it is no surprise that they expect higher yields than for non-callable bonds that are otherwise alike. Assume that an eight-year plain vanilla bond offers a 6% annual coupon and sells at its par value of £100. Since the bond trades at the par value, the yield is also 6%. A similar bond, but with a call option attached, might offer a return of, say, 6.5%. Its price would be:

$$P_0 = 6 \left[\frac{1 - [1.065]^{-8}}{0.065} \right] + \frac{100}{(1.065)^8} = £96.96$$

The bond sells at a lower price than its plain vanilla cousin. A call option is valuable to borrowers, but it isn't free. Investors accept exposure to call risk but in return demand higher yields.

The mirror image of callable bonds is puttable bonds, which give investors the right to sell the bond back to the borrower prior to the maturity date at the par value. Bonds with a put option are *less* risky than plain vanillas. The put option effectively makes the par value a minimum value. As interest rates rise bond prices fall. Investors in possession of a put option have an incentive to exercise the option, because they can realise the par value and reinvest the proceeds at the higher rates available elsewhere. However, puttable bonds, by implication, offer lower yields in general.

Stop and think 7.1

Table 7.1 indicated that there was a surge in Eurobond issues in the years following the banking crisis of 2007–8. Try to provide a rationale for why this development was at least partly due to companies borrowing money and using the proceeds to call in older bonds prior to their maturities.

5. Fixed interest securities and portfolio management

How do fixed interest securities fit into portfolio management? Much depends on the overall character of the portfolio and the underlying attitude to risk and return on the part of investors and managers.

5.1 Managing risk in equity-based portfolios

In chapter 4 on capital markets and portfolio analysis, the idea of securities offering risk-free returns plays a key role in managing the general portfolio risk-return trade-off. Wealth can be shifted in and out of risk-free assets in accordance with the priorities of the investors and their judgements concerning the scale of risk that should be taken in any given period.

Many of the risk-free assets are to be found among fixed interest securities, in particular those backed by the authority of central government. In fact, fixed interest securities in a wider sense are considered by many investors as a refuge where wealth can be held relatively safely during periods when equity markets are regarded as too speculative. Fixed interest security values are less volatile than those of equities. If held to maturity, fixed interest security values are to a great extent certain, corresponding to par values. Of course, there is still the issue of credit risk to consider, but it is generally less than the risk associated with equity investments.

5.2 Fixed interest portfolios

For some very important investment operations and portfolio structures, fixed interest securities are the most appropriate medium for maximising the prospects of achieving strategic objectives. A case in point is that of pension funds, especially those described as mature funds.

A mature pension fund is one characterised by a preponderance of retiring or near retiring beneficiaries compared to younger members. The fund finds that new contributions are in decline, while demands for payments out of the pool of accumulated investments are on the rise. This state of affairs suggests that the fund management's attitude to investment ought to be conservative, with an emphasis on safe, income-generating securities rather than speculative ventures.

The strategic investment objective is liable to stress the need to match the wealth generation side of the equation to actuarially estimated payments to the beneficiaries while reducing the possibility of shortfalls occurring. In some instances, a simple cash matching strategy may be sufficient whereby the certain proceeds from safe assets suffice to facilitate payment of predictable obligations.

In other circumstances, a more complex portfolio management strategy may be required, while still focusing on fixed interest securities. For instance, even a mature pension fund may find it prudent to take reinvestment risk into account when designing investment portfolios to meet future liabilities. A solution is to adopt what is known as an 'immunisation' approach to investment: one that is able to minimise the exposure to reinvestment risk.

5.3 Leverage and fixed interest portfolios

Chapter 6 indicated that sale and repurchase agreements (repos) provide a framework for gaining leverage exposure to the yields on fixed interest securities. In essence, repos offer the possibility of borrowing funds at 'low' short-term rates which are then used to buy higher-yielding longer-term securities. The secret is to repeatedly rollover the short-term repo-based borrowing, using the purchased securities as collateral supporting the repo agreements.

In the aftermath of the banking crisis of 2007–8, it became evident that fixed interest securities were created on a huge scale largely to facilitate trading in yield differentials. In other words, fixed interest securities (mainly asset-backed securities of various kinds) were being created not because of any underlying economic rationale, such as companies wanting to finance productive investment and adding to the stock of wealth in the process, but mainly to trade maturity-related interest rate differences.

Banks were keen to securitise assets such as mortgages, student loans and motor vehicles loans, because selling the resulting securities made the assets more liquid as well as generating more brokerage and other dealer-related fees. There is even evidence of feedback effects, with the underlying assets being created as essential raw material for fixed interest securitisation. The most notorious example was that of property-related sub-prime lending in the USA, in which concern about the ability of the borrowers to repay the loans was effectively absent.

Investors were likewise eager to borrow money short-term to buy these asset-backed securities because it seemed like easy profits. Further reassurance arrived in the form of ratings agencies prepared to assign high ratings to large components of these new issues, mostly based on theoretical models of default probabilities rather than on comprehensive empirical evidence of past performance (there wasn't any 'past performance').

The banking crisis largely grew out of the fixed interest markets – ironically, the markets normally regarded as a refuge when financial markets go awry.

Test yourself 7.8

a) What are the key characteristics of 'young' and 'mature' pension funds?

b) How is the age demographic of a fund's beneficiaries likely to influence the investment decisions of its management?

Chapter summary

◆ For large corporations, bond issues have increased in importance as a source of borrowing at the expense of reliance on bank loans.

◆ Unlike bank loans, bonds are a securitised form of debt that can be traded on secondary markets.

◆ The basic type of debt security is the plain vanilla bond.

◆ Valuing a plain vanilla bond involves similar discounting procedures to those used to value pure discount securities with the difference being that there is more than one cash flow to discount.

◆ There are many variations on the plain vanilla form of bonds which complicate the valuation process.

◆ Bonds are associated with various risks. In general, credit risk is the most significant consideration because default on repayments clearly implies significant losses for investors.

◆ There are other risks to consider such as market risk, inflation risk and call risk. Some of the variations on the plain vanilla bond offer mechanisms designed to reduce the significance of these risks.

◆ Within the context of portfolio management, bonds can be the focal point of an investment strategy in their own right, or they can form an ostensibly low-risk component of a portfolio that includes a variety of asset classes.

Note

1. A. Melnik & D. Nissim, 'Debt Issue Costs and Issue Characteristics in the Eurobond Market', International Centre for Economic Research, Working Paper No.9, 2003.

Chapter Eight
Equity markets

List of topics

1   Valuing equities
2   The dividend valuation model
3   Share prices and equity actions

Introduction

Equity capital arises when the value of a capital asset exceeds the value of liabilities incurred in the course of acquiring and using the asset. It is that part of the asset that may be said to be 'owned' by the user. For instance, the difference between the market value of a residential property and the size of a mortgage loan used to acquire the property is often referred to as homeowner equity. In the corporate environment, equity capital refers to the residual value of a business net of all its current and long-term liabilities.

Most textbooks on corporate finance state that the core objective of private enterprise is to increase the value of equity; to increase the wealth connected to ownership. It is enshrined in the declaration that the objective of the firm is to maximise shareholder wealth.

The identification of corporate equity with shareholders is explicit in business audits. The balance sheet characterises a business as an amalgam of assets used to satisfy liabilities owed to trade creditors, tax collectors, lenders and, last of all, shareholders. The latter are only entitled to any wealth remaining after all other claims have been satisfied. If there's nothing left then shares are worthless and shareholders lose their investment. They cannot seek redress in court, should companies fail to honour liabilities to shareholders.

In fact, the absence of legal recourse for shareholders means that companies are able to use shareholders' contributions as collateral to support borrowing, making equity investment riskier than lending. But the risk also appeals to equity investors. The terms of borrowing are, by and large, contractually fixed at the outset meaning that lenders' returns exhibit limited upside possibilities. But a company's liability to its shareholders is only restricted by the success or failure of its endeavours. There is an uncertain, but potentially very rewarding, upside to being an owner of corporate equity.

1. Valuing equities

The valuation of company shares is an intrinsically more taxing issue than the valuation of debt securities because the uncertainties are greater. The chapters on the money and fixed interest markets stressed that the prices investors deem worth paying in the present are equivalent to the future cash flows discounted at the required rate of return. In both markets the future cash flows are, to a great extent, contractually stipulated at the outset. There are numerous cases where an element of ambiguity is attached to the cash flows; callable, floating rate and index linked bonds spring to mind. Nevertheless:

◆ The scale of the ambiguity regarding future cash flows is generally modest.

◆ Default risk is generally a less pressing consideration because corporate debtors have equity capital as a reserve to fall back on while sovereign debtors have taxpayers to fall back on.

The upshot is that the valuation of debt securities is a comparatively routine task because the unknowns are of a lesser order. But company shares:

◆ do not offer contractually predetermined cash flows. Many regularly pay cash dividends. But there is no legal obligation for companies to pay dividends at all. And if they do, the amount is at the discretion of the board of directors;

◆ are not redeemable for specified amounts on predetermined maturity dates. Shareholders 'redeem' investments by selling shares on a market at prices that are unknown before the event; and

◆ are exposed to more default risk. Shareholders, in return for the right to share in after-tax profits, must also accept that they are the first to experience erosions of wealth if there are losses. In extreme cases where losses force a company into liquidation, shareholders are liable to lose their entire investment.

These uncertainties mean that a comparable method of valuing equities necessarily entails more reservations. Nevertheless the notion that investments ought to be worth the present value of future expected cash flows has a strong intuitive appeal. In financial analysis the discounted cash flow model of equity valuation is known as the dividend valuation model (DVM). The DVM is analogous in its approach to previous techniques used to price other types of securities, in that the stress is on the present value of future income streams.

2. The dividend valuation model

According to the DVM, share prices are dependent on three fundamental factors:

1 the stream of future dividend payments;

2 the redemption date; and

3 the expected return on equity.

Dividend payments are distributed to shareholders on a regular basis. Many UK companies declare a final year dividend (as part of the full year trading results) and an interim dividend around halfway through the annual reporting cycle. The final year dividend is normally larger than the interim. In the US it is more common for companies to pay annual dividends split into four equal quarterly payments. Dividends are unknown in advance of being announced by a company's board of directors. The equity valuation process therefore requires estimation of future dividend payments.

Shares do not specify redemption dates. But this does not mean that the maturity period is unimportant. If the value of an asset is the present value of future cash flows, company shares are dividend, generating assets in perpetuity. The term to maturity can be considered infinite.

The expected return is not known and must be estimated. Portfolio theory itself offers techniques for generating expected return estimations.

On the basis of these three considerations, the DVM states that a share price is the discounted value of all future dividend payments.

$$P_0 = \frac{d_1}{(1 + r)} + \frac{d_2}{(1 + r)^2} + \cdots + \frac{d_\infty}{(1 + r)^\infty}$$

Where:

P_0 = current share price;

d_i = each dividend payment; and

r = return on equity.

The share price is equal to the sum of the present values of all dividend payments occurring forever (∞ is the mathematical symbol for infinity). It should be obvious that trying to forecast the size of each dividend payment is futile. An expedient modification is to assume that the latest (i.e. known) dividend grows by a constant, or average, rate (g) so that:

$$P_0 = \frac{d_0 (1 + g)}{(1 + r)} + \frac{d_0 (1 + g)^2}{(1 + r)^2} + \cdots + \frac{d_0 (1 + g)^\infty}{(1 + r)^\infty}$$

This is known as the dividend growth valuation model and is the most familiar formulation of the DVM. It treats share prices as products of growth perpetuities – streams of regular dividend payments expanding at a constant rate forever. It reduces algebraically to the much more convenient form:

$$P_0 = \frac{d_0 (1 + g)}{(r - g)}$$

Worked example 8.1: Using the dividend valuation model

Imagine that a company, with an issued share capital of 10 million shares, has just paid an annual dividend of 10 pence per share. The consensus among investors is that the dividend payment is likely to grow by an annual average rate of 4% and they expect an annual return on equity of 8%. The share price, based on the dividend valuation model, should be:

$$P_0 = \frac{10(1.04)}{(0.08 - 0.04)} = 260 \text{ pence}$$

If shareholders pay 260 pence for the share and the dividend payments grow, and continue to be expected to grow, by 4% a year then the annual rate of return will be 8%.

In addition, the market value of the company's equity ought to be £26 million – the product of 10 million shares worth £2.60 each.

Test yourself 8.1

The latest dividend payment is 7 pence per share and the estimated annual dividend growth rate is 3.5%. Shareholders expect an average annual return of 9.5%. Calculate the share price based on the dividend valuation model and the market value of shareholders' equity, assuming an issued share capital of 150 million shares.

There is no need to adhere rigidly to the assumption of a constant dividend growth rate. Investment analysts might be confident in their ability to judge dividends over, say, a year or two but concede that estimates of more remote dividends are speculative and unlikely to be any more accurate than assessments that stress average growth rates.

Making it work 8.1: Dividend growth model with variable growth rates

A company has just paid a dividend of 20 pence. Analysts judge that the dividend will rise by 25% next year and 15% the year after, but concede that an average annual growth rate of 6% is as good a forecast as any for the years beyond. The expected return is 12%. The dividend payments for the next two years are:

$$d_1 = 20(1.25) = 25 \text{ pence}$$

$$d_2 = 20(1.25)(1.15) \text{ or } 25(1.15) = 28.75 \text{ pence}$$

From the end of year 2 the dividend payments become a growth perpetuity that provides an estimate of the share price in two years.

$$P_2 = \frac{28.75 \ (1.06)}{(0.12 - 0.06)} = 508 \text{ pence}$$

The current share price ought to be:

$$P_0 = \frac{25}{(1.12)} + \frac{28.75}{(1.12)^2} + \frac{508}{(1.12)^2} = 450.2 \text{ pence}$$

The share price is still the present value of all the future dividends, but the growth perpetuity component doesn't start for two years.

The example illustrates another feature of the dividend valuation model; *it implicitly accounts for capital growth*. Assume an investor buys shares for 450.2 pence and plans to hold them for two years. The investor expects to receive dividends of 25 and 28.75 pence per share, and to sell the shares for 508 pence. Part of the annual return is rooted in the growth of the asset's value from 450.2 to 502 pence.

2.1 Estimating expected return and dividend growth

In itself the DVM is not difficult to apply. The challenging feature of the model is that share price estimates are dependent upon inputs, only one of which – the latest dividend payment – is known. This makes it difficult to assess the quality of any results; an important consideration if the model is going to be used to aid investment decision-making.

The model can also be employed in relation to actual share prices prevailing in the market to 'reverse engineer' the implied return on equity and dividend growth rate. But even in this case, different combinations of return on equity and dividend growth rate can produce the same share price.

Portfolio theory offers ready-made estimations of expected returns on equity. Indeed as we saw in chapter 4, the quintessential feature of the Capital Asset Pricing Model (CAPM) is to provide risk-dependent estimates of returns on equity.

Regarding the dividend growth rate, a commonly adopted method is to infer from past dividend payments. Assume that a company has just paid a dividend per share of 20 pence and that the dividend five years ago was 10 pence. The annual growth rate needed to double the size of the dividend over five years is:

$$g = \left(\frac{20}{10}\right)^{\frac{1}{5}} - 1 = 0.149 \,(14.9\%)$$

This estimate could be incorporated into forward-looking dividend valuation estimations. The main justification for this is that many companies do in practice endeavour to pursue what might be loosely termed 'stable' dividend policies. Typically, a company's pattern of dividend payments over time exhibits more stability than the profits from which the dividends are paid. While trading profits are highly susceptible to the vagaries of economic growth and competition, dividends are subject to the smoothing influences of managerial planning. Hence there is a basis for believing that past dividend growth rates provide a useful guide to the future.

Assuming that extrapolation from past dividends payments to predict future trends is a valid exercise it still leaves open the question of a suitable timescale. In the illustration above, a five-year gap was chosen. Why not four, six, ten or any other number of years? This approach also ignores dividend payments occurring within the boundaries. An alternative approach would be to take the annual dividend growth rates and derive an average. Different approaches are liable to throw up different estimates. Finally, judgement is still required to decide whether the resulting growth rate is realistic.

Equity analysts sometimes use the DVM to derive estimates of expected returns on equities that can be compared with those given by CAPM. A little algebraic manipulation of the DVM formula produces an expected return model:

$$r_0 = \frac{d_0 (1 + g)}{P_0} + g$$

One reason for consulting the DVM-based estimate is that it is a multi-period expected return; an average periodic (usually annual) return offered by successive dividend payments. The CAPM, by contrast, is a 'single-period' return model, offering an expected return relevant to a particular holding period. This does not mean that the models are contradictory. After all, if the assumptions of CAPM hold, then the share price that goes in to a DVM-based model of expected return ought to be one that is consistent with the prediction of the CAPM.

Worked example 8.2: Dividend growth and expected return

A company has recently paid a dividend of 7.5 pence on a share that was trading at 185 pence. Six years ago the dividend was 4.8 pence. The annual dividend growth rate is:

$$g = \left(\frac{7.5}{4.8}\right)^{\frac{1}{6}} - 1 = 0.0772 \ (7.72\%)$$

The expected return on equity is:

$$r_0 = \frac{7.5(1.0772)}{185} + 0.0772 = 0.1209 \ (12.09\%)$$

Test yourself 8.2

A company has just paid a dividend of 3.5 pence on a share trading at 123 pence. Eight years ago the dividend payment was 2.1 pence. Calculate the annual dividend growth rate and the expected return on equity using the DVM.

2.2 Valuing non-dividend paying companies

Google, Yahoo, Amazon and eBay have never paid cash dividends. Moreover their corporate websites declare that they have no intention of paying dividends in the foreseeable future. Apple paid a dividend in 2012, its first since 1995. In fact, not paying dividends is common among information technology and online trading companies. Can we square the stellar status of these companies among investors with an equity valuation model that identifies the source of value with dividend payments?

From a technical vantage point, the DVM clearly breaks down when dividends are zero. It always produces a share price of zero irrespective of growth rates and expected returns; a plainly absurd result.

On the other hand, the non-dividend paying companies exemplify an important theoretical argument in finance: that the dividend decision is essentially irrelevant to company valuation. The essence of the case is that the value of a company to its shareholders is ultimately determined by how efficiently it uses capital to increase after-tax cash flows. If new investment opportunities offer appropriate expected returns, then the correct managerial response should be to reinvest existing earnings, as this offers the best prospect of increasing shareholder wealth. Dividends need only be paid if new investment opportunities are absent; dividends are merely the distribution of residual earnings that companies are unable to deploy productively on behalf of shareholders.

Paradoxically, the irrelevance thesis by no means undermines the DVM. Two points are worth stressing.

◆ Dividends can only rise on a consistent basis if earnings grow. Without earnings growth, a policy of raising dividend payments would eventually require sales of company assets and ultimately liquidation. Who would bother spending money on shares in a company whose aim is simply to sell off assets in order to hand over money to shareholders?

◆ It is not true that non-dividend paying companies offer zero dividends. Over time investors in these companies hope to experience increases in wealth in the form of rising share prices. But investors are also consumers. Much of the equity will be traded, converted into cash to spend on consumption. In other words, investors convert equity into income streams, the very definition of a dividend. This, in fact, is an important component of the dividend irrelevance case, the ability of investors to decide their own dividends through trading equities.

The dividend irrelevance argument is that corporate dividend *policy* is not the key to the enhancement of shareholder wealth. This is far from implying that income from investment is irrelevant; enhanced income is the ultimate purpose of investment. The DVM is consistent with this.

3. Share prices and equity actions

Share prices are affected by the ever-present uncertainties associated with companies producing, investing and trading in a shifting and competitive business environment. They are also affected by premeditated, equity-focused, corporate actions. Common examples include:

◆ dividend payments;

◆ company flotations;

◆ mergers and acquisitions;

◆ private placings and rights offers;

◆ share repurchase programmes; and
◆ balance sheet adjustments: stock splits, consolidations and capitalisation issues.

The study text for the 'Investment' module on the Certificate in Offshore Finance and Administration provides explanations of these corporate actions and discusses procedures and regulations affecting them. The focus in this text is on asset valuation issues arising from these actions.

3.1 Dividend payments and share prices

On 13 December 2012, Microsoft paid shareholders a dividend of $0.23 per share. The payment was announced on 18 September 2012, with Microsoft indicating that the recipients would be those registered as shareholders on 15 November 2012, known as the *record date*. What impact is the dividend payment likely to have on the share price, and when? Let's take a closer look at the key dates.

The impact of the dividend announcement on 18 September 2012 ought to have been negligible. Microsoft has for many years paid annual dividends divided into equal quarterly instalments. The payment of $0.23 was the second in the annual cycle and, therefore, would have been anticipated well before the announcement date.

The dividend was paid to shareholders registered with the company on 15 November 2012. The US Security and Exchange Commission (SEC) requires that security transactions be settled (paid for and delivered) within three business days. Hence, in order to receive the dividend, an investor must have purchased Microsoft shares by 12 November at the latest. In accordance with SEC rules shares are declared 'ex-dividend' two days prior to the record date, which in the case of Microsoft's dividend payment was 13 November.

Anyone buying shares on or after 13 November would not receive the forthcoming dividend. Shares are traded on an ex-dividend basis, meaning that they are traded without entitlement to the next dividend payment. Instead it is paid to whoever owned the share on the record date, irrespective of whether they were still owners by the payment date.

The ex-dividend date does impact on the share price. On the ex-dividend date the share price effectively falls by an amount equal to the dividend. The rationale is that new investors are purchasing stakes in a company the value of which must fall because the dividend, being paid from the company's cash reserves, amounts to a reduction of assets. The old investors are protected from the fall in the share price because they receive dividends. New shareholders are protected because they pay the reduced ex-dividend price.

Ex-dividend share prices are similar to the clean prices encountered in the discussion of bonds. Both are prices where there is no entitlement to the next cash reward: interest in the case of bonds, dividends in the case of shares. Similarly, shares also trade at dirty prices, known as 'cum-dividend' prices. In the case of Microsoft, the share price prior to 13 November is a cum-dividend price.

It is sometimes not easy to detect the shift to an ex-dividend price in the share price data because factors other than dividend payments affect prices at the same time. In the case of Microsoft, the opening share price on 10 out of the last 12 quarterly ex-dividend dates (up to 13 November 2012) was below the closing price of the previous day. This confirms what we should expect. But even in these instances the size of the difference did not necessarily correspond to the dividend payment.

Test yourself 8.3

On 1 February a company declares that its next dividend payment will be 5.5 pence. The expected annual dividend growth rate is 7%. The shares become ex-dividend on 14 February and the dividends are payable on 28 February. Assume that the risk-free return is 2% per annum, the expected return on the market portfolio is 9% and the company's beta is 1.25.

a) **Calculate the company's expected return on equity using the CAPM.**

b) **Calculate the clean, or ex-dividend, share price using the DVM (assume that the impending dividend of 5.5 pence is the latest dividend).**

c) **Given the share price in part b), what price should the shares trade at prior to 14 February?**

3.2 Company flotations

Equity capital originates from a variety of sources. There is the initial capital contributed by owners at the conception of a business. Additional equity arises from the reinvestment of annual earnings and further contributions from existing and new owners. Many company owners eventually feel impelled to supplement existing equity by 'floating' the business on a stock market with a view to accessing a wider pool of capital. Another motive behind company flotations is a desire on the part of existing owners to 'monetise' their stakes in the business – essentially to cash in on the success of the business. Whatever the motives, flotation makes company valuation a particularly pressing issue.

Corporate valuation is complex. Assets and liabilities must be valued. The valuation of land, buildings, machinery and other tangible assets is difficult, but the valuation of so-called 'intangibles' (reputation, brands, intellectual capital) present challenges of a different order. Much of the essential information arises from audits that provide data in forms not always suitable for undertaking estimates of market value. There are also a host of legal, regulatory and tax issues to consider. The following discussion provides a schematic outline of three broad approaches to corporate valuation:

◆ net asset valuation
◆ price-earnings valuation
◆ discounted cash flow valuation.

The net asset value (NAV) method uses audited accounts as a basis for assessing corporate value. The measure of equity is simply the net of assets minus liabilities.

ABC Ltd balance sheet	
Fixed assets	
Land and buildings	£9.0m
Other	£5.0m
	£14.9m
Current assets	£4.0m
Total assets	**£18.9m**
Less current liabilities:	–£2.8m
Less long-term liabilities	– £5.5m
Net capital employed	**£10.6m**
Ordinary shares (5 pence)	£1.6m
Retained profit	£9.0m
Shareholders' interest	**£10.6m**

Figure 8.1 ABC Ltd balance sheet

Figure 8.1 presents a simple balance sheet showing that the shareholder stake in the company is equivalent to the net capital employed. Assume that the owners of ABC Ltd wish to float the company and that a financial appraisal has produced the following results:

◆ The land and buildings have an estimated market value of £15,000,000.

◆ The book value of the other fixed assets is regarded as a fair reflection of the replacement cost but their resale value is estimated at £1,400,000.

◆ The current assets include unusable stock with a book value of £300,000. It has no resale value.

The case for adjusting the balance sheet numbers is compelling because the company is about to be sold.

◆ The land and buildings ought to be re-valued at £15,000,000. The current owners will not sell the business for less than could be obtained by simply liquidating the assets.

◆ In the case of the 'other' fixed assets, the replacement cost rather than the realisable value is the relevant figure. Without these assets the company cannot operate. It would cost £5,000,000 to acquire them and so they are worth that amount to owners of the company.

◆ The current assets ought to be reduced by £300,000 because the stock is both useless and worthless.

The resulting NAV is given in Figure 8.2. It is nearly £5 million higher than the shareholders' interest given in the balance sheet. Nevertheless, in most instances, the NAV understates the value that newly floated companies are sold for. One reason is that despite revisions that produce values designed to reflect how useful the assets are to a company as a going concern, it still fails to capture the earnings potential of assets owned by dynamic companies, precisely those companies most likely to undertake flotations.

ABC Ltd NAV	
Fixed assets	
Land and buildings	£15.0m
Other fixed assets	£5.0m
Current assets	£3.7m
Total assets	**£23.7m**
Less liabilities	–£8.3m
NAV	**£15.4m**

Figure 8.2 ABC Ltd NAV

A second method of corporate valuation stresses the importance of after-tax earnings and earnings potential. A straightforward version of this approach is to price a company as a multiple of its after-tax profits. Companies and shares are valued in accordance with a **price-earnings ratio** (PER).

price-earnings ratio
A company's share price expressed as a ratio of its earnings per share.

ABC Ltd income statement	
Profit after tax	£4.8m
Less dividend	–£2.4m
Retained profit	£2.4m

Figure 8.3 ABC Ltd income statement

Figure 8.3 shows that ABC's profit after tax is £4.8 million. If the PER is 10, then the value of ABC ought to be £48 million. Go back to Figure 8.1 where it states that the ordinary share capital of ABC has a book value of £1.6 million, made up of shares with a par value of 5 pence each. This means that there are 32 million shares. In the event that a flotation leaves the number of shares unchanged, the offer price per share ought to be:

$$\frac{£48 \text{ million}}{32 \text{ million}} = £1.50$$

In fact, if this is deemed by the company and its advisors to be a fair valuation, they may choose to offer the shares at a modest discount to encourage outside interest in the flotation.

The obvious stumbling block is how to determine an appropriate PER. Existing owners naturally favour a high PER since it produces an elevated flotation value, thereby making those owners wealthier. But prospective new investors take the opposite view, preferring a company to be valued on the basis of a low PER. The duty of those advising on and managing a flotation is to sell a company for the maximum possible value without putting off new investors. One option is to consult PERs for companies operating in the same industry and which are already quoted on the stock market.

Test yourself 8.4

ABC Ltd's profit after tax is £4.8 million. Three companies operating in the same industry as ABC Ltd have the following share prices and earnings per share.

Company	DEF	GHI	JKL
Share price	140 pence	375 pence	80 pence
Earnings per share	10 pence	20 pence	5 pence

a)   Calculate the PER for each company and the average of all three PERs.

b)   Value ABC based on the average PER obtained in part a).

c)   Assume that the aim is to float ABC through the sale of 32 million shares and that the management has been advised to sell the company at a 15% discount to the value calculated in part b). What is the resulting share offer price?

d)   Discuss why ABC is likely to offer shares at a discount to the estimated fair value.

A third method of valuing corporate equity involves discounting future expected net cash flows by the estimated cost of equity. The DVM is itself a method of valuing companies based on the present value of future expected net cash flows – with the net cash flows identified with dividend payments. The value of the company to the shareholders is simply the share price multiplied by the number of issued shares.

There is the practical problem in using the DVM to value newly floated companies; it is commonplace for such companies not to pay dividends for some considerable time. After all, an important impetus behind stock market flotation is to enable capital-hungry companies to access additional funds for long-term investment. Newly quoted companies tend not to be generous dividend payers but instead offer prospects of dynamic earnings growth in the future based on high levels of investment in the present.

In these circumstances, a different tack is needed to estimate future net cash flows on which to base discounting. It should be an approach that:

◆   factors in cash outlays on capital investment; and

◆   ignores non-cash flow items included in income statements.

Worked example 8.3: Cash flows to shareholders

An analysis of a company intending to float on the stock exchange has estimated that after-tax net profits for the next five years will be:

Year	1	2	3	4	5
Net profit (£ million)	30	30	200	200	300

In addition:

- the company plans to invest £100 million in each of the next two years; and

- the net profit figures include an annual charge for depreciation of £30 million in year 1, £50 million in year 2 and £70 million for each of the subsequent three years.

The net income available to shareholders will be:

Year	1	2	3	4	5
Net profit (£m)	30	30	200	200	300
Plus depreciation (£m)	30	50	70	70	70
Less capital expenditure (£m)	−100	−100	0	0	0
Shareholder net income (£m)	−40	−20	270	270	370

The depreciation charges are added back to the net profit figures because they are not an expense in the sense of cash flowing out of the company. Instead the expense of investment is recorded when money is spent on items of capital.

In practice, many more adjustments to net profits are needed to generate the shareholder net income. For instance:

- Accounts receivable (sales that have been recorded but not paid for) should be deducted and subsequent increases and decreases deducted and added respectively.

- Increases in working capital should be deducted and vice versa.

- If capital investment is financed from borrowing, it should be added to shareholder net income at the outset and subsequently deducted in accordance with the debt repayment schedule. This in turn will have knock-on effects in terms of interest payments and tax savings arising from those payments.

The upshot is that it is possible in principle to generate estimates of shareholder net income that can then be discounted in line with previously discussed principles to arrive at a value for the company. Of course, the practical implementation of these techniques is a complex exercise requiring a great deal of knowledge and professional expertise.

3.3 Mergers and acquisitions

As with company flotations, the classificatory aspects of mergers and acquisitions (M&As) have been addressed in the 'Investments' module and will not be repeated here. In addition, the basic techniques for valuing companies involved in M&As are very similar to those discussed in relation to flotations. There is, however, an important characteristic feature of M&As that is of great importance to asset managers and securities traders.

Most M&As are, in practice, acquisitions where one entity regards another as a target. The term 'takeover' perhaps better expresses the sense of the power relation at play, though there are certainly important shades ranging from takeovers verging on friendly mergers to occasions where resistance is so intense that a target launches a counter-bid for the original bidding company (the so-called 'pac-man' defence). The characteristic feature of acquisitions is that they invariably stimulate an increase in the value of the target company's equity.

A great deal of academic effort has been expended trying to explain the reasons for this 'bid-premium'. After all, if the value of a company's equity is fundamentally a product of its earnings and investor expectations about future earnings, then there is no automatic reason why company values should alter just because of the possibility of a change of corporate ownership. A common explanation consists of two key strands:

◆ Target companies offer the prospect of increased earnings because they tend to be badly managed companies whose assets are being under-utilised. In the hands of more dynamic management, earnings of target companies are liable to improve, thereby justifying the higher market values. Another formulation of the increased efficiency argument is that two companies in combination benefit from synergy effects – efficiency improvements that are not available to them when operating separately. It is a 2 + 2 = 5 argument with earnings improvements based on economies of scale and increased market power available to merged entities.

◆ Most of the putative improvements in future earnings end up with shareholders of target companies in the form of bid premiums. There is a 'rational', efficient market explanation for this. If market participants believe that a bid will be successful, then company values will immediately reflect the expected increase in future earnings. For the bidding company shareholders, any bid that allows them to obtain even the tiniest element of the premium is worth making. But the target company shareholders know this (remember, it's an efficient market) and will rationally hold out for a bid that transfers to them virtually the entire premium.

The aim here is not to engage in the wide-ranging discussion of the causal interactions that underpin M&As. Much investigation has been undertaken into the effects of circumstances on the distribution of bid premiums: the degree of hostility and resistance, the form of financing (cash or shares), dependence on leverage, industry differences, managerial ambitions and numerous other factors. Many express doubts about the explanation for bid premiums rooted in earnings improvements, citing evidence suggesting that many merged entities subsequently perform comparatively poorly.

For equity investors, the issue of immediate import is that news concerning M&As, even vaguely articulated rumours, can have significant short-term effects on equity values.

3.4 Private placings and rights offers

Table 8.1 indicates the amount of equity capital raised through placings and rights issues by companies listed on the London Stock Exchange between 2007 and 2011.

Table 8.1 Placings and rights issues on the London Stock Exchange 2007–11

Year	Private placings		Rights issues	
	Number of issues	Amount raised (£m)	Number of issues	Amount raised (£m)
2007	98	6,758	7	702
2008	89	12,288	16	27,589
2009	93	6,096	50	50,698
2010	94	4,126	7	10,134
2011	247	4,965	8	425

Placings involve the sale of new shares to selected investors (mainly institutions) rather than to existing shareholders or investors in general. Under UK company law, a board of directors is routinely permitted to undertake placings up to a maximum of 5% of the existing share capital without the need to consult existing shareholders (but restricted to a total of 7.5% of issued share capital on a three-year rolling basis). The price discounts associated with placings are also limited with 5% below the price immediately prior to the placing announcement being the normal limit. The Financial Services Authority (FSA) in the UK requires that a discount in excess of 10% of the market price would require the company to issue a prospectus. This discourages large discounts because the attraction of placings is that they allow companies to raise funds quickly at minimum cost. Issuing a prospectus undermines both of these advantages.

In principle, placings work against the interests of existing shareholders, because they are not invited to subscribe to the new shares at the discounted price. Take the case of a company that has an issued share capital of 100 million with a market price of £2, making its equity worth £200 million in total. It decides to undertake a placing of 5 million new shares at a 5% discount, giving an issue price of £1.90.

After the placing the issued share capital will be 105 million and the value of the company's equity will be £209.50 million, the increase of £9.50 million being the proceeds from the sale of 5 million shares. The new share price will be:

$$\frac{£209.50}{105 \text{ million shares}} = £1.995$$

The share price should fall slightly, by approximately 0.25% – a decline that is unlikely to provoke ire among existing shareholders. In fact, the larger among existing shareholders are likely to be invited to subscribe to the placing at the discounted value anyway and, therefore, might have received new shares at the discounted value.

The scale of placings, in terms of numbers and amounts raised, changes from one year to the next. Nevertheless they are commonly occurring, routine parts of equity raising activity in general. In fact, Table 8.1 understates the scale of placings because it does not include those by newly listed companies or those undertaken in conjunction with public offers.

Rights issues are less frequent with a somewhat greater propensity to occur in concentrated bouts followed by relatively quiet phases. For instance, Table 8.1 shows a massive surge in rights issues in the three years after the 2007 banking crisis, followed by a huge decline in 2011. Rights issues in 2011 raised less than 1% of the amount raised in 2009.

Unlike placings, rights issues offer existing shareholders the right to subscribe to the new shares on a pre-emptive basis; it amounts to them being given the opportunity to act first to ensure their interests. The characteristic features of a rights issue are as follows:

◆ New shares are offered *pro rata*, meaning that each qualifying shareholder is offered the right to subscribe to an amount of shares proportional to their existing holdings.

◆ New shares are issued at a discount to the market price of existing shares.

◆ Shareholders are entitled to trade the rights to the shares being offered.

On 14 July 2011, Pendragon PLC, a UK operator of motor vehicle dealerships, announced a nine for eight rights issue. The subscription price for the new shares was 10 pence. In addition the company declared a record date of 28 July 2011; those registered as shareholders on 28 July would be offered the opportunity to purchase additional shares.

The first thing investors needed to decide was whether they wished to take part in the rights issue. Existing shareholders not wishing to take part could sell rights to their entitlements and non-shareholders wishing to take part could buy these rights. A record date of 28 July indicates that, given the time allowed for settlement, trades up to the 25 July would affect the list of shareholders on the record date. During this time investors would have had to weigh up the general outlook towards the rights issue as it is liable to affect the share price. In fact, Pendragon's share price fell from 21.75 pence to 17.5 pence between 14 and 25 July, a decline of nearly 20%. The fact that the FTSE All-Share Index remained at around the same level over the same period gives weight to the view that factors specific to Pendragon rather than market factors were driving the share price. It suggests that there wasn't a great deal of enthusiasm for the rights issue.

On 2 August the registered shareholders received 'provisional allotment letters' (PAL) detailing their subscription rights. With receipt of the PALs, Pendragon shares began trading on an 'ex-rights' basis with the rights to the new shares to be traded separately on a 'nil paid' basis.

Ex-rights share prices are similar to the notion of ex-dividend share prices; the existing shares now trade without the rights to subscribe to the new shares attached. At the start of the ex-rights period the share price should fall to reflect the discounted subscription price of the new shares. Just prior to the start of the ex-right period, Pendragon's share price was 17.5 pence. Given the nine for eight issue ratio and the rights subscription price of 10 pence, the theoretical ex-rights price (TERP) is:

$$\text{TERP} = \frac{(17.5 \text{ pence} \times 8) + (10 \text{ pence} \times 9)}{17} = 13.53 \text{ pence}$$

Pendragon's shares opened at an actual ex-rights price of 13.25 pence on 2 August, very close to the theoretical price.

Investors and asset managers have a range of options with respect to the rights issue. They can:

◆   subscribe to their full entitlement;

◆   sell the rights to their entire entitlement;

◆   subscribe to one part and sell the rights to the other; or

◆   do nothing.

Worked example 8.4 illustrates the financial implications of each action based on the Pendragon case.

Worked example 8.4: Shareholder options

Assume that an investor owns 80,000 Pendragon shares and is therefore entitled to subscribe to an additional 90,000 at 10 pence each. For ease of illustration we will assume that immediately prior to start of the ex-rights period the share price was 17.5 pence and that it then traded at the TERP of 13.53 pence. This means that the investment prior to the rights issue was worth:

$$80,000 \times 0.175 = £14,000$$

Subscribe to the full entitlement: The investor owns 170,000 shares worth 13.53 pence each, a total investment of:

$$170,000 \times 0.1353 = £23,000$$

The stake in the company has gone up by £9,000. But don't forget, the investor has spent £9,000 buying the additional 90,000 shares. There is no *net* change in the investor's wealth, merely a change of structure.

Sell all the rights: Afterwards the investor owns 80,000 shares with a market price of 13.53 and has sold 90,000 rights. The value of each right is the difference between the TERP and the subscription price: 13.53 – 10 = 3.53 pence. The value of the investment plus the proceeds from the sale of the rights is:

$$(80,000 \times 0.1353) + (90,000 \times 0.0353) = £14,000$$

The stake in the company has fallen. But the sale of 90,000 means once again that there is no net change of wealth.

Subscribe to one portion of the shares and sell the rights to the remainder: The entitlement to 90,000 shares can be split according to the investor's preference. One possibility is to split the entitlement in such a way that the proceeds from the sale of rights generate sufficient funds to pay for the subscribed portion. The portion that must be sold corresponds to the subscription price divided by the TERP.

$$\text{Portion to be sold} = \frac{10}{13.53} \times 100 = 73.91\%$$

Sell 73.91% of the rights for 3.53 pence each and subscribe to the remaining 26.09% for 10 pence each. The net cost is:

$$(0.7391 \times 90,000 \times 0.0353) - (0.2609 \times 90,000 \times 0.1) = £0$$

The proceeds from the sold rights pays for the shares bought. The number purchased is 0.2609 x 90,000 = 23,481 meaning that after the issue the investor has a total of 103,481 shares. They are worth:

$$103,481 \times 0.1353 = £14,000$$

Yet again the investor's aggregate wealth has remained unchanged. In this case both the equity stake in Pendragon and the investor's bank balance are unaffected.

Do nothing: In the case of investors who take no action, the rights are sold on their behalf and the premiums, net of administration costs, paid to them.

Test yourself 8.5

On 15 May, shares in SCT PLC became ex-rights with shareholders receiving provisional allotment letters entitling them to subscribe to 11 new shares for each 18 owned. The subscription price for the new shares was £2.00. On the previous day SCT's share price closed on £3.1925.

a) Calculate the TERP for 15 May.

b) Assume that an investor has 18,000 SCT shares. Based on the TERP, demonstrate the financial implications of choosing to:

    i.   subscribe to the offer in full; or

    ii.   sell all of the rights.

c) Show how the investor could trade rights with a view to maintaining the value of the stake in SCT.

3.5 Share repurchases

Towards the end of chapter 5, we noted that in recent years Philip Morris has been undertaking a large-scale programme of share buybacks, effectively retiring a significant portion of its share capital. Philip Morris' initiative is symptomatic of a much broader and growing trend. In the US in recent years, share buybacks have rivalled dividend payments as the most important mechanism for distributing cash to shareholders. Not surprisingly, investors and fund managers have taken a growing interest in wealth effects of share buybacks.

In one sense, buybacks ought to have no significant impact on how companies are assessed. After all, shareholders can obtain cash from 'retiring' shares any time they wish by selling them on the open market. Furthermore, why should shareholders regard buybacks in a positive light? The act of buying shares is a choice to hold wealth in the relatively risky form, presumably in the hope of achieving better returns. A buyback converts shares back into cash: back to the riskless but low-return form of wealth that the investor had exchanged for shares.

However, share buybacks are not simply equivalent to shareholders selling shares. In the latter case the size of the issued share capital stays the same. But with buybacks the issued share capital declines. From the vantage point of the remaining shareholders, the company is riskier because there is less equity capital supporting the company's liabilities. Fewer shareholders remain to support the same level of corporate debt. And if this is the case, it could translate into companies being put under pressure to produce higher returns for shareholders. Again there is no necessary reason why buybacks would be welcomed by shareholders.

Another reason for the growth of share buybacks could be that they have, to some extent, merely provided an alternative to dividend payments as a method of distributing earnings to shareholders. In other words, the main point of interest ought to be the total amounts of cash distributed to shareholders not the mechanics of the distribution process. Buyback initiatives may appeal largely because they offer a more tax efficient mechanism for distributing earnings. Whereas dividends attract personal income tax demands, share repurchase programmes generate capital gains tax obligations. The latter are liable to be a lesser burden, not least because share values as a whole have not grown much at all over the last decade or so in the US, UK and other major markets.

Buybacks may also reflect the lack of profitable investment opportunities available to cash-rich businesses. Managers undertaking buyback schemes may simply be following textbook prescriptions to distribute funds to shareholders if they are surplus to requirements. The sobering side to this assessment is whether the lack of investment opportunities is systemic or whether we are merely witnessing a process of cash-rich but mature businesses returning capital to owners who in turn divert it towards younger, fast-growing but capital-hungry businesses. If it's the latter then there's every reason for optimism among shareholders. If not...

3.6 Balance sheet adjustments

Finally, we will take a brief look at a group of equity events that do not entail cash flowing in or out of a company. Accordingly, their impact on the value of corporate equity ought to be neutral as they do not involve additions or reductions to productive resources. The most common are stock splits, capitalisations and consolidations.

Stock splits involve a decision by the board of a company to replace the existing shares with a greater number, with the par value adjusted accordingly. For instance, assume that a company initiates a two for one split of shares with a par value of 100 pence. Each shareholder receives two shares each with a par value of 50 pence. Apple has undertaken a two for one stock split on three occasions, the first in 1987, then 2000 and then 2005.

A capitalisation issue (also known as a scrip or bonus issue) is very similar to stock split except that additional shares with the same par value are issued to shareholders. The balance sheet effect is to shift some of the shareholders' interest recorded in reserves such as retained profit or share premium accounts to the ordinary share capital account.

A consolidation is the opposite of a stock split. For instance, a one for two consolidation might involve the replacement of two shares with a 50 pence par value with single share with a 100 pence par value, thereby halving the total number of shares.

In all these instances, investors ought to appreciate that the assets of the company remain unchanged and therefore the market value of the company should be unaffected. In the case of a two for one stock split, shareholders have double the number of shares but the market price of the shares should fall by half, leaving them no better or worse off. The effect should be no different from the case of taking a £10 note from someone and offering two £5 notes in exchange.

Some evidence does hint at small value effects associated with balance sheet adjustments to equity. Stock splits and capitalisations are generally undertaken by companies that have experienced extended periods of rising share prices to a point where the price per share is very high. Stock splits increase the appeal of these shares to smaller investors. The increased demand for shares boosts prices. Another suggestion is that capitalisation issues are interpreted by shareholders as a sign that senior management is confident that reserves will not be needed to meet future dividend expectations or other expenses. The explicit incorporation of reserves into the company's long-term equity capital testifies to management optimism and this is liable to place the company in a positive light with investors.

Chapter summary

◆ Textbooks on corporate finance state the fundamental objective of corporate activity is to maximise shareholder wealth.

◆ Shareholders bear the brunt of corporate risk-taking, and therefore expect to be the main beneficiaries of corporate success.

◆ Valuing ordinary shares generally involves more guesswork than valuing debt securities because unknown factors have a greater influence.

◆ The dividend valuation model is built on similar principles to other valuation models in that it declares that an asset is worth the present value of the expected future cash flows.

◆ Investors need to understand the implications of a range of 'equity events' for share prices.

Chapter Nine
Financial risk management

List of topics

1 Financial risk, hedging and forward prices
2 Exchange-traded derivatives and risk management
3 Structured investments and options

Introduction

Investment entails a willingness to apply capital to business ventures whose outcomes, to varying degrees, are uncertain. Investors invest knowing that there is a possibility that wealth may be lost. But they quite reasonably expect to achieve positive returns, primarily because investment involves the application of capital to increase the production of wealth. The rewards for investment are ultimately rooted in the growth of aggregate wealth.

On the other hand, the process of investment includes financial risks that can be, to some degree at least, controlled. Among the most compelling are financial risks arising from changing interest rates and volatile currency and commodity markets. Furthermore, there is a strong case for arguing that businesses and investors generally should seek to minimise these risks.

The degree of business, or systematic, risk that investors choose is a question of individual preference. But the risks associated with volatile financial market prices, be they interest rates (the price of money) or exchange rates (the relative prices of different currencies), are different. Unlike investment, these factors have no inherent connection to the broader process of wealth enhancement. They bear closer comparison to games of chance with zero-sum outcomes, where the fortunate win at the expense of the unlucky.

Opportunities to mitigate the potential impact of these chance factors on business outcomes ought therefore to be seized, not as a matter of personal inclination but in general. The argument that the effects of these risk factors tend to even out over time is no argument against positive action to alleviate their effects. It is tantamount to arguing that the expected return is zero but with risk in tow. The chapter focuses on how investors can reduce financial market risks through the use of money market operations, forward agreements and exchange-traded derivatives. It also discusses how some of these tools and techniques have been used to structure and tailor investment products to particular priorities.

1. Financial risk, hedging and forward prices

1.1 Exchange rates

Take the case of a UK investment fund managing a portfolio that includes shares in a number of European companies who pay dividends in euros. Let's imagine that three months from now, the fund is set to receive a dividend of €200,000 which it intends to convert into sterling before distribution to UK investors. With a €/£ spot exchange rate of €1/£0.80, the euro-denominated dividend payment would be worth £160,000 if it were paid now, i.e.

$$200,000 \times £0.8 = £160,000$$

But the dividend is not due for three months meaning that the fund managers do not know what it will be worth in sterling terms. The euro might decline relative to sterling, making €200,000 worth less to UK investors. For instance, if a euro is worth only £0.75 when the dividend is paid, it translates into £150,000 – £10,000 less than the value three months earlier. The UK fund and its investors face the risk of exchange rate uncertainty causing a decline of wealth.

Can the fund managers do anything to fix the sterling value of €200,000 now and, thereby, avoid the exchange rate risk? Yes. They can borrow euros immediately for three months, using the €200,000 dividend to repay the loan. The borrowed euros can then be used to purchase sterling at the prevailing exchange rate. These transactions collectively dissolve the exchange rate uncertainty and fix the amount of sterling that the investment fund receives after three months. Let's examine the matter more closely.

The fund borrows an amount of euros that results in a repayment of €200,000. The scale of borrowing therefore depends on interest rates charged on three-month euro loans. Let's assume that the (annualised) rate is 2%. The fund can borrow the present value of €200,000 based on a discount rate of 2%:

$$\frac{€200,000}{\left(1 + \frac{0.02}{4}\right)} = €199,005$$

Hence the fund borrows €199,005. In three months it must pay back €200,000 using the dividend income. It is therefore free to use the €199,005 to buy sterling. Given an exchange rate of €1/£0.8, it purchases £159,204.

$$199,005 \times £0.8 = £159,024$$

This is not quite the end of the story. Just as the borrowed euros necessitate interest payments, the sterling can be deposited thereby attracting interest payments. Assume that the annual rate of interest on a sterling deposit is 3%. The future value of the bought sterling is:

$$£159,204 \left(1 + \frac{0.03}{4}\right) = £160,398$$

The upshot is that the €200,000 dividend becomes a sterling-denominated dividend of £160,398. It does not matter what happens to the actual €/£ exchange rate over the intervening period. The outcome is a fixed future exchange rate of:

$$\frac{160,398}{200,000} = £0.8020$$

The investment fund is able buy £0.8020 for each € in three months. This procedure for fixing the exchange rate is known as a money market **hedge**; a set of money market transactions that circumvent the effects of, in this instance, exchange rate uncertainty and enable the user to lock into a fixed rate.

hedge
A financial arrangement whose primary purpose is to eliminate or reduce the exposure of investments to specific types of risk.

Test yourself 9.1

Assume that a German investor is due to receive $1 million from maturing US treasury bonds in six months' time and intends to convert them into euros. The spot rate of exchange is €1/$1.31. The annualised six-month interest rates are 2% for euros and 1% for dollars.

a) How many dollars can the German investor borrow for six months on the basis of the future income of $1m?

b) How many euros does the dollar loan buy at the spot rate?

c) What is the locked in €/$ exchange rate offered by a money market hedge?

Note that the lock-in rate differs from the spot rate. In our example a euro buys £0.8020 in three months compared to £0.8 in the present. The reason for this is the difference between the interest rates applicable to the two currencies. The sterling deposit rate is 3%, while the euro borrowing rate is 2%. It means that the sterling deposit grows faster than the euro debt and, as a result, the fund receives £160,398 in exchange for €200,000 after three months – £398 more than the spot value of £160,000. A euro buys more sterling under the money market hedge than it does in the spot market.

This does not mean that the fund managers regard the hedge rate in this instance as 'better' or 'preferable' to the spot rate of exchange; the disparity is simply a mechanical result of different interest rates. What they do need to assess is whether or not a euro will be worth more or less than the hedge rate of £0.8020 in three months. If they think a euro will be worth more, they might decide not to hedge hoping to profit on the basis of a stronger euro buying more sterling. On the other hand, if they believe that the euro is likely to weaken relative to sterling, they may think that a hedge provides valuable protection. They might, of course, think it foolish of fund managers to try to predict developments in currency markets and that hedging is invariably the wisest course of action.

cost of carry
The cost of holding a financial position. It incorporates interest and other cash flows that are payable or receivable, gained or lost. There may also be custodian and storage costs.

The difference between the spot rate and money market hedge rate is known as the **cost of carry,** the cost associated with holding (carrying) financial positions over periods of time. The investment fund in our example incurs a cost in the form of the interest payment on euros, but this is more than offset by interest received on sterling. In this instance the fund's cost of carry is said to be positive because it receives more interest than it pays. This implies that another investor wanting to exchange sterling for euros in the future would face a negative cost of carry.

Test yourself 9.2

A Spanish investment fund is due to receive £300,000 in interest payments on sterling-denominated corporate bonds in six months and wishes to convert them to euros. The spot rate of exchange is €1/£0.8, while the annualised euro and sterling money market rates on 6-month arrangements are 2.5% and 3.5% respectively.

a)   Calculate how many euros the Spanish fund is able to acquire in six months using a money market hedge.

b)   What is the money market hedge rate?

c)   Consider how the cost of carry looks from the perspective of the Spanish fund.

Instead of a money market hedge, the investment fund might consider negotiating an OTC forward exchange with a bank. A forward exchange is, to all intents and purposes, a notional form of the money market hedge that avoids the need to borrow one currency, convert to another and deposit. In our example, the fund informs the bank that it wishes to convert €200,000 into sterling in three months. The bank quotes a €/£ forward rate at which it is prepared to trade three months hence. If both parties agree, they formalise the arrangement as a forward exchange. The only cash flow is after three months when the fund delivers €200,000 to the bank in exchange for the agreed amount of sterling.

There are good reasons why forward rates closely match rates implied by money market hedges. If, with reference to our example, banks quote a forward rate equal to the spot rate of €1/£0.80, it means that the investment fund is offered the opportunity to trade €200,000 for £160,000. But the money market hedge offers £160,398. The fund, and investors in similar situations, would reject forwards exchanges in favour of the money market option.

Now imagine that banks go the other way and offer considerably better terms than a money market hedge, say, a forward rate of €1/£0.81. This translates into a commitment to pay £162,000 for €200,000.

$$200,000 \times 0.81 = £162,000$$

This is an attractive offer – in fact, too attractive. Currency traders would enter the fray, eager to agree forward contracts that promise to pay £162,000 for every €200,000 delivered in three months. Using the figures from our example, a trader engages in money market transactions buying €199,005, placing them on deposit at 2% and receiving €200,000 after three months. The purchase of euros is financed by a sterling loan of £160,000 which, at 3%, results in a repayment of £160,398 to the bank.

After three months, the trader delivers the €200,000 to the bank and receives £162,000 under the terms of the forward contract. In effect, the bank sells euros to the trader for £160,398 and buys them back for £162,000, a loss of £1,602 for every €200,000 worth of forward contracts agreed. The bank's losses are inevitable from the outset, rooted in its initial mispricing of forward exchanges.

The gain realised by the trader is an example of an **arbitrage** profit which, in the strictest sense, is defined as a guaranteed profit on a zero investment. The trader recognised the inconsistency between the money market hedge rate and the forward rate, and profited entirely on the basis of funds borrowed from a bank (i.e. used others' capital). Euros were purchased from the bank with a sterling loan from the bank. They were later sold back to the bank for a greater amount of sterling under the terms of the forward exchange.

arbitrage
Financial arbitrage is the practice of exploiting price inconsistencies to generate riskless profits.

An arbitrage opportunity as stark as the one outlined above is unrealistic in practice – any bank guilty of such naive pricing of forward contracts would quickly be arbitraged into bankruptcy. The purpose of the exercise is to demonstrate that forward rates invariably bear a close correspondence to money market hedge rates; rates that preclude the opportunity for arbitrage profits. This is articulated in the concept of **covered interest rate parity**, which states that borrowing and depositing a pair of currencies and covering the outcome with a forward contract equalises the loan and deposit rates. The relation between the spot and forward exchange rates is arbitrage-free.

covered interest rate parity
The notion that forward currency exchange rates effectively neutralise interest rate differentials.

Refer again to the earlier example. Sterling interest rates are 1% higher than euro rates (3% versus 2%), or 0.25% higher in simple quarterly terms. Compare this to the difference between the spot and, what we now call, the forward exchange rates (recall that the euro spot rate is £0.80 and the three-month forward rate is £0.820). The quarterly percentage difference is:

$$\frac{(0.8020 - 0.8)}{0.8} \times 100 = 0.25\%$$

The percentage difference between the spot and forward currency rates is equal to the percentage difference between the interest rates. Significantly, the three-month forward price of euros is 0.25% higher than the spot price – euros are more expensive in the forward market.

It is entirely possible to profit from borrowing euros, converting to sterling and depositing at the higher rate. But a forward exchange is not the source of any profit. Under the forward contract the euros needed to repay the loan are 0.25% more expensive, £0.8020 instead of £0.8. The interest rate gain is therefore nullified by an equivalent exchange rate loss. The forward contract reduces the rate of return on sterling to parity with the rate of return on the euro.

carry trade
The practice of borrowing at one rate and lending the funds at a higher rate. Common examples are borrowing in low interest rate currencies to invest in higher-rate currencies and borrowing at low short-term rates to invest in higher-yielding long-term assets.

Profits from trading on interest rate differences among currencies, known as **carry trade**, occur if higher interest rate currencies (those that are deposited) appreciate in value, maintain their value or at least do not depreciate significantly. In other words, they arise if exchange rates happen to shift in ways favourable to traders engaged in speculative carry trades. Profits depend on gambles paying off. Forward exchange contracts offer deal-specific and date-specific exchange rates, but not at levels that allow for systematic arbitrage. Where arbitrage opportunities do arise, they are liable to be fleeting, slight and unnoticed by all but the most acutely observant.

1.2 Interest rate risk

An inevitable feature of ongoing investment management is the need to address short-term financing needs. In the normal course of affairs investment institutions sometimes expect to be in possession of financial surpluses for short periods, maybe cash from maturing or sold assets, or income in the form of interest and dividends. At other times institutions must plan for moments when they expect to be temporarily short of liquidity to, say, undertake a new investment, pay interest on existing loans or distribute returns to investors. In simple terms, interest rate risk arises because:

◆ those intending to borrow funds for short periods in the future, face the possibility that interest rates might rise in the interim; or

◆ those intending to place reserves on deposit for short periods in the future, face the possibility that interest rates might fall in the interim.

As with exchange rate risk, there are straightforward money market-based techniques for fixing future short-term interest rates. Assume that the management of an investment fund wishes to borrow £500,000 for three months, but starting in three months. There is a risk that interest rates rise during the time to the start of the loan period, resulting in a higher cost of borrowing for the fund. The management has an interest in fixing the interest rate.

Since the fund wishes to borrow for three months in three months' time, the money market solution is: borrow immediately for six months and hold the money on deposit for the initial three months. The effect is to fix the interest rate for the second three-month period, the period during which the loan is required. The hedge rate is a product of the prevailing annualised interest rates on three-month and six-month money market transactions. Assume that the rates are:

◆ three-month interest rate spread 1.2–1.0%

◆ six-month interest rate spread 1.6–1.4%

Stop and think 9.1

Note that the interest rates above are quoted as **spreads** with the (higher) left side being the rate at which banks are prepared to lend money and the (lower) right side the rate that banks offer on deposits. The spread is effectively the revenue in percentage terms that banks expect to earn from their dealings with savers and borrowers. In the section on hedging exchange rate risk, we refrained from using spreads (for both interest rates and spot exchange rates) in order to illustrate the principles of money market hedging in as simple a way as possible. The introduction of spreads here is simply designed to make the presentation a little more realistic.

spreads
An interest rate spread refers to the difference between the lending and borrowing rates quoted by banks for particular terms.

The investment fund needs to borrow £500,000 in three months. How much should it borrow now? This is a present value issue, with the three-month deposit rate of 1.0% being the relevant discount factor.

$$\frac{£500,000}{\left(1 + \dfrac{0.01}{4}\right)} = £498,753$$

The fund borrows £498,753 which becomes £500,000 after three months, whereupon we assume that it is withdrawn and used for its intended purpose. In effect, after three months the fund has a loan of £500,000.

The money is borrowed for six months at an annual rate of 1.6%. The total amount owed in six months is a future value.

$$£498,753 \left(1 + \frac{0.016}{2}\right) = £502,743$$

The fund repays the lender £502,743. Based on a loan of £500,000, the interest payment is £2,743 – a fixed amount for a three-month loan which is, by implication, a fixed or hedged rate. The rate, in annual terms, is:

$$\left(\frac{2,743}{500,000} \times 4\right) \times 100 = 2.19\%$$

The money markets fix the forward borrowing rate at 2.19%. If the fund managers believe there is a good chance of the actual cost of borrowing in three months' time being above 2.19%, then the hedge might be deemed a judicious choice. Of course, they might feel that an increase in interest rates of this order is a remote possibility. After all it is nearly double the prevailing three-month borrowing rate of 1.2%. They are at liberty to do nothing and pay whatever the rate happens to be at the relevant time.

Worked example 9.1: Hedging the deposit rate

Instead of the investment fund wishing to borrow £500,000 in the future, assume that it is set to receive £500,000 in three months' time, which it wishes to deposit for a further three months. In this instance, a money market hedge consists of borrowing the present value of £500,000 for three months. The loan can be paid off using the income mentioned above, thereby enabling the fund to deposit for six months. The relevant calculations are as follows:

$$\frac{£500,000}{\left(1 + \frac{0.012}{4}\right)} = £498,504$$

$$\text{Proceeds } £498,504 \left(1 + \frac{0.014}{2}\right) = £501,994$$

The proceeds of £501,994 include interest of £1,994 on the forward deposit of £500,000. This translates into a money market hedge of:

$$\left(\frac{1,994}{500,000} \times 4\right) \times 100 = 1.60\%$$

The fund can fix the three-month deposit rate at 1.6% on a deposit beginning in three months' time.

---

forward rate agreement
An OTC arrangement designed to fix the interest rate on borrowing or lending in the future.

The OTC version of a money market interest rate hedge is known as a **forward rate agreement** (FRA). Like forward currency exchanges, FRAs are constructed using notional rather than actual cash flows. The investment fund would not need to borrow or deposit money now. Instead, it borrows money when it is required in three months. If interest rates rise in the meantime the fund will be compensated when the FRA is settled.

FRAs are also similar to forward currency arrangements in that the critical factor determining forward rates are money market hedge rates. The arbitrage-free principles at the heart of this relation are similar to those that apply to currency markets.

The structure of FRAs is, however, a little different from that of forward currency arrangements. Assume that our investment fund enters into a FRA which cites a fixed three-month rate of 2.19% (the money market hedge rate) on a £500,000 notional loan starting in three months and lasting for three months. It is a '3 x 6 payer FRA': a fixed interest rate that the client pays on a notional loan starting three months from now and ending six months from now. In return, the bank pays the client the market interest rate prevailing in three months which will be the sterling Libor rate.

Let's see what happens if in three months £Libor is 2.5%. It indicates that interest rates and that the investment fund faces a higher cost of borrowing.

However, the settlement of the FRA means the fund paying 2.19% *to* the bank but receiving 2.5% *from* the bank on the notional sum. In practice there is a single net payment from one party to the other. In this instance, the bank pays the fund the equivalent of 0.31% (2.5 − 2.19), which compensates the fund for the rise in the cost of borrowing on the money markets. The fund receives the cash equivalent of 0.31% of £500,000 measured over a quarter of a year. The formula for the net payment is:

$$C = \frac{N \times (L - R) \times T}{1 + (L \times T)}$$

Where:
C = cash flow to the client;
N = notional amount;
L = Libor reference rate;
R = fixed rate; and
T = timescale of the notional transaction.

In our example the cash payment is:

$$C = \frac{£500,000 \times (0.025 - 0.0219) \times 0.25}{1.00625} = £385$$

The amounts paid on FRAs are, in fact, present values of the entitlement (hence, the division by 1.00625 in the above example). This is because FRAs are cash settled at the start of the underlying loan or deposit being hedged, whereas interest payments occur at the end of the loan or deposit term. In the investment fund's case, the FRA is settled after three months with the fund receiving £385. But it does not pay interest on the underlying £500,000 loan for six months.

How effective is the FRA in hedging the interest rate? Assume the fund pays interest at 2.5% over three months on a £500,000 loan. The interest payment is £3,125. But the money received on the FRA, after being reinvested over three months, is approximately £387. In net terms the interest paid is £2,738, which works out at an annual rate of interest of:

$$\left(\frac{2,387}{500,000} \times 4\right) \times 100 = 2.19\%$$

This is the forward rate established under the FRA.

Test yourself 9.3

Assume that the investment fund had entered into the same 3 x 6 payer FRA, fixing a borrowing rate of 2.19% on £500,000. However, instead of interest rates rising, assume that £Libor is 1.6% on the reference date.

a) Calculate the compensating payment and explain who pays whom.

b) Show how the payment fixes the fund's borrowing rate.

Test yourself 9.4

An investor is due to receive £800,000 in coupon payments on UK government bonds six months from now, and intends to hold the money on deposit for a further six months. The relevant interest rate spreads are:

- six-month interest rate spread 1.6–1.4%

- twelve-month interest rate spread 2.0–1.8%

    a) Calculate the deposit obtainable on the basis of a money market hedge.

    b) Using the rate obtained in part a), calculate the cash flow on a 6 x 12 receiver FRA in the event of the reference Libor rate being 1.2%.

    c) Demonstrate how the FRA payment fixes the deposit rate.

1.3 Hedging multi-period cash flows

Investors often wish to hedge cash flows that occur over multiple time periods. Here are some likely scenarios.

◆ Holders of fixed rate bonds are concerned that the prospect of falling interest rates will reduce reinvestment rates on many years of future coupon payments. As a result they wish to fix rates for a number of future income streams.

◆ Mortgage providers have lent substantial amounts to homebuyers at fixed interest rates extending over many years. The financial outlook has shifted towards expectations of higher rates, with the result that the cost of capital for mortgage providers threatens to rise above the rate of return on their slowly maturing assets (mortgage policies). The cost of capital is prone to increase quickly because a significant component is members' savings. If interest rates in general do rise, mortgage companies have little option but to offer higher savings rates, otherwise the savers will move their money elsewhere. Forward agreements whereby mortgage companies pay fixed rates in exchange for a series of what would be variable Libor-determined receipts could do much to alleviate the financial pressures.

◆ A UK fund has invested in European corporate bonds that pay coupons in euros at regular intervals. The issue of managing exchange rate risk over one period is extended over many periods.

◆ An American investment company, attracted by the low cost of capital in Japan, has issued bonds denominated in Japanese yen and converted the proceeds to dollars to finance investments in the US. The company wishes to avoid the exchange rate uncertainties associated with making periodic yen coupon payments on the bonds, believing that it detracts from the main business of investment. It therefore wishes to make arrangements to fix the dollar-cost of these payments in advance.

In all these cases the task of financial risk management could be carried out by agreeing a series of specific money or forward market arrangements, each applicable to a particular time-specific cash flow. The forward prices or rates of each agreement would be unique because the interest rates underpinning them differ in each case.

In fact, financial markets offer a more convenient solution – **swap contracts**. Swaps are essentially multi-period forward contracts. They provide greater economy and convenience for managing the financial risks of multi-period cash flows.

◆ A swap offers risk management for multiple cash flows bundled into a single contract. The benefits are obvious, associated with the reduced time, expense and complexity of negotiating and managing an ongoing cycle of individual arrangements.

◆ Swaps replace the series of unique forward prices associated with each hedged cash flow in the bundle with a single 'forward' price called the **swap rate**.

The explanation of how swap rates are derived from individual forward rates is a little beyond the technical level of this text. We will focus instead on how swap contracts work as risk management tools.

Assume that an investment fund owns bonds with a face value of £5 million, an annual coupon rate of 3% and a term to maturity of five years. The annual coupon payment is, therefore, fixed at £150,000. For convenience, we will also assume that the bonds are trading at par value, meaning that the yield is equal to the coupon rate of 3%.

The fund wishes to swap the five years of fixed income for variable income in the belief that interest rates are likely to increase in the coming years. This is necessary according to the management of the fund, because if interest rates do rise it will have to pay higher rates for loans used to fund investments. The interest rate swap is therefore a hedge designed to ensure that yields on assets do not fall below the cost of funding.

A bank quotes a five-year swap rate spread of 2.7–2.8%, a fixed rate spread at which it is willing to trade the variable rate, in the form of the £Libor, for five years. A client wishing to receive the Libor from the bank pays 2.8%; the client swaps a fixed rate in favour of a variable rate. On the other hand, a client wishing to pay the Libor to the bank receives a fixed rate of 2.7%; the client swaps the variable rate in favour of the fixed rate. The spread of 0.1% is the sources of the bank's fee for acting as counterparty to both.

The fund in question requires a swap under which it pays the bank 2.8% of the notional sum and receives the Libor on £5 million in return. Cash flows are determined on the basis of the Libor rate at the start of each period of the swap. Assume that at the start of the swap contract Libor is 2.0%. It means that at the end of the first year the fund pays the bank a net rate of 0.8% (the swap rate of 2.8% less the Libor rate of 2.0%). It is equivalent to a payment of £40,000 on £5 million. This reduces the investment fund's return on the bond

swap contract
An OTC arrangement that facilitates, in the case of interest rate swaps, the exchange of income streams. The most common example is the exchange of fixed rate payments for variable rate payments.

swap rate
The fixed rate quoted for a swap contract.

in the first year from 3.0% to 2.2% because £40,000 of the £150,000 coupon must be paid to the bank under the terms of the swap.

Now imagine that the investment fund's fears were justified and that by the end of the first year Libor has risen to 4%. At the second swap settlement date the bank pays the fund 1.2% (4% Libor less the fixed swap rate of 2.8%), £60,000 in cash terms. The total return on the bonds rises to £210,000 for the year, a return of 4.2%.

Test yourself 9.5

Assume that the Libor rates applicable to the three remaining legs of the five-year swap discussed above are 5.5%, 6.2% and 2.8% respectively.

a)   **Calculate the cash flows between the fund and the bank at each settlement point.**

b)   **Work out the impact of each on the bond's annual return.**

In modern financial markets swaps, interest rate swaps in particular, form the largest component of the OTC dealing in terms of the values involved, whether measured in terms of outstanding notional sums or the cash flows associated with settlement procedures. This is not surprising because, compared to other OTC techniques, swaps offer a more efficient method of managing exposures to interest rates and exchange rates in a wide range of circumstances.

2. Exchange-traded derivatives and risk management

Interest rate and currency risk can also be managed using exchange-traded contracts. Take the example of a sterling short-term interest rate (STIR) futures contract. Like other futures contracts it has standardised features:

◆   It is designed to fix a future rate of interest on a nominal sum of £500,000.

◆   The rate refers to the nominal sum deposited for three months from the specified contract delivery date. In the case of sterling STIR futures the delivery day is the first business day after the final trading day for the contract, which is normally the third Wednesday of the delivery month.

◆   The future interest rate offered by the contract is based on sterling Libor rates. In fact interest rate futures ought to be priced so that implied rates compare to those offered by similarly structured OTC forward agreements. In practice, there are liable to be small divergences between forward and futures rates due to differences in counterparty risk, market liquidity and the fact that forwards are bilaterally negotiated. But any significant difference would rapidly disappear due to arbitrage by alert traders, who would contract to borrow at the low rate and deposit at the high rate.

In early October 2012 the sterling STIR futures contract with a delivery date of 20 December 2012 was trading at a price of 99.48. The Libor rate offered by the contract is obtained by subtracting the futures price from 100:

$$100 - 99.48 = 0.52\%$$

The contract provided an annualised Libor rate of 0.52% on a three-month deposit of £500,000 starting on 20 December. It offered a *fixed* rate in the future.

To illustrate how it would work, assume that in early October 2012 an investor planned to deposit £500,000 on 20 December for three months and decided to hedge against the possibility of a decline of the interest rate by purchasing a sterling STIR futures contract. Suppose that by 19 December (the final trading day for the contract) the sterling Libor rate was 0.3%, indicating that short term interest rates had fallen. The futures contract would have closed at 99.7 (100 − 0.3) because on the final trading day the interest rate implied by the futures price must be the same as the actual Libor rate.

Stop and think 9.2

Referring back to the earlier discussion about the relation between the current and forward rates of interest, explain why the futures price on a contract's final trading day gives a rate of interest corresponding to the Libor for that day.

The contract was bought at 99.48. A sale on 19 December at 99.7 closes the position with the investor gaining financially. How much? The cash difference between 0.52% and 0.3% on £500,000 over three months:

$$\frac{500,000 \ (0.0052 - 0.003)}{4} = £275$$

If the investor undertook the planned deposit of £500,000 at the Libor rate of 0.3%, it would have produced interest of £375 after three months which, when added to the £275 on the futures contract, produced an annualised return of 0.52% (it is worth recalling that the £275 would have accrued as credits to a margin account over the period that the contract was open, not as a single credit on closure).

Test yourself 9.6

Take the case of the investor who intended to deposit £500,000 on 20 December and hedged against exchange rate risk by buying a futures contract at 99.48.

a) **If three-month sterling Libor was 0.8% by 19 December, what were the implications for the cash flowing in and out of the investor's margin account?**

b) **Demonstrate how the deposit rate was fixed using the futures contract.**

Instead of a deposit of £500,000, assume that the investor wished to borrow £500,000 for three months on 20 December and was concerned that interest rates might rise. A hedge would have been possible by *selling* a sterling STIR future. Determine the pay-offs and the resulting borrowing rate if by 19 December:

a)   Libor was 0.25%;

b)   Libor was 1.00%.

The standardisation of futures is a potential obstacle to their use in hedging financial risks:

◆   At any moment there are parties planning to deposit reserves and borrow funds at different moments over diverse periods. Likewise there are parties planning to trade currencies at different times. Yet interest rate and currency futures available for hedging financial risks typically operate on quarterly cycles implying just four delivery dates per year. Some futures markets, especially in the area of interest rates, supplement the quarterly cycle with contracts offering delivery dates for the immediate two succeeding months. Even so, it still means that delivery dates are scarce. It would be the exception rather than the rule for a planned transaction to mirror exactly the temporal features of a futures contract.

◆   The same goes for the relation of the fixed notional amounts characteristic of futures and the sundry amounts being hedged. It is unlikely that the latter can be bundled into exact futures contract-sized packages.

In fact, standardisation is less problematic than it might seem at first. Suppose that the investor in the example above intended to deposit £500,000 on 1 December rather than 20 December and had purchased a STIR future as a hedge. Because futures are marked to market (see chapter 2) any price increases arising from a fall in interest rates is credited immediately to the investor's margin account. On 1 December the investor sells a future, effectively closing the position and taking the gain as compensation for the lower interest rate.

basis
The difference between a futures price and the spot price of the asset to which the futures contract refers.

In these circumstances the gains or losses from futures may not exactly offset changes in the value of the underlying asset due to **basis** risk. The basis refers to the difference between the actual price of the underlying asset and the futures price at any moment. It is similar to the difference between the spot and forward prices (or rates) associated with OTC arrangements. In fact, the use of futures to hedge financial risks largely consists of replacing the financial risk with basis risk, the latter being a small fraction of the former. A detailed analysis of basis risk is, unfortunately, beyond the scope of this text.

3. Structured investments and options

3.1 Derivatives and leveraged risk taking

Aside from hedging financial risk, forward contracts, futures and swaps enable leveraged risk-taking. Take the example of the £/$ currency future. With an initial margin of $1,320 and an ability to meet margin calls, a trader can buy a currency future on a notional value of £62,500. Based on the March 2013 futures prices of £1/$1.6250, this amounts to trading $101,562.5. Every 1 cent decline in sterling is a loss of $625, meaning that total losses can end up being much greater than the initial margin staked on the outcome. A mere 3 cents fall to £1/$1.5920 more than wipes out the margin. The attraction is that small increases in sterling magnify profits; a 3 cent increase to £1.6550 produces a gain of $1,875 – a return equal to 142% of the initial margin.

The trader in this simple scenario takes a stance on the future direction of a particular market and uses a derivative to augment potential gains. Other derivative arrangements, both OTC and exchange-traded, can be used to create the possibility of leveraged profits, but at the cost of piling up large losses in the event of being wrong. An alternative is to deploy strategies that can prove highly profitable in the event of asset prices moving in one direction while limiting the scale of losses should prices shift in the opposite direction. Implicit within this idea is the use of hedging to restrict the scale of downside outcomes while retaining exposure to the upside advantages. This demands a type of derivative different to those discussed so far. Welcome to options.

Stop and think 9.3

Before proceeding, think about the discussion of forwards and futures contracts and how they offer protection against damaging movements in market prices – the protection costs. In the event that asset prices move favourably for those hedging, they cannot expect to gain in net terms. The asset price movements will be offset by losses on forward/ futures contracts. The essence of hedging is certainty of outcome whatever happens.

3.2 Options and risk

An option is exactly that; an option to buy or sell a specified asset at a fixed price in the future. The option to buy the underlying asset is known as a call option, while an option to sell is a put option. In essence:

◆ Call options increase in value if the underlying asset price rises. Being able to buy something at a set price when the actual price is higher is intrinsically valuable.

◆ Put options increase in value if the underlying asset prices falls. Being able to sell something at a set price when the actual price is lower is also intrinsically valuable.

Option contracts occur in OTC and exchange-traded forms. They cover a broad range of financial arrangements, including fixed interest securities, equities, interest rates, currencies and traded commodities. There are also options on futures and swaps.

An option combines a hedge against the effects of an adverse movement in the price of the underlying asset with a leveraged stake on a favourable movement. Contrast this with a futures contract. A future can be used to shield an investor from potential losses on an asset, but at the expense of profiting on the asset. Alternatively, it can be used to establish a leveraged trade in the future price of the underlying asset, but at the expense of large losses if the asset price shifts in the 'wrong' direction. It does not provide protection and profit potential at the same time. Options do.

Take the example of FTSE 100 Index options, traded on the Euronext exchange in London. At the time of writing the FTSE 100 stood at 6,122. Index option contracts were available with exercise prices ranging from 3,200 to 8,800 and exercise dates up to December 2014. As exchange-traded contracts, FTSE 100 index options are standardised:

◆ One index point corresponds to a cash flow of £10. For instance if a trader had bought a call option with an exercise price of 6,125 and, on the exercise date, the FTSE 100 was 6,126, it results in a gain of £10. It is as if the trader pays £61,250 (6,125 x £10) for something that is actually worth £61,260.

◆ Index options are cash settled rather than an underlying product being delivered (with an index option, the 'product' doesn't actually exist in a readily transferable form). On the exercise date the contract mentioned above would be priced at 1 point and would, therefore, be sold for £10.

Most types of option contract command an upfront purchase price, referred to as the option premium. The term 'premium' is no accident because options display similarities with insurance. To demonstrate the point, assume that the FTSE 100 Index stands at 6,125 and that two investors have the following positions:

1 A diversified portfolio of FTSE 100 shares with a market value of £61,250.

2 A one-month FTSE 100 call option with an exercise price of 6,125, which cost the investor the equivalent of 64.5 points, i.e. £645.

Imagine that after a month the FTSE 100 has collapsed to, say, 5,000 – a decline of over 18%. The loss on the diversified portfolio is likely to be in the region on £11,250. But the loss for the option holder is limited to £645, the price paid for the call option contract. The £645 is effectively a premium that buys protection against the effects a decline in the FTSE 100.

Test yourself 9.7

Take the two investment positions outlined above and assume that the FTSE 100 rises to 7,500 by the end of the month.

a) Calculate the total financial gain for each investor.

b) Calculate and compare the rates of return of the two investors.

3.3 Structured investments

Structured investment products occur in a wide variety of forms. However, they generally have three elements:

1 a capital preservation feature normally identified with straightforward saving;

2 a risk-taking feature normally identified with equity-style investments; and

3 a leveraged approach to the equity component designed to raise the overall return. The leverage is usually based on options, or in some cases swaps, because they restrict potential losses to the equity investment element.

Structured investments can be adapted to particular preferences. The capital protection side can be stressed to generate products that appeal to more conservative investors. Other products incorporate levels of 'capital at risk' and offer the possibility of higher, leveraged-based, returns. Nevertheless some mix of the two is an inherent feature of structured investment.

The banking crisis has stimulated more interest in structured investments. Nowadays well-known banking and asset management groups routinely advertise structured investments as alternatives to straightforward savings products. There are a number of reasons for their popularity.

Historically low interest rates (1 or 2% in many circumstances) make simple preservation of capital costly with yields not even providing compensation for inflation.

Many investors also remain wary of riskier investments. The potential downsides appear sizeable and intimidating.

Structured products seem to provide a compromise; a safe haven together with the prospect of significant gains. A typical product, which we will call a 'Four-year Growth Plan', might state:

◆ a return on capital of 35% after four years if the FTSE 100 is at or above the level at the start of the Plan;

◆ if the FTSE 100 is below this initial level there will be no return, but capital net of expenses will be returned to investors;

◆ if the FTSE 100 is 50% or more below the initial level, capital returned will be reduced on a 1:1 basis. For example, if the FTSE 100 finishes 51% below the initial level, investors will repaid just 49% of their net investment; and

◆ withdrawal of capital is allowed but will incur penalties which might result in monies returned being less than the amounts invested.

The manager advertises the Plan with the aim of attracting funds from investors. Once a predetermined level is reached, the Plan is closed to further investment. Let's assume that the Plan in question raises £1 million.

Most of the proceeds are lent to a bank for the entire term. This is the capital preservation part of the product. Let's assume that the bank pays an annual return of 3%. In order to realise £1 million in four years, the Plan must invest:

$$\frac{£1,000,000}{(1.03)^4} = £888,487$$

The Plan manager spends £888,487 on, say, four-year zero coupon bonds issued by the bank. The bank repays £1 million in four years with the result that the initial investment is recovered. The bank is presumed to be a safe investment because it has an A2 credit rating by Moody's.

This leaves £111,513 (ignoring operating expenses) to produce the positive return of 35% on £1 million over four years, a cash return of £350,000. The implication is that the Plan manager needs to more than treble the value of the £111,513 being risked on the FTSE 100 over four years. The money is used, in the main, to purchase FTSE 100 call options.

Pricing an option is a complex matter incorporating the current asset price, contract exercise price, the length of time to the exercise date, estimates of the underlying asset price volatility and interest rates. In order to demonstrate how the 35% return can be funded, we make a number of simplifying assumptions:

1. The FTSE 100 currently stands at 6,000.
2. The company spends £111,513 on four-year call options with an exercise price of 6,000.
3. The four-year options cost the equivalent of 600 index points, or £6,000 each.
4. The risk capital therefore buys approximately 18.6 call options.

Now assume that the FTSE 100 grows by an average of 8% per annum over the next four years. It will reach:

$$6,000(1.08)^4 = 8,163$$

In exercising the contracts the Plan manager pays the equivalent of 6,000 points but receives 8,163 points. The 2,163 difference translates into income of £21,630 per contract or £402,318 on 18.6 contracts. The £1 million repaid by the bank makes a total value of over £1.4 million – more than enough to ensure the promised 35% return on £1 million.

There is no assurance that the FTSE 100 will achieve an average growth rate of 8% per year. But what the exercise does show is that an 8% growth rate for the FTSE 100, which is a far from fanciful expectation, is enough for the structured product to provide capital protection *and* generate the 35% return on total capital.

Of course in the event that the FTSE 100 growth rate is less than 8%, the Plan management will be obliged to cover any resulting shortfall. If the FTSE 100 finishes below 6,000, the options will be worthless and the management will be obliged to find £350,000 from elsewhere to make good on the promise of a 35% return. This is a risk to the management company. But the potential reward is that it keeps any gains in excess of the 35% commitment.

The Plan states that even the initial investment ceases to be protected in the very unlikely event that the FTSE 100 index falls by more than half, effectively to below 3,000 in this example. A possible reason for this is that the Plan manager might also have *sold* a four-year put option with an exercise price of 3,000, receiving a premium in return. Should the FTSE fall below 3,000 the owner of the put will exercise it, effectively forcing the Plan manager to pay the equivalent of the difference between 3,000 and the actual index level. The terms of the Plan mean that it will be paid from the investors' capital.

The motive for the sale of the put is that it generates additional income (though it will be a small amount) which can be used to increase the risk capital with a view to further boosting the Plan's returns. The assumption is that it is extremely unlikely that the FTSE will fall to such a disastrous extent.

Finally it should be stressed that despite the apparent assurances regarding the protection of capital, investors are not protected from the effects of default by the bank on the zero coupon bonds or by the Plan manager with respect to the promised 35% return.

Chapter summary

◆ The risks associated with volatile financial market prices have no inherent connection to the broader process of wealth enhancement. Opportunities to mitigate the potential impact of these chance factors on business outcomes ought to be seized.

◆ Interest rate and exchange rate uncertainty can be alleviated through the use of money market hedging.

◆ Financial institutions offer organised alternatives to money market hedging in the form of OTC forward transactions and exchange-traded futures contracts.

◆ The use of derivatives to hedge price risks requires that participants give up the advantages of favourable price movements.

◆ The relationship between spot prices and forward prices is assumed to be arbitrage-free. In practice, skilled traders are able to uncover opportunities to arbitrage.

◆ Swap arrangements offer a method for hedging interest rate and other risks in relation to series of underlying cash flows.

◆ Like forwards and futures, option contracts offer a hedge against downside developments. But, in exchange for the payment of an option premium, they retain an exposure to the benefits of favourable price movements.

◆ Options are used to create structured investment products that purport to offer investors some degree of capital protection, while offering returns well above market interest rates.

Part Four

Performance measurement and assessment

Overview

Throughout the previous sections of this text, there are references to returns on individual assets, asset portfolios and associated financial arrangements such as forward transactions. It could hardly be otherwise, given that the fundamental themes are investment management and financial markets. The aim of this final part is to examine some of the most common methods used to appraise the qualities of different investments, to form opinions about future prospects and to assess outcomes in the context of prior objectives.

Chapter 10 focuses on how returns on assets are represented in relation to debt and equity investments. Chapter 11 concludes the text by examining criteria by which the returns on portfolios of assets can be assessed, stressing that the methods employed are dependent on the investment philosophy and strategic thinking behind given initiatives.

Learning outcomes

After reading this part, students should be able to:

◆ explain the significance of the concept of duration in relation to debt securities and market risk;

◆ tackle basic exercises involving the measurement of duration and bond price variations;

◆ demonstrate an understanding of the concept of a yield curve and its significance in asset management;

◆ explain the strengths and weaknesses of accounting ratios to interpret the prospects for equity investments;

◆ use data to calculate price to earnings ratios, dividend yields and dividend cover, and interpret the results;

◆ appreciate the nature of the modern world of investment and the pivotal role of asset management institutions;

◆ articulate the significance of the distinction between active and passive fund management for investment styles and the assessment of fund performance;

◆ demonstrate knowledge of various methods and perspectives that inform the pursuit of investment fund management, such as replication strategies, fundamental analysis, stock picking and views concerning market psychology; and

◆ explain the meaning of alpha returns and their significance for the assessment of the performance of actively managed funds.

Chapter Ten
Asset performance analysis

List of topics

1　Debt securities and performance analysis
2　Equity and performance analysis

Introduction

Many techniques for measuring asset performance can be applied in a straightforward manner to readily available data. But easy application does not imply easy interpretation. Results do not tell their own story. They must be placed in context; maybe through comparison with historic results, current peer group results or preset targets. Furthermore, all appraisal techniques involve distillation, with some things ignored or sidelined for ease and clarity of representation. How can we be certain that excluded aspects are unimportant and that, therefore, the resulting technique is appropriate for the task in hand?

This chapter examines a range of performance measurement tools used in the analysis and management of investments. It highlights how they provide useful means of summarising developments and revealing future possibilities. But it also underlines the potential pitfalls of over-reliance on 'the numbers' at the expense of thoughtful assessment and judgement. We start with appraisal techniques related to the risk and return on debt securities, and then shift on to those relevant to the appraisal of equity.

1. Debt securities and performance analysis

In chapters 6 and 7 on money market and capital market debt securities, the general approach was to posit a return, or yield, and address the implication for the asset price. Take the case of a corporate bond that matures in five years, offers a coupon of £3.00 per annum and on which investors require a 4% yield. The price is:

$$P_0 = 3 \left[\frac{1 - [1.04]^{-5}}{0.04} \right] + \frac{100}{(1.04)^5} = £95.55$$

But why is the yield 4% and to what extent can we expect it to stay at 4%?

The first part of the question is the most intractable. Chapter 7 showed that yields on debt securities are affected by a range of risk factors; credit risk, market risk, reinvestment risk, inflation risk and call risk. Normal practice is to regard any given yield as consisting of a risk-free component, corresponding to the yield on government bonds, plus a premium (or spread). If the yield on a government bond maturing in five years is 3%, the corporate bond offers a premium of 1% because investors require compensation for the extra risk. The 1% premium is due primarily to credit risk (and possibly call risk) since even 'risk-free' bonds are not immune to market, reinvestment and inflation risk.

This is not an explanation of the 4% yield. The question is merely restated. Why is the risk-free rate 3% and why is the credit spread 1%? Economic analysis is necessary. The risk-free rate reflects the impact of central bank lending rates, inflationary expectations, government fiscal policy, exchange rate considerations and economic growth prospects. The spread might be regarded as a market consensus based on prevailing perceptions of the scale of credit risk, past debt default rates and credit ratings afforded by ratings agencies. A definitive explanation will always be elusive, not least because many of these issues are the subject of debate among economists regarding their causal significance.

The second element to the question, can we expect yields to remain constant, is easier to answer – no. Both the general level and structure of yields on debt securities shift over time. It is difficult to anticipate the direction in which yields change and far more difficult to correctly anticipate when and on what scale changes occur. Nevertheless, the fundamental relation between yields and prices is known.

1. Debt security prices move in the opposite direction to yields.
2. Prices of long-term debt securities are more volatile relative to yield changes than the prices of short-term securities.
3. Prices of low coupon rate debt securities are more volatile relative to yield changes than are the prices of high coupon rate securities.
4. Yields tend to be positively related to the term to maturity.

These characteristics enable asset managers to assess market risk and, in principle, act to alleviate the effects of unfavourable market developments or take advantage of promising developments.

1.1 Market risk and debt security management

Points 1 and 2 above were presented in chapter 7. An increase in yields causes debt securities to fall in value. However, while this relation holds generally, it is less significant in the case of securities set to mature in the short-term and more noteworthy the longer the term to maturity. The interdependence of yield and price produces a host of potential asset management dilemmas. Here are just a few possible scenarios:

◆ Managers of money market funds, holding assets such as treasury bills and commercial paper, ought not to be too concerned by the prospect of rising yields. Prices of short-term assets do not fall significantly in the event of higher yields. Furthermore, short-term securities are likely to be held to maturity, meaning that investors receive fixed principal amounts irrespective of yields. In fact money market fund managers might regard rising yields as good news, because money from regularly maturing assets can be used by buy new (slightly) lower-priced assets offering higher yields.

◆ Shift to the opposite end of the maturity spectrum, investors holding long-term bonds. The prospect of rising yields could be unwelcome news because long-term bond values are liable to fall by significant amounts. Higher reinvestment rates on coupon receipts may not be sufficient to compensate for the decline in bond values.

Test yourself 10.1

Two funds manage the following portfolios:

- **Fund 1 holds 20,000 pure discount securities each with a par value of £100 and maturity of 31 days. The current annual yield is 2%.**

- **Fund 2 holds 20,000 securities each with a par value of £100 and maturity of 10 years. They pay an annual coupon rate of 4% and offer investors an annual yield of 5%.**

  a) **Calculate the market value of both portfolios.**

  b) **Calculate and compare the effects of a 1% increase in the yield on the market value of both funds.**

  c) **Assume instead that yields fall by 1%. Compare the outcomes for the two funds.**

How fund managers and other investors address these and other dilemmas depends to a considerable extent on circumstances. For instance, a fund manager intending to hold long-term assets to maturity might not be unduly concerned by the prospect that rising yields might cause asset values to fall in the meantime. By contrast, an active bond trader, anticipating an increase in yields, might choose to short sell long-term bonds in the hope of profiting from significant price falls.

Investors must take a view on whether potential yield changes are temporary or signal the start of a trend. For some, the trade-off between capital gains/losses and reinvestment gains/losses associated with yield changes might not be clear-cut. An added, but profoundly significant, difficulty is that most of these decisions must be taken in anticipation of developments as 'after the event' is often too late. If anticipated developments do not transpire, it can prove just as costly as not doing anything when they do occur.

Stop and think 10.1

At the start of 2013 the annual yield on UK three-month treasury bills stood at around 0.36%, while the yield on ten-year UK government bonds was approximately 2%. Yields this low are unprecedented. Even after factoring in generous credit spreads on corporate bonds, the general scale of yields on sterling denominated bonds is exceptionally low by historical standards. The pattern was also true of debt securities traded in many other jurisdictions at the time.

Assume that you are asked for advice on the direction in which yields are most likely to shift over the next few years. How would you respond?

1.2 Duration and price volatility

duration
A measure of bond maturity based on a weighted average of the individual constituent cash flows. It is useful in the assessment of bond price volatility.

The concept of **duration** offers a mechanism for measuring the price volatility, and hence market risk, of debt securities. At one level, the duration of a bond is simply an alternative method of measuring its maturity. Let's begin by presenting the idea at an intuitive level, using the example of the two bonds in Table 10.1.

Table 10.1 Cash flows and prices for four-year zero coupon and coupon paying bonds

	Year				Price (5% yield)
	1	2	3	4	
Zero coupon cash flows	£0	£0	£0	£100	£82.27
Coupon paying cash flows	£5	£5	£5	£105	£100.00

Both bonds have the same term to maturity of four years. Owners of the zero-coupon bonds receive a single cash flow of £100 in four years; 100% of the return occurs after four years. By contrast, owners of the coupon paying bonds receive some of the total reward after one year, two years and three years as coupon payments; parts of the bond's value 'mature' in less than four years. Therefore its maturity, seen from a weighted average perspective, is less than four years. This perspective is the basis for the concept of duration.

Duration takes the maturity of each individual cash flow (one year, two years, etc), multiplies it by the present value of the cash flow and sums the results. Dividing by the bond price gives the duration (*D*).

$$D = \frac{\Sigma t\left(\frac{C}{(1 + y)^t}\right)}{P_0} + \frac{t\left(\frac{100}{(1 + y)^t}\right)}{P_0}$$

Taking the prices and yield from Table 10.1, the duration for the zero coupon bond is four years. For the coupon paying bond it is:

$$D = \frac{\dfrac{1 \times 5}{1.05} + \dfrac{2 \times 5}{(1.05)^2} + \dfrac{3 \times 5}{(1.05)^3} + \dfrac{4 \times 5}{(1.05)^4}\ \dfrac{4 \times 100}{(1.05)^4}}{100} + \frac{}{100} = 3.72 \text{ years}$$

Unlike the zero coupon bond, the duration of the coupon paying bond is less than its term to maturity. The significance of this observation has less to do with the observation itself than with its implicit properties. A simple modification to duration provides a mechanism that can be used to determine how much the prices of different bonds change in response to variations in yields. Modified duration (*MD*) is:

$$MD = \frac{D}{1 + y}$$

The modified duration measures the sensitivity of a bond's price to changes in yield. The higher the modified duration of a bond the more its price shifts in response to yield variations. The price change, in cash terms, is determined in the following way:

$$\text{Change in } P = \text{Change in } y \times \frac{D}{-1 + y} \times P_0$$

Table 10.2 Modified duration

	Duration	Modified duration
Zero coupon bond	4.00 years	3.81
Coupon paying bond	3.72 years	3.55

Table 10.2 indicates the modified durations for the two bonds. It shows that the zero coupon bond is more sensitive to changes in yield than the coupon paying bond; its modified duration is higher. Hence the price change associated with a yield change is greater relative to the prevailing price. Assume that the yield on both bonds rises by 0.25% to 5.25%. The changes in price will be:

Change in *P* (zero coupon) = 0.0025 × –3.81 × £82.27 = –£0.78

Change in *P* (coupon paying) = 0.0025 × –3.55 × £100.00 = –£0.89

The new bond prices are £81.49 and £99.11 respectively; both have fallen in value. The zero coupon bond has fallen by more in relative terms, though less in absolute terms.

Test yourself 10.2

A bond has three years to maturity and pays a coupon of 12% per annum and a redemption payment of £100. Assuming that the annual yield is 4%.

a)   Calculate the market price and the modified duration of the bond.

b) **By how much would its price change in the event of a fall of 0.3% in the yield?**

c) **What is the new bond price?**

The concept of duration provides a means of measuring the price sensitivity of bonds that exhibit all manner of combinations of coupon rates, maturities and yields. It is, in effect, a useful technique for analysing the price implications of market risk.

1.3 The yield curve

It was stated earlier that yields tend to be positively related to the term to maturity; longer-term bonds tend to offer higher returns than short-term bonds. The discussion of duration provides a clue as to why. Long-term bonds have larger durations, indicating that their prices are more sensitive to changes in yields; they are more volatile. This is the same as saying that they are more exposed to market risk. Hence capital markets tend to offer higher yields on long-term bonds as compensation for market risk.

yield curve
A depiction of the relationship between yield and maturity for debt securities issued by central government.

The structure and scale of the risk premium is customarily depicted as a **yield curve**, a graphical representation of yields on securities that differ only with respect to their maturity. They are usually plotted using yields from government bills and bonds with different terms to maturity. Techniques are employed to rid the data of effects from different coupon rates so that all that is left is the relation between yield and maturity. Given the effects of market risk, yield curves are normally upward sloping.

Yield curves based on government securities are especially significant for bankers, financial analysts, fund managers and securities dealers.

◆ They facilitate the measurement of credit risk premiums on non-government debt securities. Imagine that the yields on two corporate bonds with five years to maturity are 5% and 8%, while the five-year risk-free return is 2%. We could conclude that the corporate bonds offer credit risk premiums of 3% and 6% respectively. We could also conclude that the company paying an 8% yield is regarded by investors as considerably more likely to default.

◆ As time passes, the maturities of issued debt securities naturally decline. So even if yields in general remain unchanged, yields on individual securities will change in line with their declining maturities. This will affect bond prices.

Test yourself 10.3

Assume that a bond that has four years to maturity pays a coupon of 6%. The annual yield on four-year bonds is 4%, while the yield on three-year bonds is 3%.

a) **Calculate the current price of the four-year bond.**

b) **Calculate what its price should be in one year, assuming that yields overall remain constant.**

2. Equity and performance analysis

2.1 Ratio analysis

The Accounting Fundamentals module on the Certificate in Offshore Finance and Administration programme devotes a chapter to the use of accounting ratios in the assessment of company performance. This section therefore presumes familiarity with accounting ratios associated with the assessment of profitability, liquidity, working capital and financial leverage.

Financial analysts and investment managers take a keen interest in the financial statements of companies and use ratio analysis as a tool to form assessments of performance and opinions about prospects. However, they are also aware that ratio-based assessment has its limitations.

Firstly audit methods produce valuation and performance measures that are often not suitable for use in investment appraisal without qualification and adjustment. For example, according to Apple Inc's October 2012 accounts, annual operating profit after tax was $41.7 billion. Shareholders' equity was valued at $118.2 billion. With no long-term debt capital to consider, the capital employed can be identified with the shareholders' equity, meaning that the return on capital employed (ROCE) was just over 35%. Yet Apple's share price at the end of October 2012 stood at around $600, implying a market value for the company's equity of around $560 billion. The market value of equity was nearly five times greater than the audited value.

In this case, the capital employed does not offer a meaningful measure of the capital that shareholders have invested in Apple. Investors and traders will be much more interested in market values because they reflect the economics of investing and dealing. This does not make the ROCE necessarily redundant. Even if the figures are inaccurate in a strict economic sense, persistent trends in one direction or the other are usually indicative of important underlying developments.

The questionable suitability of ratios in investment appraisal arises in other areas such as measuring companies' financial leverage and, by implication, the financial risk that shareholders face. If equity capital is significantly lower in the accounts than in the market, it can lead to an exaggerated impression of the scale of leverage, especially because items of debt capital are less prone to being 'understated' in company accounts (although it is also true that certain liabilities may not appear in the accounts). Another example is reported profits, which incorporate non-cash flow items such as capital depreciation into the calculation. From an investment appraisal perspective, what matters fundamentally is the relation between cash coming in and cash going out.

A second drawback of ratio-based assessment is that it records what has happened while investors necessarily look forward to what might happen.

Other investment appraisal techniques (an example being the dividend valuation approach discussed in chapter 8) begin from estimates of futures cash flows to establish whether it is worth investing in the present. They can incorporate consideration of the uncertainties associated with future cash flows in a seamless fashion through the use of risk adjusted discount rates.

By comparison, the inspection of profit margins and leverage ratios from previous years looks somewhat archaic. Efforts to adapt accounting data to the priorities of investment analysis are symptomatic of this. Take the example of EBITDA: earnings before interest, tax, depreciation and amortisation. It aims to get closer to the idea of a net operating cash flow for a business. It excludes depreciation (on fixed capital) and amortisation (of intangible assets) in order to arrive at a measure of the surplus available to reward lenders (interest), the state (taxes) and shareholders (dividends and reinvestment). Likewise, formulations of corporate free cash flow exclude depreciation and amortisation but seek to incorporate estimates of future spending on the replacement of existing fixed capital to arrive at more shareholder-focused measures of earnings.

2.2 The price-earnings ratio

The price-earnings ratio (PER) expresses a company's share price as a multiple of its earnings per share. Among stock traders and fund managers, it is the single most keenly monitored accounting ratio though, strictly speaking, it is not a pure accounting ratio because it measures *market* price against *audited* earnings. The PER can offer very useful insights if employed judiciously as part of a comprehensive analysis.

Assume a company whose shares are trading at a high PER compared to either companies in general or to companies operating in the same sector. There are a number of potential reasons for this:

◆   The company may be prominent in an especially dynamic part of the economy where innovation and growth are happening at a fast pace. The high share price relative to earnings reflects a widespread expectation that the company's future earnings will grow very rapidly. What shareholders are paying for is not current earnings, but future earnings possibilities.

◆   The company may be in a powerful position in a stable and profitable but mature market; a market where demand is reliable, competition minimal but growth prospects more limited than elsewhere. In this case, shareholders are paying for what they see as a safe, low-risk stream of earnings. Remember the tobacco producer Philip Morris? At the time of writing, Philip Morris' PER was higher than that of Apple, 17.66 compared to 11.47.

◆   The company may simply be overvalued based on estimates of current and future earnings.

An important lesson highlighted by the PER is the importance of context. The significance of a particular value is dependent on circumstances at the moment. In fact many traders monitor PER trends, believing that they offer insights into how investor sentiment, and therefore market conditions, is evolving.

Test yourself 10.4

A company's shares are trading at a low PER. How might this be explained?

2.3 Dividends

In chapter 8 there was a suggestion that corporate dividend policy isn't necessarily a critical factor in determining corporate value. Nevertheless, it is certainly the case that for many investors, dividend policy is a key factor influencing their decisions. In fact, dividend policy is the cornerstone of a particular equity investment philosophy that stresses the importance of dividend yield and dividend payout ratios. The two ratios are very straightforward.

$$\text{Dividend yield } (DY) = \frac{\text{Annual dividend per share}}{\text{Share price}} = \frac{d_0}{P_0}$$

$$\text{Payout ratio } (PR) = \frac{\text{Annual dividend per share}}{\text{Earnings per share}} = \frac{d_0}{EPS}$$

Test yourself 10.5

A company has annual earnings of £280 million and has announced that it intends to pay a dividend of 15 pence per share. Its equity capital is made up of 940 million issued shares and the current share price is 420 pence.

a) Calculate the dividend yield.

b) Calculate the earnings per share and payout ratio.

As with all financial ratios, care is needed in how they should be used to guide investment decisions. Take the dividend yield. A 'high' dividend yield could occur simply because of a fall in the share price. If a company pays a dividend of 10 pence and its share price is 250 pence, the dividend yield is 4%. If the share price falls to 125, the dividend yield rises to 8%. This is plainly bad news for existing investors, since they experience a significant decline in wealth. For prospective investors, the fall in the share price ought to command more attention than the high dividend yield.

In contrast, even a high dividend payment translates into a reduced dividend yield if the share price rises significantly. This is good news for existing investors. Prospective investors would need to assess whether it is wise to pay the higher price for the dividend yield.

A useful method of assessing the 'quality' of a dividend yield is by reference to the dividend payout ratio. Assume that a company has generated earnings per share of 40 pence and intends to pay a dividend of 12 pence. The payout ratio is 30%. Furthermore, the dividend represents a yield of 5% on the prevailing share price of 240 pence. Shareholders might reasonably believe that this is a 'good' dividend yield. Why?

◆ In circumstances when bank saving rates and government bond yields are generally below 2%, an annual yield of 5% compares very favourably.

◆ The payout ratio of 30% suggests that the company is reinvesting a significant portion of current earnings which ought to result in earnings growth in the future. In these circumstances, even a constant dividend payout ratio implies rising dividend payments in the future (as well as rising share values).

◆ The payout ratio of 30% might also persuade investors that the dividend policy of the company is well protected. Only a dramatic decline of earnings would result in the company being unable to afford to sustain the existing dividends.

Of course, other factors would need to be considered such as the level of debt and the underlying risk of the business before deciding whether the company is a suitable part of a dividend-seeking investment strategy. Note also that the emphasis on dividend yield does not mean a failure to appreciate the fact that the sustainability of the dividend policy depends to a considerable extent on reinvestment of earnings. Advocates of dividend centred investment are not necessarily all that distinct from those who place greater emphasis on capital growth.

In fact the difference is mainly one of risk. In general, companies that fit the dividend yield bill tend to be large, well-established, publicly quoted companies with long track records of reliability. Companies in newer areas where innovation proceeds at an intense pace necessarily emphasise reinvestment of earnings in expansion and product development. They have no choice because they face intense competition from other companies. For many of these companies, dividend 'policy' amounts to a corporate website declaration that they have no plans to pay dividends in the foreseeable future.

To some extent therefore, the focus on dividend yield testifies to a relatively conservative attitude towards risk. In the current business climate there has been a revival of interest in dividend payments among investors. Companies such as Philip Morris and Wal-Mart have increased dividend payments at significant rates and supplemented them with further payouts via share buyback schemes. Dividend payments by S&P 500 companies totalled $281 billion in 2012, an increase of 17% on the previous year and a record high.

cash rich
A description of a company with stable earnings that significantly exceed its long-term capital reinvestment requirements.

Many of the companies in question are **cash rich** operations. This has added to their appeal because it encourages investors to believe that rising dividend payments will continue for some time yet. As a result, the share prices in many instances have risen more than the S&P 500 as a whole. Wal-Mart's share price at the start of 2013 was 48% higher than at the start of 2008, whereas the S&P 500 was only about 7% higher. One irony, therefore, is that companies that have attracted investors with high dividends have also produced high capital growth. A further irony is that this has driven down dividend yields.

Chapter summary

◆ Investors in bills, bonds and other debt securities appreciate that variations in yields and prices affect actual returns over time. They will therefore seek to measure the wealth implications.

◆ The concept of duration plays an important role in risk assessment of debt securities, especially in relation to market risk.

◆ Generally longer-term and low coupon paying bonds exhibit more price volatility than short-term and higher coupon paying bonds. They are more prone to the effects of market risk.

◆ The fact that yields on debt securities tend to be higher when terms to maturity are longer is due to the higher degree of market risk.

◆ Ratio analysis is an important part of analysing the performance and prospects for equity investments. However, ratios are not always presented in forms wholly suitable in an investment appraisal environment.

◆ The price-earnings ratio (PER) has a pivotal status in equity analysis.

◆ Many investors regard companies' policies towards dividend payments as a key consideration informing their investment decisions. Other investors place greater importance on capital growth. The contrast, while important, is not as significant as it sometimes appears.

Chapter Eleven
Portfolio performance analysis

List of topics

1   Institutional asset management
2   Passive asset management
3   Active asset management

Introduction

A report published by the UK Office for National Statistics (ONS) in 2012 estimated that individuals held just 11.5% of UK publicly quoted shares at the end of 2010. UK financial institutions owned 41%, with a similar portion being held by overseas organisations (Ownership of UK Quoted Shares, 2012). In effect, most of the trading and investment decision-making related to UK company shares is carried out by persons in institutional roles rather than by individuals in their own names. This is typical of modern day markets in stocks, bonds and other financial securities around the globe. Institutions tend to predominate in the areas of asset allocation and investment decision-making.

Headlines about unscrupulous institutions costing clients dear occur often enough to encourage deep cynicism in some quarters regarding the motives of financial institutions. Yet investors (individuals and organisations) are more likely to put their faith in the financial acumen of fund management institutions rather than to tackle the challenges of investment analysis and asset management directly. This cannot be down to naivety about institutional motives. Many investors view institutions as providers of invaluable services, while expressing robust opinions on matters such as hidden fees and the opacity of some financial products. Heavily consulted, investor-oriented websites urge vigilance in the face of the marketing claims of fund managers and financial advisors for new products. They ably dissect these claims and expose misleading, overpriced and gimmicky features if deemed justified.

The initial aim of this final chapter is to briefly indicate why institutions are important in investment and wealth management. The main purpose is to examine how institutional asset managers articulate fund objectives and the methods that can be used to assess the performance of asset management funds.

1. Institutional asset management

How the relation between investors and asset managers plays out is contingent on many factors. But investors are inclined to entrust the management of capital to institutions such as investment companies, pension funds and hedge funds for a number of compelling reasons:

◆ Institutions acquire information about the risks and returns of a huge array of investment opportunities across different markets and are therefore in a better position to deliver these opportunities to investors, and to advise on the associated uncertainties. In the absence of institutional arrangements, investors would lack much of the essential information needed to make judgements on many types of investment.

◆ Institutions offer knowledge of the trading customs for different markets and expertise in dealing with legal and regulatory issues. They therefore help to overcome many technical obstacles to security trading and investment that most individuals would find insurmountable.

◆ By pooling capital from many individuals, investment institutions reduce the transaction costs per investor since it is much cheaper, relatively speaking, to trade large blocks of securities.

◆ Pooling also makes spreading risk more economically viable than it would be for an individual with limited resources. It thereby alleviates the exposure to non-systematic risk for each investor.

◆ Institutions can more readily securitise investments into tradable claims, thereby offering investors a relatively convenient method of adjusting asset portfolios in accordance with changing views or needs.

None of these justifications for the central role of institutions in trading and asset management are problem-free. To cite just one case: securitisation was an important facet of the financial market debacle of 2007–8. The ability to quickly securitise and sell on risky assets to other parties provided funds to create even more risky assets to securitise and sell on in what, to many participants, seemed a virtuous circle. In a corruption of the conventional notion that spreading risk makes it easier to absorb and confine the effects of any losses, the process metamorphosed into one of spreading certain losses. Securitisation was an important element of this so-called 'contagion effect' in which the troubles of one institution infected others just as badly.

Nevertheless, securitisation did not cause the financial crisis. Nor does the crisis invalidate the idea that securitisation by financial institutions, in principle, has important advantages for both providers and users of capital.

Financial institutions can also tailor asset management to different client tastes. Over many years of doing so one of the most striking differences to emerge is between strategies designed to replicate returns on a particular market, or other benchmark, and strategies that emphasise the prospect of asset managers using superior knowledge and insight to outperform a benchmark. The former is sometimes referred to as passive fund management, in contrast to an active management style associated with the quest to outperform.

To some extent, the two approaches exemplify rival investment philosophies. Partisans of passive fund management argue that consistently outperforming the market is a quest that the vast majority of fund managers fail. The additional time and expense of active fund management is unwarranted because it does not produce gains for investors. In contrast, advocates of active management believe the 'passivists' to be overly in thrall to the precepts of efficient market theory and contend that there are plenty of opportunities for skilled investors to profit systematically.

In practice, the majority of investors and asset management funds tend to be broadly non-committal on these points of principal. Many investors incorporate market replication and actively managed components within their overall portfolios. Many financial advisors venture that this is a wise thing to do. Meanwhile, big fund management institutions offer both passively and actively managed investment products. This chapter keeps to the broadly non-committal stance and concentrates on illustrating the key characteristics of both styles and the corresponding methods used to assess the performance of asset portfolios and, by inference, asset managers.

2. Passive asset management

The Capital Market Line (discussed in chapter 4) epitomises the philosophy of passive fund management. It states that returns are dependent on the degree of exposure to the risk of the market portfolio. Conservatively minded investors can hedge against market risk by directing some portion of their capital into risk-free securities. The price of hedging is a lower return. Those seeking higher returns adopt a leveraged stance towards the market portfolio, borrowing additional capital to buy more of the market portfolio.

The style is passive in the sense that investors do not analyse and then choose from a multitude of assets. There is only one factor to decide: the balance between the risk-free asset and the market portfolio. The content of the market portfolio is already defined in terms of its component parts and optimal weightings. Investors do not study the individual components of the market portfolio. They must merely ensure that they are held in the correct portions.

As time goes by the structure of the market portfolio alters and requires investors to adjust their asset holdings accordingly. But adjustments are also passive; automatic responses to changed circumstances rather than willed actions rooted in judgements about uncertain situations.

2.1 Equity index tracking funds

It is no accident that the passive approach is most readily identified with index tracking funds, where the aim is to replicate the performance of a benchmark index. Common examples are FTSE 100 and S&P500 trackers. In the former case, a fund manager uses investors' money to buy shares in the 100 companies included in the FTSE 100 Index, in proportion to their respective weightings. For instance, at the end of 2012 the largest company in the FTSE 100 was HSBC Holdings, which accounted for 7.97% of the total market value of the 100 companies. The manager of a tracker fund ought, therefore, to spend 7.97% of the fund's money on HSBC shares.

Test yourself 11.1

Assume that an equity index consists of five companies with the following market values:

Company	Market value
A	£128,450,950
B	£468,123,938
C	£63,457,412
D	£377,288,562
E	£833,429,667

a) Calculate the aggregate market value of the five companies.

b) Calculate each company's value as a portion of the total value.

c) Assume that a fund with £1 million to invest wishes to track the index of the five assets. How much should the fund manager invest in each company at the outset?

Asset management organisations offer trackers both narrow and broad in scope. Some track indices that embrace relatively small numbers of companies confined, for example, to a particular sector within a particular national economy. Others track broad, globally oriented, indices such as those maintained by MSCI Inc, a provider of performance analysis and risk measurement services. The Developed Market Index Fund run by the investment management company Vanguard replicates the performance of the MSCI-EAFE (MSCI Europe, Australasia and Far East) index of more than 1,000 companies.

Tracker funds make a simple promise to investors: a rate of return equal to the percentage change of the relevant index. If an index rises, investors in a linked tracker fund gain to an equivalent degree. But if the index falls, investors lose to the same degree.

There are three basic methods that asset management funds use to replicate the performance of an index: full, partial or synthetic replication.

◆   Full replication involves holding all the assets in an index in the required proportions. In effect, full replication creates a scaled model of the index.

◆   Partial replication occurs where a fund manager chooses to track an index by investing in a representative sample of the constituent assets.

◆   Synthetic replication uses equity swaps to imitate the performance of an index.

Making it work 11.1: Synthetic index tracking

Rather than buy the underlying securities, a fund managing a FTSE All Share (FTSE-AS) index tracker wishes to use synthetic replication. It does so by negotiating an OTC equity swap with an investment bank. Let's assume that:

- the swap is for five years with annual settlement dates;
- the fund aims to earn the FTSE-AS return on an investment of £100 million; and
- the fund pays the bank £100 million and receives a basket of securities, consisting of bonds and equities, from the bank worth £100 million.

If the return on the FTSE-AS exceeds the return on the basket, the bank makes a payment to the fund (in cash or more securities). The opposite occurs if the basket produces a better return than the FTSE-AS. Either way, the fund receives the return on the FTSE-AS index.

For ease of comparison it is best to represent the basket as an index. Assume that at the outset of the swap agreement the basket and the FTSE-AS are assigned an index value of 100, and that on the first annual settlement date the FTSE-AS stands at 109.2 and the basket at 106.5. The FTSE-AS has earned 9.2% while the basket has earned 6.5%. The basket of securities held by the fund has underperformed the FTSE-AS index by 2.7%. Under the swap the bank is obliged to pay the fund £2.7 million (2.7% of £100 million) to bring the basket index up to 109.5.

Assume that on the second annual settlement date the FTSE-AS index is 113.5 while the basket index has risen to 117. Calculate the size of the settlement payment and explain which party is obliged to pay.

There are advantages and disadvantages with each replication method.

◆ The main advantage of full replication is that the fund tracks the index with a high degree of accuracy. But full replication incurs higher transaction costs because asset portfolios must be frequently rebalanced in order to sustain accurate replication.

◆ The principal advantage of partial replication is that it enables fund managers to economise on trading costs. There are fewer assets to manage and rebalancing is less frequent. The disadvantage is that it offers a less reliable mechanism for tracking indices. Aside from the risks arising from the performance of the reference index itself, investors in tracker funds deploying partial replication face the possibility of a fund's performance deviating significantly from that of its reference index.

◆ Synthetic replication avoids tracking inaccuracy because it does not require a fund manager to purchase underlying securities. The disadvantage is that equity swaps incur fees associated with the arrangement of contracts and the custodianship of collateral used to manage counterparty risk.

Full replication might sound like a straightforward exercise. Find out which shares are included in the index, establish their respective weightings and invest clients' money accordingly. In fact, index tracking is complicated by a number of factors:

◆ The values of index components, and therefore their weightings within the index, change. Hence, index funds need frequent rebalancing to sustain tracking accuracy.

◆ The level of capital invested in a fund varies. Funds create new units for investors contributing new capital and retire existing units as investors liquidate holdings. Net purchases of new units by investors results in the fund having to invest in additional assets. Net liquidations of units mean capital flowing out of the fund resulting in a need to dispose of assets. Acquisitions and disposals must be undertaken while also maintaining the appropriate asset weightings.

◆ The accrual of income from investments complicates the tracking process. In the case of equity index trackers, the underlying shares pay dividends. Some funds distribute dividends to investors, others reinvest dividends on behalf of investors. Many offer investors a choice of **distribution units** that pay dividends or **accumulation units** that reinvest dividends. Both the scale of dividends and investors' dividend preferences complicate the administration of the tracking process.

◆ Intermittent corporate events are liable to affect tracking accuracy. Mergers, acquisitions, rights issues, de-listings, bankruptcies and other occurrences require portfolio adjustments from tracker fund managers.

◆ Index constituents change. Companies that decline in value relative to others may be replaced by other companies in an index. The constituents of FTSE indices, for example, are reviewed and modified on a quarterly basis. Alterations of index components naturally demand adjustments to tracker funds

◆ Many funds lend assets for short periods to brokers who offer them to other clients for settlement and short-selling purposes. Funds can therefore earn interest that the index cannot.

distribution units
Units sold by investment funds that distribute dividends or interest on underlying assets to holders of the units.

accumulation units
Units sold by investment funds that reinvest dividends or interest in additional assets. It results in accumulation units having higher prices than comparable distribution units.

The return on a tracker fund depends on three factors: the performance of the index, the accuracy of fund tracking and fund operating costs. The first factor is obvious and doesn't require explanation. However, the issues of tracking accuracy and operating expenses merit attention. In fact they are doubly important in the case of passive investment funds like trackers because the underlying investments are so alike. For instance, asset management groups offering FTSE All-Share tracker funds are selling the same investment portfolio. Hence for investors interested in FTSE-AS trackers, the tracking accuracy and operating costs of different providers are issues of primary concern. Even modest differences can have a significant cumulative effect on investment returns over time.

Worked example 11.1: The effects of management fees on fund returns

Assume that you place £10,000 in a fund that levies an annual management charge of 2% in advance on the outstanding value of your investment. Hence the amount actually invested, the net investment, is £9,800 in the first year. Furthermore, assume that the annual return on the net investment is 10% so that after one year your investment, before management charges, is worth £10,780 (£9,800 x 1.1). After four years, your wealth would have grown to £13,234, as follows:

	Now	Year 1	Year 2	Year 3	Year 4
Gross investment	£10,000	£10,780	£11,620	£12,527	£13,504
2% charge	£200	£216	£232	£251	£270
Net investment	£9,800	£10,564	£11,388	£12,276	£13,234

What if the annual management charge is 1% rather than 2%?

	Year 1	Year 2	Year 3	Year 4	Year 5
Gross investment	£10,000	£10,890	£11,859	£12,914	£14,063
1% charge	£100	£109	£119	£129	£141
Net investment	£9,900	£10,781	£11,740	£12,785	£13,922

The investment is worth nearly £700 more – a considerable difference that illustrates the cumulative impact that fund operating expenses can have on investors' wealth.

2.2 Tracking error and the total expense ratio

Tracking error is a statistical measure of the extent to which the risks of investing in managed funds exceed the risks of benchmark investments. With actively managed funds, sizeable tracking errors may be warranted. Given that such funds aim to outperform a benchmark it is no surprise that they might be comparatively risky. With index funds, on the other hand, tracking error should in theory be zero. Allowing for the fact that there are practical reasons why index tracking cannot work perfectly, tracking errors for index funds should nevertheless be marginal. Large errors indicate that investors are exposed to considerable risk over and above the risks of investing in the index itself. Large tracking errors, in effect, negate the fundamental rationale for tracker funds – the avoidance of non-market risk. They indicate poor fund management.

Hence, in the context of index funds, the tracking error is an estimate of the additional risk that investors face due to the quality of fund management. A low tracking error suggests that an index fund is being managed effectively. It can be estimated as the standard deviation of the difference between a fund's returns and benchmark index returns. Table 11.1 shows quarterly returns for a tracker fund and its reference index.

Table 11.1 Fund and index returns

Period	Fund return (%)	Index return (%)	Difference (%)
1	1.25	1.30	−0.05
2	2.50	2.40	0.10
3	−0.50	−0.25	−0.25
4	0.30	0.40	−0.10
5	3.60	3.60	0.00
6	7.65	7.80	−0.15
7	−2.80	−3.10	0.30
8	4.60	4.70	−0.10
Average	2.075	2.10625	−0.03125

The final column indicates whether the fund over- or underperformed the index during each period. On average the fund return deviates from the index return by −0.03125% each quarter, equivalent to an average of −0.125% per year. The tracking error is the standard deviation of the return differences and can be calculated in the same fashion as the standard deviation of a security's return outlined in chapter 3. We replace return with the return difference, signified by the Greek letter Δ (delta).

$$\text{Variance} = \sigma_\Delta^2 = \frac{\Sigma(\Delta_t - \bar{\Delta})^2}{N}$$

$$\text{Tracking error} = \sigma_\Delta = \sqrt{\frac{\Sigma(\Delta_t - \bar{\Delta})^2}{N}}$$

Where:

Δ_t = return differential for each period; and

$\bar{\Delta}$ = average return differential.

The tracking error is approximately 0.16%. Normally it is annualised. Given that the data in the table above is quarterly then the annual tracking error would be:

$$\text{Tracking error} = 0.16\% \times \sqrt{4} = 0.32\%$$

An annualised tracking error of 0.32% is fairly typical of index trackers. According to the data, the fund underperforms the index by 0.125% per year on average. The standard deviation of 0.32% suggests that underperformance on a significant scale will be a rare event.

tracking difference
The difference between the return on an investment fund and the return on a benchmark against which it is compared.

It can be difficult to calculate tracking errors due to lack sufficient data for estimating the risk. An easier method of assessing tracking performance is the measuring **tracking difference**, which is simply the difference (individual, average and cumulative) between the index return and fund return over a given time period.

Worked example 11.2: The tracking difference

Period	1	2	3	4	5	6	7	8
Return difference (%)	−0.05	0.10	−0.25	−0.10	0.00	−0.15	0.30	−0.10

The average tracking difference is -0.03125% and the cumulative is 0.25%. While this is a straightforward method, it requires some care when comparing the tracking differences for various funds, because it does not measure the risk associated with the estimated tracking difference.

The tracking error provides some insight into the efficiency of fund management but it does not highlight the operating costs of fund management. The most obvious cost is the annual management charge (AMC) which, in the case of conventional funds, is normally a fixed percentage of the assets under management. The AMC is an explicit cost deducted annually from investors' capital by the fund manager. Nowadays the AMCs for tracker funds are normally below 0.5%. However, there are other costs charged to funds that are not as clear cut. Figure 11.1 lists the annual expenses of a UK FTSE-AS tracker fund that was managing assets with a net worth of £3.866 billion in 2012.

Annual management charge	£13,453,444
Registration fees	£4,537,387
Trustee's fees	£243,427
Safe custody fees	£37,434
Audit fee (inc VAT)	£8,160
FSA fee	£144
Total expenses	**£18,279,996**

Figure 11.1 Annual expenses of a UK FTSE-AS tracker fund

Aside from the AMC, the fund pays additional charges of nearly £5 million. The total expenses divided by the net assets being managed produce a total expense ratio (TER). The TER for the fund was 0.473%, compared to an AMC charge of 0.348%. The TER offers a truer measure of the cost to investors of having wealth managed by funds. Under pressure from investors and financial regulators, asset management groups nowadays state TERs alongside AMCs. Nevertheless, assessing the merits of similar funds solely on the basis of which offers the lowest TER has its pitfalls:

◆ The TER does not include transaction costs on security dealings, such as brokerage commissions and stamp duty. Nor does it consider interest on borrowing or taxes on capital gains and earnings.

◆ More importantly if funds offering comparatively low TERs exhibit the highest tracking errors, the apparent cost savings could prove illusory. Differences in TERs are liable to be in the order of one or two tenths of a per cent. It does not take much of a difference in tracking error to undermine any operating cost benefits.

2.3 Exchange traded funds

At the end of 2008 there were 305 exchange traded funds (ETF) listed on the London Stock Exchange. The number of trades in ETFs in 2008 came to just over 700,000, involving the turnover of nearly £55 billion of securities. By the end of 2012 the number of ETFs had grown to 1,026, with more than 1.6 million trades and turnover in excess of £111 billion. In four years the scale of business has more than doubled. ETFs represent one of the most dynamic arenas of growth in managed investments post financial crisis.

ETFs are close cousins of index trackers funds. Most are passive investments designed to replicate an index. And like tracker funds they variously employ full, partial and synthetic replication methods. A key difference is that funds issue units while ETFs issue shares.

Index and actively managed funds issue 'units' in exchange for investors' capital. In fact such funds are still sometimes referred to as unit trusts in the UK, although as a result of regulatory reforms in the late 1990s most unit trusts have converted to open-ended investment companies (OEICs, or 'oiks' to use the market vernacular). 'Open-ended' refers to the fact that there are no strict legal limits on the number of units that a fund is entitled to create. The limit is economic, dependent upon the amount of capital that investors are willing to invest in a fund.

With the number of issued units dependent on the level of capital invested in a fund, liquidation of holdings by investors causes the number of units to fall. In other words, ownership of units cannot be traded with third parties; they can only be bought from and sold to the issuing fund (either directly of via a broker).

ETFs are also, in the main, open-ended funds but they issue shares instead of units. Initially ETF shares are not offered to the general public but sold in large blocks of shares called 'creation units' to institutional investors who, in exchange, offer securities that ETFs need to form replicating portfolios. Similarly institutions can redeem ETF shares in exchange for securities held by funds. The transactions are 'in kind' rather than in cash.

Some institutions hold on to the shares as investments in their own right. Others, such as large brokerages, divide creation units into smaller amounts that can be offered to retail investors on the secondary market.

One consequence of the tradable character of ETF shares is that deals are agreed at whatever price the market deems them to be worth at the time of a transaction. This differs from OEICs and similar funds, which normally declare a dealing price for units each day that remains fixed until the next dealing price declaration the following business day. Hence there is a greater degree of trading flexibility with ETFs compared to unit funds.

Another typical claim in favour of ETFs compared to conventional tracker funds is that they are able to operate with lower overall costs. One reason is connected to the in kind character of much of the dealings between ETFs and institutions. It allows ETFs to avoid many of the brokerage expenses associated with having to convert cash contributions into equity purchases and unit redemptions into equity sales. Furthermore, redemption in kind means that ETFs can afford to operate with lower cash reserves than unit funds, thereby facilitating higher investment rates.

However, the value of these saving should not be exaggerated. While ETFs can avoid some brokerage expenses, retail purchasers of ETF shares cannot. Transactions in ETF shares incur brokers' fees, an expense that does not occur with dealings in unit funds. This tends to reduce the value of trading flexibility offered by ETFs relative to index trackers, especially for retail investors, because regular buying and selling of ETFs will generate brokerage charges that exceed the implicit brokerage savings of the ETFs themselves.

Synthetic replication using equity swaps, which is more common with ETFs than conventional tracker funds, also offers investors potential operating cost benefits. Synthetic ETFs avoid many of the expenses of managing a portfolio of assets. However, it should be stressed that the expense is transferred to counterparties rather than nullified; counterparties must manage portfolios of assets to hedge their exposures to index movements under the swap arrangements. Not surprisingly, counterparties to swap arrangements will charge ETFs fees for assuming the burdens of asset management. Whether synthetic ETFs offer cost benefits, and whether benefits pass to investors, are complex matters.

The truth of whether or not ETFs offer consistently better returns than comparable unit-based tracker funds is an issue that is difficult to assess. Even observers with considerable expertise find that the information available lacks sufficient detail and reliability to come to definitive judgements.

2.4 Risk and passive fund management

Passive investment products such as index tracking funds and ETFs are marketed as straightforward and cost-effective mechanisms allowing individual investors with relatively modest amounts of capital to obtain the risk reduction benefits of asset diversification. But this doesn't mean that passive investment strategies constitute low risk choices.

Refer back to the discussion of the Capital Market Line in the section on portfolio theory. An index fund tracking, say, the S&P 500, displays some similarities with the theoretical market portfolio whose risk is measured as a standard deviation of returns. Or think of the Capital Asset Pricing Model which states that the systematic risk of the theoretical market portfolio is represented in a beta value of 1. Again, broader index funds exhibit certain parallels with the market portfolio of the CAPM.

Market risk is considerable. At the turn of the new millennium the FTSE-AS index stood at around 3,200. By spring 2003 it reached a low point of around 1,600 – a drop of 50% in a period of just over three years. Yet by July of 2007 the FTSE-AS was in touching distance of 3,500. In other words, the values of the constituent companies more than doubled over approximately four years. But less than two years later it had again fallen precipitously to around 1,800, an average decline of over 40% in constituent company values. Even by late 2012 the FTSE-AS index still stood below its 2007 peak. Plainly, investing in securities that purport to offer the most efficient risk-return trade-offs is risky because market risk can reach considerable proportions.

The risks can be hedged or leveraged depending on the tastes of individual investors. In fact, if we adopt the perspective that individuals routinely accumulate various assets that can be collectively described as asset portfolios (remember Joe in the introductory chapter?), then most investors hedge to some degree without necessarily thinking about it in those terms. The simple act of holding cash in a savings account offers some protection against the effects of risky components of portfolios turning sour.

Buying an index tracker, while also depositing funds in a savings account, is not dissimilar from an investor in a CML environment moving down and left along the line towards the risk-free return.

An investor could instead move up and right along the CML by borrowing money to invest in the same index tracker. The result is a leveraged investment that offers a higher potential return, but which is riskier because the investor is obligated to pay interest on a loan on top of the uncertain performance of the tracker. A more probable, but essentially analogous, course of action would be to buy shares in an ETF on margin. The investor puts up a portion of the initial capital needed to buy the shares, say 50%, with the rest being borrowed from a broker (see chapter 2 for a commentary on margin trading). Alternatively, the investor could buy shares in a leveraged ETF, one that itself borrows money and uses derivatives in an effort to amplify returns. A riskier option still would be to buy shares in a leveraged ETF on margin.

3. Active asset management

Passive fund management aims to replicate the return on a benchmark such as an equity index. Therefore, active fund management must offer investors returns that on average surpass those achieved by some benchmark, otherwise passive investment will suffice. Why undertake the extra work, bear the extra costs and endure the extra risks of active fund management if the results are liable to be no better than those offered by index replication?

However, simply exceeding the return on an index does not, by itself, prove the efficacy of activism. Passively managed funds can expect to outperform benchmarks by deploying financial leverage. Assessing the accomplishments of active fund management by reference to benchmarks is, therefore, not as straightforward as it might sound. Let's employ the CAPM framework to illustrate the point.

The CAPM states that the expected return for a portfolio is determined by its exposure to systematic risk, represented by the portfolio beta. Recall the CAPM model of expected return.

$$E(r_p) = r_f + \beta_i [E(r_M) - r_f]$$

Assume a risk-free return of 1% and an expected return for the market portfolio of 7%. The expected return for an investment with a beta of 1.5 (an investment that carries more systematic risk than the market portfolio) is:

$$E(r_p) = 1 + 1.5[7-1] = 10\%$$

The expected return of 10% betters the 7% offered by the benchmark market portfolio. The investment is expected to outperform the benchmark. But this does not require active fund management. In theory a 10% expected return on an investment with a beta of 1.5 can be achieved by leveraging a fund that tracks the market portfolio. Active fund management is valid only if it offers the prospect of outperforming benchmark expectations *after* adjusting for risk. If, referring to the example just outlined, a fund manager expects to generate an average return of 13% on an investment carrying a beta of 1.5, then the manager's discretionary decision-making is effective. And so long as the fund manager charges less than a 3% premium over passive fund charges, investors are better off with the active manager.

excess return
The percentage by which the return on an investment beats the benchmark return after adjustment for risk.

Active fund management is thus about managers beating the benchmark on a risk-adjusted basis. Furthermore, they need to beat the benchmark by more than the additional management costs. Fund managers who produce an average **excess return** of 3% on capital but charge an extra 3% of capital are no good to investors.

Making it work 11.2: Leverage, betas and passive portfolio management

The market portfolio offers an expected return of 7% and the risk-free return is 1%. Suppose an investor is looking for a 10% return on capital of £100,000 but wishes to invest only in a tracker fund that replicates the market portfolio.

A target return of 10% on £100,000 is £10,000. It is achievable if the £100,000 is supplemented with a loan and the total is invested in the tracker. Assume that the cost of borrowing is 3%. Given the target return of £10,000, how much does the investor need to borrow? Set the total amount invested to equal x and solve for the expected return of £10,000:

$$£10,000 = 0.07 \,(x) + 0.03(£100,000 - x)$$

$$x = £175,000 = \text{total investment}$$

$$£100,000 - x = -£75,000 = \text{amount borrowed}$$

The investor borrows £75,000 and places a total of £175,000 in the tracker fund offering 7%. The *rate* of return after paying the cost of borrowing:

$$(1.75 \times 0.07) - (0.75 \times 0.03) = 0.1 \text{ i.e. } 10\%$$

What is the investment beta? It is a weighted average of the replicating fund beta minus the debt beta. We know from the CAPM that the market portfolio beta is 1, and hence so is the replicating fund beta. The debt beta is derived from the risk premium. The market risk premium of 6% (7%–1%) corresponds to a beta of 1. The loan pays a risk premium of 2%, which is one third of the market risk premium, making the loan beta 0.3333. The beta for the leveraged investment is therefore:

$$(1.75 \times 1) - (0.75 \times 0.3333) = 1.5$$

The loan beta is subtracted because the lender effectively assumes some of the risk associated with the performance of the investment (which is why the borrower is prepared to pay a premium over the risk-free rate for the loan). The key point is that we have an essentially passively managed investment that is expected to 'beat' the benchmark, but only on the basis of accepting a greater level of risk.

Test yourself 11.2

The market portfolio offers an expected return of 7% and the risk-free return is 1%. Assume that an actively managed fund is expected to earn an average return of 6% per annum and that its beta is 0.4. Explain whether or not the fund offers benefits to investors if the fund manager charges 2% of capital.

Active fund management encompasses investment styles that differ from one another in a host of ways. But one thing that unites them, at least loosely, is scepticism towards notions of financial markets being efficient, certainly to the extent suggested by EMT. This is necessarily the case because EMT effectively states that no investor or investment strategy can consistently produce an excess return. Any disproportionately successful strategy is quickly copied by others and, once widespread, ceases to offer market-beating performance.

In broad terms, active asset management can be categorised into three types:

1   strategies that are founded on fundamental analysis of the economy, financial markets and securities;

2   strategies based on identifying traits other than risk that appear to be consistently associated with risk-adjusted excess returns; and

3   strategies rooted in views on human behaviour and market psychology.

These types of active management are not mutually exclusive. There are many ways in which elements from each are incorporated into an overall approach to investment. However, the categorisation does help to clarify key features of active fund management.

3.1 Fundamental analysis and fund management

In the aftermath of the 2007–8 banking crisis there was a widespread reluctance to hold company shares. Fears about the scale of economic recession discouraged risk-taking, to the extent that investors chose to invest large amounts of wealth in government securities offering yields barely above zero. Paradoxically, given that the financial crisis was primarily associated with credit-based securities gone bad, many companies deemed reliable found that they were able to borrow funds quite easily on very favourable terms and set about issuing bonds to, among other things, retire shares. In effect, there was a significant shift among investors in favour of holding one asset class, debt securities, at the expense of another, equities.

top-down
An investment approach that starts from an assessment of broad economic fundamentals to inform investment decisions and wealth allocation.

This process could be characterised as the workings of **top-down** asset management, a style of fund management that starts from the analysis of broad economic fundamentals and works down towards specific investment decisions. In this scenario, asset managers calculated that the banking crisis would herald a period of falling equity prices, with even the shares of companies not complicit in the crisis suffering the fallout. In an effort to minimise losses, managers embarked on strategic reallocations of capital in favour of high grade debt securities.

The classic top-down asset allocation strategy relates to the business cycle. Fund managers attempt to predict peaks and troughs in economic growth and modify asset holdings accordingly.

If fund managers expect the economy to emerge from recession, the typical recommendation is: shift investment in favour of producers of consumer durables such as cars and household appliances. During recessions consumers concentrate on funding essentials and cut back on buying expensive durable goods. Hence a return to economic growth unleashes pent-up demand for durables, resulting in rapid increases of earnings for companies in these sectors. In theory, this ought to offer the prospect of excess returns.

When economic growth is properly underway, a top-down strategy might suggest asset reallocation in favour of producers of capital goods. In the early stages of an economic revival, companies meet extra demand by using up existing spare capacity. But at some point new fixed capital will be required to sustain expansion. By monitoring data on spare capacity, fund managers seek to anticipate when demand for fixed capital is likely to surge.

Top-down managers also try to predict the top of an economic boom – the point at which the economy starts to slow. The standard top-down recommendation is to reweight portfolios in favour of producers of essential consumer goods and utilities such as power providers, the so-called 'counter cyclical' sectors. The rationale is that these sectors are the least prone to the effects of an economic downturn and should, therefore, offer relatively better returns.

The key to the success of top-down asset management is timing. Asset reallocations in response to expectations that prove to be unfounded are costly and cause comparatively poor performance. So do asset reallocations after the event. A manager must be correct more often than not for investors to profit from the manager's activity. Not surprisingly, being able to anticipate extremely complex trends often enough to profit systematically is a daunting task.

Top-down investing is not limited to timing the economic cycle. Advocates attempt to anticipate other broad shifts of investment: between established and emerging markets; between equities and fixed interest securities; between large and small companies and from old to new sectors.

In contrast to the top-down management of assets, other managers adopt a **bottom-up** approach. The hallmark of the bottom-up style is to search markets for assets that are undervalued or overvalued irrespective of the prevailing economic circumstances. It is often called 'stock picking'.

bottom-up
An investment approach that seeks to identify under- and overvalued securities, irrespective of the state of the broad fundamentals.

Over-/undervaluation assessments can be based on *absolute* measures of what an asset is worth. For instance, a fund manager could use dividend valuation techniques (see chapter 8) to estimate what the shares of particular companies ought to be worth and then compare these 'fair values' to actual prices. If a price is significantly less than the fair value estimate, and a rigorous search for reasons yields nothing, the fund manager concludes that the asset is underpriced and should be bought in expectation of the price rising towards the fair value.

Stock picking is also based on *relative* measures. A straightforward example involves examining price-earnings ratios (PERs) of companies in a particular economic sector. The rationale is twofold:

◆ The PER measures the expense of acquiring the earnings produced by a company. A low PER suggests that the earnings are cheap while a high PER means that investors pay a high price for the earnings.

◆ Companies in the same sector, being of approximately the same risk, ought to operate on the basis of roughly comparable PERs.

Constituent companies with PERs well below the sector average might be considered candidates for investment because they are deemed cheap. Their prices ought to rise to reflect the sector average PER. And those with above average PERs might be considered candidates for short selling (if the fund rules permit short selling). Of course companies must be carefully screened to check for other factors that justify atypical PERs.

3.2 Excess return traits

A good deal of research into equity markets suggests associations between excess returns and certain corporate characteristics. Among the most important are:

- a small firm effect whereby companies with smaller market capitalisations tend to offer higher risk-adjusted returns than larger companies;
- companies with low PERs tend to outperform those with high PERs; and
- companies with relatively low share price to book value (PBV) ratios tend to offer superior returns when compared to those with high ratios.

The inference is obvious. Active fund managers should favour investments that exhibit one or more of these traits. It should be equally obvious that outperforming a benchmark requires a lot more than simply conducting a trait search. Take the example of the small firm effect. Even if we accept the favourable evidence, there simply aren't sufficient small firm investment opportunities to make them a significant option for most funds, and therefore investors in those funds. Even large numbers of small firms collectively represent only a minor fraction of the capital at the disposal of large asset management groups. The problem can be compounded because orders placed by large funds for small firms' shares sometimes drive up purchase prices; investment institutions become price makers rather than price takers.

There tends to be a significant overlap between shares that exhibit low PERs and those with low PBVs. A low PER indicates that a share is trading at a price which is a small multiple of earnings. In most cases the same prices will also be relatively low multiples of equity book values. These ratios are important reference points for what is nowadays called value investing, a style that is contrasted with growth investing.

Value-oriented asset managers, as the terms suggests, search for value. They look to acquire assets that they deem to be cheap. Low PERs and PBVs are regarded as powerful indicators of 'cheapness'. There is a clear intuitive sense to this perspective. A dollar of earnings is a dollar of earnings irrespective of which company it comes from. Hence the lower the price of buying those earnings, the better. Value investors are well aware that low PER companies are often higher-risk companies, but contend that there is still excess return even after accounting for additional risk. Low PER investments really are, or at least tend to be, cheap.

Test yourself 11.3

Explain why companies with low PERs are often higher-risk companies.

Growth-oriented investors are less interested in current asset prices and more interested in the earnings side, more specifically the future earnings prospects. In principle growth funds are more willing to pay high multiples if they believe that earnings potential justifies the expense.

3.3 Investment and market psychology

Most financial market professionals broadly accept the view that in the long run, asset returns tend to reflect asset risks. However, many suggest that over shorter periods, asset prices can deviate significantly from true values and that this presents profitable trading opportunities. It offers the prospect of excess returns from **contrarian investing** and **momentum investing**.

Contrarian trading is rooted in the belief that investors, including professional fund managers, systematically overreact to new information that contains some element of surprise or shock. Overreaction to 'positive' surprises causes prices to overshoot fair values and results in investors being prepared to pay over the odds. Overreaction to 'negative' surprises causes values to undershoot and results in investors being willing to sell too low. The contrarian strategy is, thus, to trade against the crowd. Sell assets to the over-excited masses on positive news and buy assets from the panic-stricken masses on negative news. Await the 'reversion to the mean', the eventual shift of asset prices back to fair asset values once everyone has calmed down. Pocket the excess returns.

Momentum investing is based on the view that price movements have a propensity to build on themselves for reasons other than information about economic fundamentals. Again observations from behavioural analysis are used to explain the phenomenon, in this instance the notion of confirmation bias (see chapter 5). Individuals form opinions about investments which harden into convictions that become difficult to dislodge due to a psychological urge to see reality confirm one's initial stance. Undue importance is placed on information that bolsters an opinion, while conflicting evidence tends to be downplayed. If enough individuals cohere around a particular perspective, it can gain traction. In the world of investment, it results in asset prices acquiring momentum.

The momentum investor aims to ride the wave of momentum-driven assets, buying into an upward price impetus and shorting in the case of a downward impetus. The skill is to have ceased surfing by the time the process runs its course and shifts into reverse. At that point the ideal is to be in contrarian mode.

contrarian investing
An investment version of 'going against the crowd', rooted in the belief that market prices tend to overreact to new information and that excess returns arise due to mean reversion.

momentum investing
Based on the belief that asset prices can acquire momentum beyond levels justified by fundamental information. Momentum traders seek to identify opportunities to profit from these price trends.

3.4 Making alpha

How can the performance of active fund management be measured? Investors are interested in fund managers being able to generate average excess returns after accounting for the additional management costs of active funds. Another term for the notion of a risk-adjusted excess return is alpha return. It brings to mind the CAPM which states that average returns depend solely on the scale of a portfolio's systematic risk represented by a beta coefficient. Alpha returns ought to be zero on average because any risks other than systematic risk can be neutralised through asset diversification and, therefore, should not command a return.

In the realms of active fund management, alpha returns act as a standard of managerial capability. Alpha measures the ability of fund managers to defy the market and extract returns in excess of those consistent with the scale of risk. A number of ratios are employed to assess the quality of actively managed funds.

The Sharpe ratio takes the average premium that an investment earns over the average risk-free rate and expresses it as a ratio of the total risk of the portfolio (as represented by the standard deviation of portfolio returns).

$$S_p = \frac{\overline{r}_p - \overline{r}_f}{\sigma_{r(p)}}$$

The ratio for a managed fund is compared to the Sharpe ratio for the market portfolio. If a fund's Sharpe ratio is higher, it suggests that the manager is generating an alpha return. The return per unit of risk is greater than the market return per unit of risk.

Worked example 11.3: Sharpe ratios

Assume that the risk-free rate has averaged 2% per annum in recent years and that the average return on the FTSE-AS index has been 7% with a standard deviation of 17%. Over the same period an actively managed fund that concentrates on value stocks has earned an average annual return of 12% with a standard deviation of 24%. The Sharpe ratio for the market portfolio is:

$$S = \frac{7\% - 2\%}{17\%} = 0.294$$

In comparison the Sharpe ratio for the managed portfolio is:

$$S = \frac{12\% - 2\%}{24\%} = 0.417$$

The managed fund is more risky in absolute terms. However, it delivers more return per unit of risk than the FTSE-AS index. It suggests that the actions of the manager have made a difference because a passively managed tracker type fund is liable to have the same Sharpe ratio as the market, irrespective of the absolute level of risk.

Test yourself 11.4

Assume that the risk-free rate has averaged 2% per annum in recent years and that the average return on the FTSE-AS index has been 7% with a standard deviation of 17%. Two actively managed funds have the following earnings and risk profiles:

1. An average rate of return of 15% and annual standard deviation of 52%.

2. An average return of 6% and an annual standard deviation of 7%.

   a) Calculate the Sharpe ratios for the FTSE-AS index and the two managed portfolios.

   b) Explain which (if any) of the two portfolios is acceptable to investors seeking excess returns.

The Treynor ratio is similar to the Sharpe ratio except that it uses beta instead of total risk as the denominator.

$$T_p = \frac{\bar{r}_p - \bar{r}_f}{\beta_p}$$

If the Treynor ratio for a managed portfolio exceeds that of a benchmark, it indicates that the management is generating returns in excess of those consistent with the exposure to systematic risk. It suggests that there is a positive alpha return.

Worked example 11.4: Treynor ratios

Assume that the risk-free rate has averaged 2% per annum in recent years and that the beta for the FTSE-AS index, taken as a proxy for the market portfolio, is 1. Over the same period an actively managed fund has earned an average annual return of 12% and has a beta value of 1.4. The Treynor ratio for the market portfolio is:

$$T = \frac{7\% - 2\%}{1} = 5\%$$

In comparison the Treynor ratio for the managed portfolio is:

$$T = \frac{12\% - 2\%}{1.4} = 7.14\%$$

The Treynor ratio for the market portfolio is 5%. For the managed portfolio it is 7.4%, indicating that the portfolio has earned a return that exceeds the level that is consistent with the portfolio's systematic risk.

Test yourself 11.5

Assume that the risk-free rate has averaged 2% per annum in recent years and that the average return on the FTSE-AS index has been 7% with a beta of 1. Two actively managed funds have the following earnings and betas:

1.   An average rate of return of 15% and beta value of 3.

2.   An average return of 6% and beta of 0.5.

   a)   Calculate the Treynor ratios for the FTSE-AS index and the two managed portfolios.

   b)   Explain which (if any) of the two portfolios are acceptable to investors seeking excess returns.

The Sharpe and Treynor ratios are commonly used methods for assessing the performance of managed funds. They offer methods of comparison that are intuitively quite straightforward.

Research into the performance of managed funds generally shows that at any particular time large numbers of actively managed funds fail to outperform market-wide indices. Some commentators conclude that this proves that active fund management in general fails. There isn't scope here to do justice to all the details and nuance of the debate. We will simply conclude with a few points for you to ponder:

◆ Many actively managed funds approximate tracker funds. The 30 largest UK companies quoted on the London Stock Exchange account for approximately 85% of the total market value of the FTSE 100 index of companies. Funds dominated by stakes in a small number of the very largest companies are, therefore, unlikely to consistently outperform a benchmark because they too closely resemble the benchmark. Indeed, factor in the higher management charges and it becomes virtually inconceivable that they can consistently outperform benchmarks.

◆ Is the notion of investment increasingly dominated by tracker-like management behaviour desirable? The hallmark of tracker funds is passivity with respect to the content of what is being invested in. The quest is merely to ensure the proper portioning among given securities. It is antithetical to the idea that it is important or worthwhile to assess the specifics and prospects of businesses seeking to attract capital.

Chapter summary

◆ Investment decision-making and asset management are dominated by institutions.

◆ Passively managed funds emphasise replicating the returns of benchmarks on a risk-adjusted basis and for minimal cost.

◆ Actively managed funds justify higher charges on the basis that they aim to better the performance of benchmarks on a risk adjusted basis.

◆ Passively managed funds seek to minimise tracking error. Actively managed funds seek to maximise the ratio of excess returns to tracking error.

◆ The total expense ratio is gradually succeeding the annual management charge as the main measure of the cost of fund management.

◆ Active fund management consists of a variety of investment philosophies, rooted in attitudes to fundamental analysis, market anomalies and market psychology.

◆ Actively managed funds seek to generate alpha returns.

◆ Alpha returns measure investment acumen of fund managers.

Glossary

Accumulation units Units sold by investment funds that reinvest dividends or interest in additional assets. It results in accumulation units having higher prices than comparable distribution units.

Actively managed funds Investment funds that involve managers adopting trading and investment strategies that aim to exceed the performance of predetermined benchmarks as opposed to merely achieving the benchmark outcome.

Arbitrage Financial arbitrage is the practice of exploiting price inconsistencies to generate riskless profits.

Basis The difference between a futures price and the spot price of the asset to which the futures contract refers.

Basis point In finance a basis point is equal to one hundredth of 1% and is a widely used method for quoting interest rate changes and differences.

Bottom-up An investment approach that seeks to identify under- and overvalued securities, irrespective of the state of the broad fundamentals.

Callable bond A bond that entitles the issuer to repay the debt earlier than the specified redemption date.

Capital repayment mortgage A mortgage payment method where the monthly instalments include two components, one directed to repaying the debt and the other to paying interest on the debt.

Carry trade The practice of borrowing at one rate and lending the funds at a higher rate. Common examples are borrowing in low interest rate currencies to invest in higher-rate currencies and borrowing at low short-term rates to invest in higher-yielding long-term assets.

Cash cow A business that consistently produces earnings well in excess of those needed to grow the business to its maximum potential.

Cash rich A description of a company with stable earnings that significantly exceed its long-term capital reinvestment requirements.

Contrarian investing An investment version of 'going against the crowd', rooted in the belief that market prices tend to overreact to new information and that excess returns arise due to mean reversion.

Cost of carry The cost of holding a financial position. It incorporates interest and other cash flows that are payable or receivable, gained or lost. There may also be custodian and storage costs.

Coupon payment A term that is often used to describe interest payments on bonds.

Covered interest rate parity The notion that forward currency exchange rates effectively neutralise interest rate differentials.

Defined contribution pension A type of pension scheme in which payments into the plan are specified, but the scale of benefits depends on the returns accruing to the scheme's assets.

Deposit insurance scheme A mechanism, normally government sponsored, for protecting depositors' funds in the event of a bank failure.

Derivatives A general term describing financial arrangements whose values derive from some underlying asset. A futures contract is an example of a derivative.

Disintermediation Financial disintermediation describes a growing tendency for large corporations to bypass banks and borrow money directly from investors by selling bonds to them. It constitutes an erosion of the traditional intermediary position of banks between savers and borrowers.

Distribution units Units sold by investment funds that distribute dividends or interest on underlying assets to holders of the units.

Duration A measure of bond maturity based on a weighted average of the individual constituent cash flows. It is useful in the assessment of bond price volatility.

Equity growth fund An asset management fund that places particular emphasis on the objective of acquiring shares deemed likely to offer significant capital growth.

Excess return The percentage by which the return on an investment beats the benchmark return after adjustment for risk.

Floating rate note A bond whose periodic interest payments vary in line with changes in a specified benchmark rate such as Libor.

Forward rate agreement An OTC arrangement designed to fix the interest rate on borrowing or lending in the future.

FTSE 250 Index A stock market index that expresses developments in the value of the 250 companies below the FTSE 100 constituents by market capitalisation.

Futures contract An agreement to transact a specified amount of an asset at a predetermined price on a specific date in the future.

Haircut The difference between the market value of an asset and the value assigned by a broker lending a client funds to purchase the asset.

Hedge A financial arrangement whose primary purpose is to eliminate or reduce the exposure of investments to specific types of risk.

Index-linked bond A bond whose coupon and principal payments vary in line with changes in a specified index of inflation.

Initial margin The proportion of a margin-based investment that must be financed from the investor's resources.

Interest rate swaps An OTC agreement between two parties to swap streams of interest payments. The most common type involves swapping a stream of fixed rate payments for variable rate payments.

Interim dividend A dividend payment paid prior to a company's end-of-year financial statements and, technically, paid from past years' earnings. It is distinct from the 'final' dividend, which is declared in conjunction with the full year financial statements.

Investment grade A term that applies to debt securities deemed by ratings agencies to be of high quality and low risk.

Maintenance margin A minimum level of collateral that an investor must maintain in a margin account.

Margin account A dealing account in which a broker permits a client to trade on credit in return for the deposit of a margin.

Margin call An instruction to deposit additional capital into a margin account that occurs when collateral falls below the maintenance level.

Marked to market The practice of marking down profits and losses at the end of each trading day based on market prices.

Median The middle value in a sample as distinct from the mean, which is the average of a sample.

Momentum investing Based on the belief that asset prices can acquire momentum beyond levels justified by fundamental information. Momentum traders seek to identify opportunities to profit from these price trends.

Nominee account A security trading account where the nominated account holder (normally a broker) administers assets on behalf of clients defined as the beneficial owners.

Option contract A right to transact a specified amount of an asset at a predetermined price on a specific date in the future.

Over-the-counter A generic term for financial market transactions undertaken directly between willing parties rather than on securities exchanges such as the London Stock Exchange.

Payment protection insurance A type of insurance designed to offer the policyholder some protection from the burden of loan repayments in the event of loss of income.

Price-earnings ratio A company's share price expressed as a ratio of its earnings per share.

Principal In the case of bonds, the principal refers to the amount repayable on the maturity date of the bond.

Pure discount See **Zero coupon**.

Retail bond The retail bond market is an electronic trading system launched by the London Stock Exchange in 2010. It is designed to facilitate trading in both corporate and government bonds in denominations small enough to appeal to retail investors.

S&P 500 index A performance index based on the securities of 500 US companies publicly traded on either the New York or National Association of Securities Dealers Automated Quotations (NASDAQ) stock markets.

Secondary market A market for trading already existing financial securities, in contrast to the primary market where new issues take place.

Settlement date The day on which the terms of a trade are completed with cash and assets being credited to and debited from participants' accounts.

Settlement price The 'market' price at the close of trade that is used to mark down profits and losses.

Share-buyback The use of liquid reserves by a company to buy, and effectively retire, a portion of its issued share capital.

Special purpose vehicle A subsidiary operation set up for a specific financial undertaking. In some cases the aim is to reduce tax payments by registering the SPV in a tax haven. They also offer mechanisms for removing liabilities from sponsors' balance sheets.

Spot price Refers to the prices of assets such as currencies and traded commodities involving immediate settlement. In practice immediate settlement normally means two to three business days.

Spreads An interest rate spread refers to the difference between the lending and borrowing rates quoted by banks for particular terms.

Swap contract An OTC arrangement that facilitates, in the case of interest rate swaps, the exchange of income streams. The most common example is the exchange of fixed rate payments for variable rate payments.

Swap rate The fixed rate quoted for a swap contract.

Top-down An investment approach that starts from an assessment of broad economic fundamentals to inform investment decisions and wealth allocation.

Tracking difference The difference between the return on an investment fund and the return on a benchmark against which it is compared.

Tracking error A measure of the difference between the actual return on an investment fund and the return on a benchmark. In the case of funds set up to track a market index, the tracking error ought to be negligible.

Treasury bills A type of financial security issued by central governments seeking to borrow funds on a short-term basis.

Yield curve A depiction of the relationship between yield and maturity for debt securities issued by central government.

Zero coupon Term that describes financial securities that offer a single payment on maturity, with no interim reward. Also known as pure discount.

Index